Andersonville Raiders

Yankee versus Yankee in the Civil War's Most Notorious Prison Camp

Gary Morgan

STACKPOLE
BOOKS

Guilford, Connecticut

Published by Stackpole Books
An imprint of The Rowman & Littlefield Publishing Group, Inc.
4501 Forbes Blvd., Ste. 200
Lanham, MD 20706
www.rowman.com

Distributed by NATIONAL BOOK NETWORK
800-462-6420

British Library Cataloguing in Publication Information available

Library of Congress Cataloging-in-Publication Data

Names: Morgan, Gary, 1961– author.
Title: Andersonville raiders : Yankee versus Yankee in the Civil War's most notorious
    prison camp / Gary Morgan.
Other titles: Yankee versus Yankee in the Civil War's most notorious prison camp
Description: Guilford, Connecticut : Stackpole Books, [2020] | Includes bibliographical
    references and index. | Summary: "In July 1864, six Union soldiers were hanged
    at Andersonville, a Civil War prison camp notorious then and now for its harsh
    conditions. But the hanged men's crimes had nothing to do with the war against
    the Confederacy; they weren't spies or saboteurs. They were the leaders of a gang-
    known as The Raiders-who terrorized their fellow Union prisoners in the hell of
    Andersonville. By June 1864, prisoners had had enough, and camp commandant
    Henry Wirz (executed after the war) sanctioned the formation of a quasi-police force,
    the Regulators, with permission to arrest, try, and punish offenders. In less than two
    weeks, the Raiders were broken up and arrested and hanged. Andersonville is one
    of the most notorious aspects of the Civil War, and this is one instance in which
    brother-against-brother chivalry did not prevail, not even amongst inmates from the
    same side. Gary Morgan has dug deep into the historical record to tell this story,
    which is at once dramatic and historically important."— Provided by publisher.
Identifiers: LCCN 2019046256 (print) | LCCN 2019046257 (ebook) | ISBN
    9780811738842 (cloth) | ISBN 9780811768917 (epub)
Subjects: LCSH: Andersonville Prison—History. | United States—History—Civil War,
    1861–1865—Prisoners and prisons. | Military prisons—Georgia—Andersonville—
    History.
Classification: LCC E612.A5 M67 2020 (print) | LCC E612.A5 (ebook) | DDC
    973.7/71—dc23
LC record available at https://lccn.loc.gov/2019046256
LC ebook record available at https://lccn.loc.gov/2019046257

To Frederic Augustus James, United States Navy, who was there but chose not to watch the execution "Having no relish for such scenes," and to Jefferson Hammer and Rita Arthur for keeping James's story alive and entrusting me with his memory. Requiescant in pace.

Contents

Acknowledgments

$\mathcal{A}$lthough only one name appears on the front of this work, this book would not have been possible without the assistance and support of a great many people. This book is theirs as much as it is mine.

First and foremost, I have to acknowledge my good friend Gail Abbott, who first handed me copies of the letters of the only known sailor to have kept a diary at Andersonville, Frederic Augustus James. "Fred" was a sailor on the *Housatonic*, was captured at the ill-fated Second Battle of Fort Sumter, a designated hostage, and kept a diary that he wrote in every day from February, 1864 until shortly before his death at Andersonville, just 5 days before he would have left that place. Trying to fill in the blank in Fred's diary where he would have listed the names of the six raiders (the only blank in the entire diary!) was the question that launched me on my voyage into the world of the raiders.

Secondly, I must acknowledge and publicly thank the pair who kept Fred James's memory alive and passed the keeping of that legacy on to me. Father Jefferson J. Hammer and Sister Rita Arthur were both members of the Catholic clergy and dedicated historians. Jeff bought Fred's diary from legendary antiques dealer Norm Flayderman in 1967, and it became his lifelong obsession. In 1973, ably assisted by Rita, his edition of the *Frederic Augustus James's Civil War Diary* was published. Jeff was a remarkable man; he was one of the Freedom Riders in the Deep South in the early 1960s, and he was the chaplain on duty at Saint Vincent's Church in New York City on 9/11 when the planes hit the towers. I wish I had known him longer. When he passed away, Rita, who had a doctorate in French literature, worked for the United Nations at part of a nongovernment organization, and served as a trustee at both Marymount Manhattan College and Marymount Loyola

University, asked me if I would like to have both the notes for Jeff's book and Jeff's collection of books dealing with Civil War prisons. I gladly accepted both. Jeff's books and Fred's words are the foundation on which *this* book was constructed. Rita passed away not long after Jeff, and again and again while writing, I dearly missed being able to pick up the phone and tell her what new information I had uncovered.

This book would have been quite different without a research grant from the Friends of Andersonville, a nonprofit organization dedicated to supporting Andersonville National Historic Site and the National Prisoner of War Museum. Because of the grant, I was able to not only use the resources at the National Prisoner of War Museum's archives, but had the rare opportunity to stay in Andersonville National Historic Site's guest residence for several nights, and it was a rare privilege to be able to stand alone in the stockade site at dawn and watch the sun rise, or breathe in the soupy August air and imagine what it was like not to be able to move to someplace cooler, and to stand alone there at night and look up at the stars and think about my family so far away, just as the men there did back in that awful summer of 1864.

I would also be remiss if I did not mention the rangers, staff, and volunteers at Andersonville National Historic Site, who gladly shares their knowledge and expertise. First and foremost among these is lead ranger Jennifer Hopkins, who cheerfully answered every question, sent me hot leads about the raiders when she came across them, and who makes sure that what happened at the prison is understood and remembered. Thank you to the Barr family, father Wade, and sons Chris and Charles. Chris, I'm looking forward to reading your book one day. Also to Rangers Jake Koch, Jimmy Culpepper, Ryan O'Connell, Jody Mays, and retired ranger Allen Marsh. Thanks to college professor and former seasonal ranger Evan Kutzler, who I wrote looking for information on sailor William Ritson. He in turn wrote back to say that there was no Ritson in the database of known prisoners, but that the name was remarkably similar to that of W. Rickson—Evan, you were right! Thanks to Regina Marsh, for recording my talk at the National POW Museum for me. And most particularly to park volunteers Jerry and Rosemary Higgs, whose spirit of adventure I admire and whose friendship I cherish.

Thank you to Kevin Frye, who took me on a tour of the prison and cemetery and helped me trace the footsteps of the prisoners. If you ever have a chance to take a tour with him, take it!

Thanks to Ed Worman, for sending me information about men who may have been raiders.

Thanks to Robert Scott Davis, the author of *Ghosts and Shadows of Andersonville* and retired National Archives historian Mike Musick for the discovery of the transcript of the raiders' trial. I'm glad I was able to verify its authenticity. And thank you to William Marvel, the author of *The Last Depot*, for letting me bounce an idea off of him

Thank you to noted Civil War historian Stephen B. Oates, who I was fortunate enough to have taken a year-long class with during his final year of teaching.

Thank you to retired history professors Mario DePillis and Constance M. McGovern, who would graciously offer me advice as I went along.

Thanks to Major Michael Ayoub, regimental historian and author of *The Campfire Chronicles: The Words and Deeds of the 88th Pennsylvania 1861–1865*, for answering my questions and for discovering William Collins's name listed on the Pennsylvania Monument at Gettysburg and for walking me through William Collins's footsteps on the fields of Gettysburg.

Thank you to Brian Bennett, author of *Sons of Old Monroe: A Regimental History of Patrick O'Rorke's 140th New York Volunteer Infantry*, for the information on John McGraw's letters describing the crime wave on board the ship taking him to join his regiment, and to McGraw's descendants Ted McGraw and Julie Brown for sharing information with me and for donating his letters to the University of Rochester where they can be studied. Thank you to Richard Holmes Anderson and Margaret Brown for permission to quote from the diary of their ancestor Harmon Anderson.

A big thanks to Tom Lowry of the Index Project, for checking to see if any of the raiders had been formally court-martialed.

Thank you to Sherrill Willis and the members of the Three Porches Writing Group; and to my friend and critique partner Heidi Luchterhand— I hope we get to actually meet someday!

Thank you to the Connecticut Historical Society in Hartford, Connecticut, which holds about a dozen original Andersonville diaries, including the original diary of Robert Kellogg, who, along with Fred James and Eugene Forbes, I found to be an extremely trustworthy source of information. I hope someday they publish the original diary as a companion piece to Kellogg's memoir. Thank you to the Fenimore Art Museum in Cooperstown, New York, particularly Special Collections Librarian Joe Festa. Thank you to the Massachusetts Historical Society, where Frederic James's diaries and letters are reunited for the first time in a century and a half. Thank you to the New York State Military Museum, and particularly archivist Jim Gandy. Thank you to the New England Civil War Museum and the hardcore staff of volunteers who keep it going. Thanks to the Civil War Navy Museum in Columbus, Georgia, for letting me go through their files on the USS *Water Witch*, where I found a hitherto unnoticed disciplinary record of Andrew Muir in the ship's deck log. And thanks to the National Archives and Records Administration in Washington, DC, which helped me both when I traveled to Washington and by mail when I needed copies of pension records and compiled military records that probably hadn't been looked at in the past 100 years. Thank you to E. Kathleen Shoemaker of the Rose Library at Emory University for helping me track down one of the scattered prisoner's diaries. And particular thanks to librarian Paul Friedman of the Brook Astor Reading Room at the New York Public Library, for helping me track down the *Sunday Mercury* article that provided one of the foundations of this book. Thanks to Christina Lucas of Navarro College for help with the Edwin Marsh papers. Finally, thank you L. Eileen Parris of the Virginia Museum of History and Culture for assistance with the remarkable collection of Robert Knox Sneden papers.

Every writer should have a librarian like Shelley Gayler-Smith, of the University of Dallas. I overheard her talking in the seat behind me at a symposium in North Carolina in 2015 and turned around and introduced myself. She went on to become a good friend, sounding board, resource, and occasional travel buddy, and if an institution did not want to grant me access to their holdings because I'm not affiliated with a university, she used her credentials to get it for me. She is also the instigator of the infamous "Gary Experiment." Thanks, Shelley. I owe you!

Thank you to the members of the Salisbury Confederate Prison Association for sharing your vast knowledge with me and for keeping the memory of those who served alive. Particular thanks to Ed and Sue Curtis, who organize a most interesting symposium every year. Thank you to Larry Knight for graciously letting me quote from his ancestor's diary. Thank you to John and Mike McCully for help finding references to raiders at other prisons. Thank you to my travel buddy and friend Dianne Hall and her husband Doc; to Mark Brelsford; to Navy vet and my sometimes roommate Caroline Hancock; and particularly to my friend Mike DuMont; thank you for the information on deserters, Mike, and for coming down to Georgia to hear me speak.

Thank you most particularly to the patrons and staff of the Sunderland Public Library in Sunderland, Massachusetts, particularly to former director Adam Novitt and to librarian Kelly Baker, who jumped through all kinds of hoops to locate an obscure master's thesis for me. Thank you to the staff of the Forbes Library in Northampton, who let me into their historical collection even though I arrived on a day when it was not open to the public. Thank you to former head librarian Leslie Lomasson and current head librarian Ella Stocker of the Amherst Regional High School Library, who wouldn't bat an eye when I'd wonder into their office in the middle of the day and say things like, "I need to see Philadelphia court records from the 1890s."

I was lucky enough to have had teachers who grew up in the 1960s, and they taught us to not only question authority, but to question everything. This book is very much a result of their teachings. Thank you to my earliest history teachers: Bob Jones, Peter Twomey, Ed Miller, David Dore, Maurice Donnelly, Gerry Beals, and Jerry Saval. You see? I was listening! And much love and gratitude to my second grade teacher, Dr. Ruth Albert, for showing us all that learning is fun, and who taught me to read. Dr. Albert, I am proud to have been your student.

Thank you to the rest of the faculty and staff at Amherst Regional High School in Amherst, Massachusetts. Particularly to the paraeducators, who are front line supporters of those facing challenges—both mine and the students! These include Emily Coelho, Mary O'Connell, Mary Catherine Mukimba, Yvonne Michaels, Oscar Hernandez Daguer, Stephen Bechtold (who always makes me laugh and whose obscure bits of knowledge fascinate me!), Susana Brena, Nazrin Sahabdeen-Miskin, and Spencer McIntyre. A special thank you to the social studies faculty, particularly Jim Elliott (Go, Red Sox!), Simon Leutz, Tom Fricke, Gloria Davis, Becca Leopold, Chris Gould, Sarah Bourbeau (thank you for the motivational chocolate!), and Sam Camera (whose phrase "shining the light of truth" on the story of John G. Doud I am very grateful for). Thank you Ken Jacque for repeatedly finding me a desk to work at. Thank you to Mary Kiely for letting me test the explanation of why Curtis wasn't Curtis with her A Period Math class (you're right, kids! It is like "CSI Civil War!"). Thanks to former principal Mark Jackson and former acting principal Miki Lee Gromacki for their support and encouragement. With an extra special thanks to Candace Wells and Marilyn Mish for (literally!) holding my hand when I submitted this.

Thanks to Shihanna Maradiaga, Kira Thomas, and Melanie Burt for technical support. And particular gratitude goes to Dave and Robin Cleland for hunting down and photographing John G. Doug's grave for me.

And finally to my family. For Kiki Gorman, thank you Mom for everything. Thanks to my cousins Maureen and David Vann, Martha and Larry Eaton, and Luke and Rachel Eaton for putting me up during the course of my travels south. Thanks to my children Katie Fox and Beth Gorman Duncan—I love you both exceedingly! And particularly, I would like to thank my father, Tucker Gorman, who knew that I was writing this book, but unfortunately passed away the week before my first trip to Andersonville National Historic Site to research it. I hope I made you proud, Dad.

Gary Morgan

* 1 *

The Raiders in History

$\mathscr{I}$t was the most witnessed execution in US history.

On a sweltering July evening in 1864, in a remote corner of southwest Georgia, in a foul and overcrowded prison stockade, six men, all Union prisoners of war, surrounded by guards and accompanied by a Roman Catholic priest, followed behind the prison commandant as he rode into camp mounted on a pale horse. They stopped at the foot of a hastily constructed gallows, and the commandant made a short speech disavowing himself from the proceedings before he ordered the guards to leave the stockade and rode out in their wake. The six prisoners seemed stunned, and several witnesses would later write that they had the impression that the six had not actually believed that they were about to die until that moment. They seemed to have been under the impression that their arrest, trial, and sentence had been part of some elaborate charade intended to frighten them into changing their ways. Once they'd been handed over to the other prisoners by the prison commandant, however, the awful reality that they were about to be killed began to take hold of them. One of the men tried to flee just as he was about to mount the gallows' steps, wading through the swampy, filth-filled stream that served as both the prison's water supply and its latrine. By the time he was recaptured and brought back to the place of execution, the other five men had already mounted the gallows. Meal sacks were slipped over their heads in the place of hoods, and the nooses were affixed around their necks. At a signal, the prop holding up the platform on which they stood was knocked away and the men fell into the void. Within minutes, one of the men, a large six footer, crashed back to earth, the rope he'd been hung with, broken. He was hastily revived, and although he pleaded piteously for mercy, he was hanged again, this time fatally. The bodies hung for about fifteen or twenty minutes, long enough to

1

make sure that the last sparks of the six lives had been snuffed, and then they were cut down and removed from the prison stockade for burial. The 26,000 plus Union prisoners who had witnessed the execution went back to the business of struggling to survive the deprivation and depravations of life in Camp Sumter, more commonly known as Andersonville Prison.

No one disputes this scenario. Nearly everything else about what happened that day is up for debate. Like a nineteenth-century game of "telephone" where a whispered sentence becomes more and more unrecognizable with each repetition, the details surrounding those six men and their deaths were obscured by perspective, memory, and exaggeration. Witnesses who wrote about the incident disagreed on the crimes that led to the executions, the role the prison officials played, specific details about the trial and subsequent hanging, and even the names of the men who were killed. So just who were these six prisoners who were killed by men on their own side? What crimes were they guilty of? Where did they come from? Why, out of thousands of prisoners, were these six singled out for punishment? Did they deserve to die?

The six men killed were part of a larger group of thieves and ruffians who preyed on their fellow prisoners at Andersonville. These "raiders" got their name from the short, effective attacks that they would make on their fellow prisoners. They would single out prisoners who were new to the prison, or who were sick or weak, or injured, and thus unlikely to fight back effectively. They frequently targeted men who had been brought into the stockades without comrades, because their friendless state made them more vulnerable. The raiders would attack, and then withdraw to their small neighborhood in the southwest corner of the stockade before help could be summoned. They may have worked individually, or in loosely organized bands, occasionally headed by an individual. They stole whatever they could of value—food, cash, watches, clothing, and other forms of personal property. They were not above using violence when they met with resistance. Many of the raiders had begun their criminal careers before they ever set foot in Andersonville, robbing fellow prisoners in places like Belle Isle, Virginia, where many of them had been held as prisoners before their transfer to the Georgia stockade. The first mention of "raiders" in Andersonville prisoners' diaries began not long after the prison camp opened. Although the men they preyed on were vulnerable, raiding was nonetheless a dangerous occupation, and men who were caught raiding were subjected to prison justice, where they might be beaten or flogged or have half of their heads and beards shaved as a visual warning to the rest of the prison population.

Following the hanging, the six bodies were removed to the "dead house," which is where the dead were kept until their burial in the nearby prison cemetery. The names of the dead, if known, were recorded in the prison's Register of Deaths, along with their rank, regiment, and cause of death. Anger over the fact that these six men had preyed on their fellow prisoners led the burial detail to bury them separately from the rows of graves where the other prisoners lay. The six men were buried dozens of yards away from the loyal dead who died of starvation, wounds, and disease. When the graves were marked by an expeditionary force after the war ended, the six raiders' graves were marked but not numbered. They are not counted among the honored dead, a sentiment that continues to this very day; when the thousands of graves at Andersonville National Cemetery are decorated with individual American flags on Memorial Day, the six graves that are set off to the side are left unmarked.

According to the grave markers, the executed raiders included four soldiers and two sailors. Going from left to right, the dead men are identified as "Pat'k Delaney PA.," "Chas. Curtis R.I.," "Wm Collins PA," "Jno. Sarsfield NY," "W. Rickson U.S.N.," and "A. Munn Sea US Navy." But from the very start, there was controversy about the identifications. Not a single diarist who witnessed the event mentions either "W. Rickson" or "A. Munn." Nearly every prisoner who recorded the names of the executed men in their diaries mentioned that one was named "Sullivan," a name that doesn't appear on the grave markers. John McElroy, who would write a best-selling memoir of his prison experiences a decade and a half later, claimed that their names didn't matter because they were probably aliases anyway. "These names and regiments are of little consequence, however, as I believe all the rascals were professional bounty-jumpers, and did not belong to any regiment longer than they could find an opportunity to desert and join another," wrote McElroy in his prison memoir, 15 years after the fact. The generally unreliable "diarist" John L. Ransom took the question of identity a step farther in his book, claiming that as he stood on the gallows, raider Patrick Delaney announced that he was using an alias: "He said his name was not Delaney and that no one knew who he really was, therefore his friends would never know his fate, his Andersonville history dying with him."

This refutation of the names of the doomed men dehumanizes them and makes them seem more like shadows and cardboard figures than living, breathing human beings. The angry mob of witnesses was definitely not interested in the details about the individual raiders, and later writers, in particular, relished relegating the raiders to the role of "bad guys" whereas they cast themselves firmly in the role of "good guys" and heroes to the starving, suffering victims of the raiders' crimes. By refuting their names and taking away their identities, all that is left of these men is the knowledge that they were the worst kind of predators. Unfortunately, the accusation that the raiders were all bounty jumpers who used assumed names does not always stand up. William Collins served with his regiment for over two years before he was captured and had earned a field promotion to corporal at the battle of Gettysburg. J. Sarsfield fought with his regiment for eight months before he was captured and was a good enough soldier that he was carried in the muster rolls as having been captured rather than as a deserter. Andrew Muir, the sailor misidentified as "A. Munn," had completed his year's enlistment as a sailor on the USS *Water Witch* and was awaiting transport back home to New York when his ship was captured. Looking at their compiled service records, it quickly becomes apparent that the story of the six raiders is much more complicated than the one history tells about them.

To untangle the real story of the Andersonville raiders, one needs to be conscious of how the story of the raiders has evolved over time. Over 26,000 prisoners witnessed the execution, as did an unknown number of guards and other Rebels. Dozens of eyewitnesses wrote about the event the day it happened in their prison diaries, but the diaries are only as good as the information available at the time. While most diarists present mention the hanging, the majority dismissed it in a single sentence or two. For example, Adelbert Knight of the 11th US Infantry wrote, "Their was 6 of our men hung inside of the stockade at 5 P.M. for murder and robery [*sic*] by our men." The difficulty in studying the Andersonville raiders is that the different witnesses frequently disagree in the details. For example, many diaries mention the last-minute escape attempt and the broken rope, while others do not. Most put the date of execution as July 11, but some state that it happened on July 12, likely because the execution happened late in the day and so they saved writing about it until the next day's journal entry. One of the sailors who was killed is variously identified as Munn, Muir, Meever, Murray, or Buer. Few letters home were sent from Andersonville, and it seems as if few, if any, of the letters that survive mention the execution, possibly because the idea of the prisoners turning on their own and the details of the hanging were just too ghastly to be shared with the tender folk at home. Despite these inconsistencies, the surviving diaries are the best primary source of details available to scholars, even if they are flawed accounts.

Wartime newspapers did not, for the most part, make mention of the raiders' reign of terror or the executions, although there were exceptions. One major exception was when 16th Illinois Cavalry Sergeant Leroy L. Key gave an interview to the Christian Commission after his exchange detailing how he organized and orchestrated the raiders' downfall. That interview was published in several newspapers, including the *Boston Journal* and *New York Times*, in late 1864 while the war was still going on and the prisoner-of-war camp at Andersonville was still in operation. While the prison was covered only sporadically in the press while it was in operation, the raiders' story featured widely in the press during the 1865 war crimes trial of Henry Wirz, when the bloodthirsty press took great delight in writing about the depravities of "Demon Wirz" and sought to exploit the worst stories about him, true or not, in order to help sell newspapers.

Within the first two years after the war, there were several prisoner memoirs published, and most, but not all of them, referenced the raiders. The best of these publications was *Life and Death in Rebel Prisons* by 16th Connecticut Sergeant Major Robert H. Kellogg. Not surprisingly, Kellogg drew on his prison diary, a remarkably detailed document now in the possession of the Connecticut Historical Society. But none of these books sold particularly well, and by five years after the war, both the nation and the former prisoners began to look forward rather than backward at a particularly difficult period in their history, and there were no more prisoner memoirs published.

By 1870, the nation was moving on from the Civil War and very little was written in the press about the prison or the raiders for nearly a decade. Then, in 1879, a reporter and former Andersonville prisoner of war (POW) named John McElroy, reportedly drawing from a popular series of prison sketches that he'd written for the *Toledo Blade*, published a four-volume memoir of his wartime experiences titled *Andersonville: A Story of Rebel Military Prisons*. McElroy was nothing if not a good storyteller, and he wrote about how, as a young man, he served as one of the regulators, the ad hoc police force responsible for attesting, court-martialing, and punishing the raiders. The book became an instant best seller and has remained in print ever since.

McElroy devoted two entire chapters to the crimes, arrest, and punishment of the raiders, providing rich detail, even dialogue, from the remembered incidents 15 years before. The story of the Andersonville raiders and the epic struggle within the prison walls between the forces of good and evil became part of the American consciousness. McElroy became the definitive source of information for what life was like at the Andersonville stockade, although he wrote it as a man in his 30s, looking back on events that had occurred over a decade before. His success spawned a glut of prison memoirs, although none of them matched his book for style or sales. In fact, many of the books that came later clearly drew on McElroy for information, and repeated his remembered details, dialogue, and drama. Some incidents, such as a battle royal between the raiders and the regulators, and Captain Wirz screaming at his men to open fire on the prisoners during Charles Curtis's failed escape attempt, were never mentioned either in diaries or earlier memoirs, but appear in several memoirs published after McElroy's.

These later books not only suffered from the vagaries of memory, but in some cases from authors who refused to let the facts get in the way of a good story. Particularly notable among these is John Ransom, who claimed to be publishing his "diary," but when questioned about the whereabouts of the original diary, he claimed that it had been burned in a fire, but only after he had copied it first. A typical example of the faults in Ransom's account is the "diary entry" that allegedly gives details of the hanging. Ransom claims that the hanging took place on July 12 (prison records show that the date was July 11); that Sarsfield fought with the 144th New York (it was the 140th); and that the two sailors were named A. Munn and W. R. Rickson (these names do not appear until after the war when the grave markers were erected in the National Cemetery). Ransom claims that "Munn" was captured four months before, when in fact Andrew Muir was captured on June 3, 1864, just under six weeks before the hanging. Ransom claimed that Sarsfield had studied law before the war, had been with his regiment for three years, and had been wounded in battle before being captured, when his compiled service records indicate that Sarsfield worked as a shoemaker, was never injured, and had been with his regiment for just eight months before being captured. Ransom claimed that the hangings took place at 11 o'clock in the morning when most other accounts say they occurred in the early evening, and Ransom never mentions the aborted escape attempt, instead claiming that Curtis, the man who most accounts say tried to bolt at the last minute, tells them to hurry the execution along and not spend all day talking about it. Ransom claims that Delaney announced that he would rather hang than live on small rations, which seems unlikely at best. Ransom reports blood spurting from Collins's ears, mouth, and nose after his hanging is botched and he falls to earth, details found in no other account. In short, it looks like Ransom was more interested in telling a thrilling story than the truth when he published his book under the title *Andersonville Diary* in 1881.

Accurate or not, McElroy's book with its rich details became the definitive account of Andersonville in general and the arrest and hanging of the raiders. Since its publication, the story of Andersonville prison has stayed in the public eye and become part of the American mythos, serving as an inspiration for novelists, playwrights, and filmmakers. Almost a century after the events, a writer named McKinlay Kantor would draw heavily on McElroy's and Ransom's accounts to craft his own novel, *Andersonville*, which would win a Pulitzer prize for fiction in 1956. In 1959, *The Andersonville Trial*, a play by Saul Levitt depicting the trial of Andersonville prison Commandant Henry Wirz, would have a successful run on Broadway before being filmed in 1970 in an Emmy-winning PBS presentation starring Richard Basehart and William Shatner. Finally, in 1996, a made-for-TV movie from Turner Pictures titled *Andersonville* won several Emmy awards, including Outstanding Miniseries or Special. But each retelling and artistic representation takes us one more level of removal from the truth.

The first scholarly book on Andersonville was written over a century after the last prisoner left the stockade. In 1968, *History of Andersonville Prison*, written by a college professor from Morehouse College in Atlanta named Ovid L. Futch, was published. Although Futch did a credible job sifting through the documents and accounts of Andersonville Prison, he was nonetheless looking back across a century and had to contend with accounts that were, occasionally, at odds with each other.

Time and memory are strange things. Both are cherished, fleeting, and difficult to capture. Looking back, mountains are higher, challenges become greater, and death and losses turn bittersweet. There is a tendency to categorize and to simplify. Both good men and bad become caricatures, details get hazy, and mistakes are made. In the hands of later writers, the prison and its men become literary devices; stand-ins for hell and the epic struggle between angels and demons. Truths are manipulated, facts are tweaked, and literary license is taken for the sake of telling and selling the story. A century and a half later, it's difficult to wade through the layers of time and treatment and discover the substrate that lies beneath the detritus.

Despite their limitations, contemporary and near-contemporary accounts must be considered more reliable than later memoirs written decades after the fact. The best we can do is to look for details that are consistent between accounts and examine them critically. Using contemporary and close-to-contemporary accounts, as well as records from the prison camp and the compiled service records of the individual men involved, we now attempt to go beyond the caricatures that history has given us and answer the question: Who were the Andersonville raiders?

NOTES ON CHAPTER 1

A Roman Catholic priest—The priest was Father Peter Whelan, who is noteworthy for having regularly entered the prison stockade in order to attend to the spiritual needs of the Roman Catholic prisoners. He later recounted his experiences on the day the raiders were hung at the war crimes trial of Captain Henry Wirz. Although he was assisted at times by other priests, Father Whelan ministered to the prisoners longer than his clerical brethren, some of whom became ill from their exposure to the prison. Father Whelan was the priest who attended the condemned men at their execution. He would later go on to testify at the Wirz trial.

The six prisoners seemed stunned, and several witnesses would later write that they had the impression that the six had not actually believed that they were about to die until that moment—Robert Kellogg wrote, "They themselves seemed strangely unconcerned, apparently thinking it was simply an affair got up thoroughly to frighten them, and they appeared to cling to the idea, even until they had ascended the platform erected for their execution." John McElroy wrote, "For a moment the condemned looked stunned. They seemed to comprehend for the first time that it was really the determination of the regulators to hang them. Before that they had evidently thought that the talk of hanging was merely bluff." McElroy also reported that, upon seeing the gallows, one of the condemned men gasped, "My God, men, you don't really mean to hang us up there!" Prisoner Warren Lee Goss recalled that "up to this time the murderers did not seem to view the proceedings in a serious light, but rather as a joke." And the *Sunday Mercury* reported that, "It was evident that the culprits themselves did not believe they were to die; although a worthy priest named Father [Peter] Whelan, from Florida, who had been attending the prisoners for several months before was unceasing in his labors in trying to impress upon them the real nature of their position."

The 26,000 plus Union prisoners—Prisoners varied in their estimates of the size of the crowd, but according to the Morning Report entry for July 11, 1864, there were 26,464 prisoners within the prison stockade that day, with another 1,517 in the prison hospital, making an official total of 28,685 prisoners. Of this number, those in the prison hospital outside the stockade walls would probably not have been able to see inside the stockade fence, and some within the stockade would have been too sick or disabled to get to a vantage point where they could witness the proceedings. A few, such as sailor Frederic Augustus James, opted not to watch, "having no relish for such scenes."

No one disputes this scenario—Although most of the prisoners agreed on the essentials of the story, there is occasional discrepancy over the details, such as some diaries recording the execution as being on July 11, rather than July 12, likely because the hangings happened in the evening after that day's diary entries had already been completed, and a few much later memoirists, looking back, combined the story of the broken rope with the memory of a man trying to bolt, and recorded that it was the same man involved in both incidents. However, most accounts are essentially as given here.

Robbing fellow prisoners in places like Belle Isle, Virginia, where they were held as prisoners before their transfer to the Georgia stockade—The first prisoners at Andersonville were transfers from other Confederate prisons, such as Belle Isle. A Belle Isle prisoner named J. Osborn Coburn wrote in his diary about having four loaves of bread stolen by men he identified as "Raiders." Memoirist Gilbert Sabre wrote in his 1866 memoir that "The system of 'raiding,' which was carried on with so much annoyance at Belle Isle, was practiced, with even greater industry, at Camp Sumter."

The first mention of "raiders" in Andersonville prisoners' diaries began not long after the prison camp opened—Robert Kellogg specifically mentions one of the men who would later be hanged in his diary on May 5, 1864, just three days after his arrival at Andersonville, when he wrote that "The Moseby gang [*sic*] tried to raid it on us last night, but we were out in a twinkling, ready to give them a pounding. Unfortunately, they escaped." At this point, the prison had been open just over two months.

Anger over the fact that these six men had preyed on their fellow prisoners led the burial detail to bury them separately from the rows of graves where the other prisoners lay—At the time of their deaths, burial workers were still placing bodies in what would later become known as Section K of Andersonville National Cemetery. As more and more prisoners died, the area between Section K and the raiders' graves was used to accommodate more burials, creating Section J. This makes it appear today as if the raiders were placed much closer to the other prisoners than they originally were, although their graves are still set off to one side of the rows containing the honored dead.

The generally unreliable "diarist" John L. Ransom—Ransom, reportedly a first sergeant with the 9th Michigan Cavalry, Company A, was the author of a book called *Andersonville Diary*, which was published in 1881. He died in Pasadena, California, on September 23, 1919.

Adelbert Knight—Knight's unpublished diary is currently owned by his descendant, Larry Knight.

One of the sailors who was killed is variously identified as Munn, Muir, Meever, Murray, or Buer—This man is identified as A. Munn on his grave marker; as Muir in the prison death register (which was likely misread when the grave markers were being made) and in the diary of prisoner Robert Knox Sneden; as Meever in the 1866 prison memoir of Gilbert E. Sabre; as "Murray" by Eugene Forbes's diary; and as Buer in the diary of Albert Shatzel.

Leroy L. Key gave an interview to the Christian Commission after his exchange detailing how he organized and orchestrated the raiders' downfall. That interview, was published in several newspapers, including the *Boston Journal* and *New York Times*, in late 1864 while the war was still going on and the prisoner-of-war camp at Andersonville was still in operation. An account of Key's interview appeared at the bottom of a long article on war happenings that first appeared in the *Boston Journal*, and later ran on the front page of the December 11, 1864, *New York Times*.

As a young man—John McElroy's age is difficult to determine. His death certificate gives his date of birth as August 25, 1844, which would have made him a little more than a month shy of his twentieth birthday at the time the raiders were hanged. But his gravestone at Arlington National Cemetery clearly states that John McElroy, a private in the 16th Illinois Cavalry, was born in 1846, which would have made him approximately 18 years old during his summer as a POW. The 1900 US census lists him as a 50-year-old journalist and gives his month and year of birth as August 1849, which would have made him a month shy of his 15th birthday when the raiders were hanged. On the other extreme, the 1880 US census, taken on the second day of June, was the first census taken after his book on his wartime experiences was published, and lists him as a 38-year-old journalist, meaning he'd have been 22 years old in July 1864.

Ransom reports blood spurting from Collins's ears, mouth, and nose after his hanging is botched and he falls to earth, details found in no other account—Diarist John L. Hoster reported Curtis bleeding from the ear as a result of being beaten during his aborted escape attempt, but Ransom is the only one to describe William Collins this way.

In 1968, a college professor from Morehouse College in Atlanta, named Ovid L. Futch published his book, *History of Andersonville Prison*—Sadly, Ovid Futch died in March 1967, and his book was published posthumously.

The Trial Transcript?

*O*n June 30, 1864, prison commander General John Winder issued General Order Number 57, authorizing the proceedings against the raiders and dictating that, "The whole proceedings will be properly kept in writing, all of the testimony will be fairly written out as nearly in the words of the witnesses as possible." Although many prisoners reported that a transcript of the trial was kept and sent to Washington, DC, no such transcript was ever reported as having been received, and for a century and half it was assumed that such a record of the raiders' trial had been lost, if it had ever existed at all.

But languishing in archives such as the National Archives in Washington, DC, and the New York Public Library was a newspaper article from page 3 of the August 20, 1865, *Sunday Mercury*. Published just over a year after the executions and just four months after Andersonville Prison ceased operations, the article gave a long account of the trial of the Andersonville raiders. It was published along with a brief editorial introduction urging the readers to have an open mind regarding Henry Wirz, then on trial for war crimes. The article gave a day-by-day account of the trial, naming the men accused, the jury members, prosecuting and defense lawyers, court reporter, and witnesses. It seems to be, if not the long-lost court transcript, then something quite similar.

Does the *Sunday Mercury* show the actual, assumed-to-be-lost account of the raiders' trial? At first glance it seems promising. Details that can be checked, such as the names and regiments of the men taking part in the trial do, for the most part, match with men who are known to have been held prisoner at Andersonville. Where there are errors, they appear to be minor, such as a wrong company or an apparently misheard name, such as juror J. Western Dana of the 56th Massachusetts, who is more likely J. Weston Dana of the 56th Massachusetts. Likewise, the mentioned name of a Confederate officer, "Bush" matches the name of Second Lieutenant Warren S. Bush, who served at Andersonville. The *Sunday Mercury*'s account of the trial mentions that Sarsfield was found guilty on the first day of the trial, an event confirmed by prisoner Eugene Forbes's diary entry for June 30, the day after the arrests of the raiders, which states that "towards night news came in that Sarsfield, one of the principals, who said he would 'Cut out Dowd's heart and throw it in his face,' had been convicted and sentenced to be hung." Prisoner James Vance of the 5th US Cavalry wrote on July 1 that three raiders had been sentenced to hang, which coincides with the *Sunday Mercury*'s assertion that Delaney, Sullivan, and Muir were sentenced on the second day of the trial. Similarly, a man named Richard Allen of the 83rd Pennsylvania, Company E, is reported to have been found guilty of robbery and assault, raising the possibility that this is the same "Dick Allen" who, according to John McElroy, swore vengeance over Patrick Delaney's body (Delaney was also a member of the 83rd Pennsylvania, Company E). And finally, the *Mercury* reveals that the man named "Dowd," whose assault led to the arrest and downfall of the raiders, was a member of the 97th New York, a detail never mentioned in any diary or book, and indeed, a man named "Doud" served with the 97th New York, was captured, and sent to Andersonville.

It would have been all but impossible for someone with no connection to Andersonville to come up with the names, regiments, and details listed in this article. So how could the transcript of the raiders' trial have ended up published in a New York City newspaper rather than being forwarded to Washington, DC?

There is a clue in the article itself: "Edward Wellington Boate, Forty-second New York, was unanimously appointed official reporter of the Court." Boate, an Irish native, had already had a long newspaper career before enlisting in the 42nd New York under the alias "Edward W. Bates." He'd worked as a journalist for the *Waterford Chronicle* and *Wexford Guardian* before moving to London and working as a foreign correspondent. He then worked as a Parliamentary correspondent before moving to the United States with his family sometime around the beginning of the War of Rebellion.

In 1863, Boate joined the 42nd New York and was captured at the Battle of Bristoe Station at roughly the same place and time as condemned raiders Patrick Delaney, William Collins, and John Sullivan. Like them, he was sent to Belle Isle, and then to Andersonville. Interestingly, Boate left the prison within a month of the execution of the raiders. Perhaps because he held the belief that the US government was responsible for the horrific condition at Andersonville due to its refusal to resume the exchange of prisoners, Boate was one of six prisoners selected to carry a petition calling for the resumption of prisoner exchanges and for the Union government to allow supplies to be sent through enemy lines for the relief of the men held at Andersonville. It seems logical that as the court reporter, Boate would have been an ideal choice to bring the trial transcript to Washington, perhaps with the intention of giving it to Abraham Lincoln personally. But it was not to be. Much to Boate's consternation, "the representatives of thirty-eight thousand Union prisoners were treated with silent contempt, the President declining to see them or have any communication with them!" Unable to present the transcript to Lincoln, Boate apparently kept it. Given the difficulties Dorence Atwater later had with the federal government over the list of names of the dead who had died at Andersonville, Boate's keeping the transcript may have been a good choice.

Boate went on to testify on behalf of Henry Wirz at his trial—a very unpopular position, but one that is in line with the exhortation not to rush to judgment of Wirz at the beginning of the *Mercury* article. So how did the transcript go from Boate's possession to the pages of the *Mercury*? Simple. According to his 1871 obituary, Edward Wellington Boate had been a reporter for the *Sunday Mercury*. It appears, then, that Boate was the court reporter at the raiders' trials and took the transcript with him to Washington, DC, when he was paroled as part of a delegation of prisoners on August 7, 1864. Because Lincoln declined to meet with the delegation, Boate was unable to present the transcript to Lincoln, and so he kept it, then saw it published in the newspaper that he worked at during the war crimes trial of Henry Wirz. Boate probably hoped that by revealing Wirz's role in stopping the raiders, he might improve the public's perception of Henry Wirz and help the man get a fair trial.

Given this information, it's very likely that the *Mercury*'s account of the raiders' trial *is* the long-lost account mentioned by several different prisoners. It seems to have been accepted as a legitimate account by some sources in Washington as well; all four of the executed soldiers' compiled service records contain the notation: "See Bookmark AMO-433-1865." That "bookmark" refers to a document at the National Archives that is inside a file on Dorence Atwater—a newspaper clipping that's misidentified as being from the *New York Mercury*, but which is from the August 20, 1865, *Sunday Mercury*.

The *Sunday Mercury* article is both a fascinating and frustrating document. The section on the trial is framed by two episodes of questionable veracity. In one, hearing about the situation created by the raiders, Henry Wirz enthusiastically takes immediate action, calling for his gun so that he can presumably settle the issue personally. In the other, condemned prisoner Curtis claims to have taken the Oath of Allegiance to the Confederacy and appeals to General John Winder for clemency (Winder reportedly responds by offering Curtis the choice of being shot as a Rebel or hanged as a Yankee). In both cases, it's questionable whether either event happened; it's never explained how the reporter, a prisoner, would have been present in Wirz's office before the arrests and there's no record of a prisoner named "Charles Curtis" ever taking the Oath of Allegiance.

The central portion of the article is a day-by-day account of the trial, although it only records a portion of the proceedings. Phrases such as "Other witnesses testified to other charges" and "There were several others tried, and found guilty, and sentenced to wear ball and chain for terms varying from ten days to the remainder of their imprisonment" tantalize, but unless Boate's original trial notes become available, the *Sunday Mercury* article is likely as close as we can come to knowing the specific details of the Andersonville raiders' crimes and the testimonies lodged against them.

NOTES ON CHAPTER 2

But languishing in archives such as the National Archives in Washington, DC— The file in the National Archives can be located at AMO-443-1865, interfiled with file APZ-479-1865; Letters Received, 1862–Dec. 1889; Enlisted Branch, 1848–1889; Records of the Adjutant General's Office, Record Group 94; National Archives Building, Washington, DC.

Although many prisoners reported that a transcript of the trial was kept and sent to Washington, DC—Henry Davidson wrote in his 1865 book, *Fourteen Months in Southern Prisons*, "A full account of the proceedings from the beginning of the trial to the burial was written by the Clerk of the Court, and transmitted by flag of truce to the Government at Washington." Charles H. Knox claimed that the transcript had been sent to General Sherman in Atlanta with a request to ratify the sentence.

Languishing in archives such as—The article exists as a clipping in the National Archive and was initially discovered by Mike Musick and reprinted as an appendix in Robert Scott Davis's book, *Ghosts and Shadows of Andersonville*, but the National Archives incorrectly identified the article as coming from the *New York Mercury*. However, the *New York Mercury* published on Saturdays, and the article was published on August 20, 1865, which was a Sunday. Once this error was discovered, other copies of the article could be found. At the New York Public Library, the issue of the *Sunday Mercury* containing the article in question is preserved on microfilm.

The article gave a day-by-day account of the trial, naming the men accused, jury members, prosecuting and defense lawyers, court reporter, and witnesses—See Appendix A for a complete transcript of the *Sunday Mercury* article.

J. Weston Dana of the 56th Massachusetts—James Weston Dana, formerly a corporal with the 1st Massachusetts.

Likewise, the mentioned name of a Confederate officer, "Bush"—The highest ranking Confederate named Bush at Andersonville Prison, and thus the one most likely referred to in the article was Second Lieutenant Warren S. Bush, of the Third Georgia Reserves, Company D. Other Bushes who served at Andersonville include E. B. Bush, 55th Georgia Infantry, Company C; Calvin Bush, 2nd Georgia Reserves, Company A; and Nathan Bush, 3rd Georgia Reserves, Company E.

A man named "Doud"—The name in question is always spelled "Dowd" in prisoner accounts, but the name appears to be "Doud" in pension documents provided by the man's mother following his death. Boate and the men who wrote in their diaries used the more common spelling of the name Dowd/Doud, and were likely not aware how the severely beaten man spelled his surname. See chapter 11, "Dowd."

In 1863, Boate joined the 42nd New York—For unknown reasons, perhaps to protect his identity as a reporter and get an "undercover" look at the life of a Union soldier, Boate enlisted under the pseudonym "Edward W. Bates."

Boate was one of six prisoners selected—The other prisoners selected were Henry C. Higginson of the 19th Illinois, Company K, the man who, according to the *Mercury* article, acted as defense attorney for the accused raiders; Prescott Tracy of the 82nd New York, Company G; and Sylvester Noirot or Norrit, of the 5th New Jersey, Company B. Two other men, William N. Johnson and either F. Garland or a man named Dennison, also reportedly left the prison stockade with the others, but did not arrive in Washington, DC, with them. Although the original intent may have been for these men to return to the prison after delivering their message, none of them returned to Andersonville.

"The representatives of thirty-eight thousand Union prisoners were treated with silent contempt"—Boate recounting of his experiences as part of the failed delegation appeared in the 1882 edition of the *Southern Historical Society Papers*, volume 10, nine years after his death. The piece was originally the sixth in a series of articles by Boate published in the *New York News* in July 1865, a month before his account of the raiders' trial appeared in the *Sunday Mercury*.

Given the difficulties Dorence Atwater later had—Nineteen-year-old Dorence Atwater, a private with the 2nd New York, Company D, served as a clerk at the prison hospitals at both Belle Isle and Andersonville. One of his jobs was to keep the prison's Register of Deaths, a duty he shared with several other clerks. Fearing that when the war ended, the Confederates would destroy the list rather than hand it over to the Union, Atwater began to secretly make his own copy of the list, which he took with him when he was exchanged in February 1865. The War Department initially offered Atwater $300 for the list upon learning of its existence, but Atwater wanted the list to be published so that the families of the dead would know what had happened to their loved ones. Atwater negotiated with the War Department saying that he would give them the list, but that they, in turn, must either provide him with a copy or allow him to make another copy. They agreed and Atwater turned the list over to the War Department, but as weeks passed, it became clear that they did not intend to honor their side of the bargain. At this point, Clara Barton, a popular figure because of her assistance to the sick and wounded of the war and who later founded the American Red Cross, learned of the existence of the list and persuaded the War Department to give it to her so that the dead of Andersonville might be identified and their graves marked. Atwater returned to Andersonville and assisted in this effort, and it's thanks to him that only 460 of the nearly 13,000 prisoners' graves had to be labeled "unknown." At the end of the expedition establishing the National Cemetery, Atwater simply took his list back when he left. Because of this "theft," he was court-martialed, convicted, and sentenced to eighteen months hard labor and a $300 fine! This was just a year after his release from Andersonville and, like most of the prisoners, Atwater's health was still quite fragile. Fearing that he would not survive this latest prison experience, Clara Barton again intervened, and Atwater was released. His list of Andersonville dead was finally published in the *New York Tribune* in 1866.

Boate probably hoped that by revealing Wirz's role in stopping the raiders, he might improve the public's perception of Henry Wirz and help the man get a fair trial—Wirz's guilt seems to have been a foregone conclusion even before his trial. Some witnesses perjured themselves and had never actually been at Andersonville, and the trial judges did not allow some witnesses for the defense to testify.

There's no record of a prisoner named "Charles Curtis" ever taking the Oath of Allegiance—Nor is there any record of an Oath of Allegiance taken by a man named Rickson, Wrixon, or Ritson.

• 3 •

Beyond John McElroy

It's not possible to talk about the Andersonville raiders without discussing John McElroy, a private with the 16th Illinois Cavalry, Company L, and a prisoner of war who wrote a best-selling memoir about his wartime experiences. McElroy enlisted as a teenager in 1863, and was captured near Jonesville, Virginia, in January 1864, along with over 400 other members of his regiment. McElroy spent a month imprisoned in Richmond before being sent to the newly opened Camp Sumter (more commonly referred to as Andersonville Prison) in late February 1864, where he remained until the following October. After the war, McElroy became a newspaper reporter for the *Toledo (Ohio) Blade*, eventually becoming that publication's editor. What began as a short series of sketches of prison life for the *Blade* and was so well-received that McElroy went on to write a memoir of his experiences as a POW, titled *Andersonville, A Story of Rebel Military Prisons*, with the subtitle, *Fifteen Months a Guest of the So-Called Southern Confederacy: A Private Soldier's Experience*. The book, published in 1879, was an instant best seller and is still in print to this very day.

McElroy's book is one of the definitive books on the subject of Andersonville. Other prisoners wrote memoirs as well, but none caught the public's imagination the way McElroy's did. His prose is eminently readable and exciting, his characterizations are vivid, and his accounts are both dramatic and thrilling. His is the longest, most detailed and most often cited account of the arrest and punishment of the raiders.

This is not to say that McElroy is unbiased. By his own account, he was a part of the "regulators," the self-appointed police and judicial force behind the arrests and punishments. One of his primary purposes in writing his account is to justify the prosecution of the raiders to the reading public.

Another motive was to sell books and newspapers. For an engaging account of the events of late June and early July 1864, John McElroy's is hard to beat. But just how well does his account hold up?

Although McElroy places the raiders as a key force within the prison's walls, the story of their rise and fall within the prison stockade is just a very small incident in the history of Camp Sumter. The execution of the raiders accounts for just six deaths out of nearly 13,000, and, if one defines the execution as the end of their story, they were only active for about four months out of the prison's 14 months as a functioning prisoner-of-war camp. Crime inside the prison rose drastically beginning on May 1, 1864, with the arrival of the "Plymouth Pilgrims," a large contingent of prisoners captured at the Battle of Plymouth, North Carolina. Many of these men arrived at the stockade having just received three months back pay and their enlistment bounties, which they could keep as part of their terms of surrender. This new influx of wealth into the prison stockade brought in by the 2,364 men captured at Plymouth raised the stakes for those already willing to commit crimes inside the prison, and attacks became more frequent, more brazen, and more violent. But the time between the arrival of this influx of wealth and the arrest of the raiders was a mere two months. In terms of the number of people affected, the number of deaths, and the duration of the raiders' activity, the raiders' story makes up only a small part of the history of Camp Sumter.

It's much more interesting to read about heartless men stealing from their fellow prisoners and being caught and punished than it is to read about men slowly starving, suffering lingering deaths from scurvy or chronic diarrhea, or simply going through the motions of trying to survive day by day. John McElroy's book, which told the story in a thrilling fashion, captured the imagination of the reading public. His version of all things Andersonville was widely accepted as the authoritative version. Even in the writing of the book you are now reading, whenever the author would contact a potential source of information, almost invariably the answer would come back with some variation of "According to John McElroy . . ."

Exactly how large a threat were the raiders? Trying to establish the number of raiders actively preying on their fellow prisoners, McElroy tells us, "We never estimated that the raiding N'Yaarkers, with their spies and other accomplices, exceeded five hundred." It's worth noting that in coming up with this figure, McElroy is also assigning "spies and other accomplices" to the number. Indeed, there were instances when a prisoner would be accused and punished by the other prisoners for offenses other than raiding, such as revealing information on tunnels to the Rebel authorities in exchange for extra rations or tobacco or other forms of payment. Although both raiders and informants were contemptible according to the prison's moral code, it can't automatically be assumed that all "spies" were raiders, and therefore 500 is likely inflated. In fact, it is more than twice as high as almost all other prisoners' estimates as to the number of raiders.

In comparison to McElroy's estimate, Sergeant Leroy L. Key, who McElroy identifies as the chief organizer of the arrests and executions, said in an 1864 interview, "'Raiders' numbered, about the 20th of June, 150 or 200." Eugene Forbes wrote in his diary the day the arrests began that, "About 50 were taken outside," and added that more were arrested the following day. John L. Hoster wrote in his diary that Henry Wirz put the number much lower still, "He remarked that it was no more than right that we should suffer if we allowed 50 men to rule 26,000." Most of the prisoners, writing about the arrests of suspected raiders at the end of the first day, mentioned numbers between 50 and 120. McElroy's estimate is likely too high.

McElroy also exaggerates the number of bands of raiders that were at large in the camp, attributing a separate group of cutthroats and thieves to most of the six men hanged, omitting only Sullivan, Muir, and Rickson or Ritson, although these might also be implied by his use of the term "etc." "We now called them 'Raiders' and the most prominent and best known of the bands were called by the names of their ruffian leaders, as 'Mosby's Raiders,' 'Curtis's Raiders,' 'Delaney's Raiders,' 'Sarsfield's Raiders,' 'Collins's Raiders,' etc." This is contradicted by the transcript of the raiders' trial in the *Sunday Mercury*, which relates testimony that shows that at least four of the six men who were executed (Delaney, Sarsfield, Sullivan, and Munn) worked together in a small group rather than each one having a band of his own. Even if the *Mercury* article is in error, McElroy mentions Collins's raiders and Mosby's raiders as being two separate entities; however Collins and Mosby are the same person, a fact McElroy acknowledges later when he mentions "Collins, alias Mosby." Prior to McElroy's book, the prisoners all seem to consider the raiders to be part of a single gang, and many of them refer to it as "Mosby's Gang" or "Mosby's Raiders."

How great a threat the raiders posed to the general population also seems to be exaggerated. Even if McElroy's assessment of the number of raiders was accurate, and the number of raiders within the camp stood at approximately 500, this is still a very small number compared with the general prison population. There were approximately 26,000 prisoners held at Andersonville when the raiders were arrested and hanged, so if there were 500 raiders, the ratio of prisoners to raiders is approximately 52 prisoners for every raider. Given that the prisoners were turned into the stockade without guns, the only weapons that would have been available to the prisoners would have been knives, razors, makeshift clubs, and brass knuckles. For this reason, the raiders tended to single out victims who were alone; it's also the reason the raiders frequently worked in small groups. The raiders did not live scattered among the general population, but instead clustered in the southwest corner of the stockade, protected, to some extent by the prison walls on two sides, and the swampy, filth infested creek on a third. For both criminals and victims, having allies to watch your back increased your chances of survival. The raiders preyed on the weak and the solitary. The idea that, outnumbered 52 to 1, they dominated the prison population simply does not make sense.

McElroy asserts that the raiders were not afraid to commit murder in the commission of their crimes, and he states that they did so quite often. He writes, "If the victim resisted, there was always sufficient force on hand to conquer him, and not seldom his life paid the penalty of his contumacy. I have known as many as three of these to be killed in a night, and their bodies—with throats cut, or skulls crushed in—be found in the morning among the dead at the gates." This dreadful assertion, however, is not substantiated by the prison's Register of Deaths, which was kept by Union clerks at the prison's Dead House, where bodies were stored while awaiting burial. Looking at the death listings for the period when the raiders were at their peak, from the arrival of the wealthy "Plymouth Pilgrims" in early May until the day the arrests began on June 29, not a single cause of death is listed as slit throat or skull fracture, and only two prisoners—both African American—are listed as having died of "unknown" causes. Nor are there any prisoners during this period who are reported to have died of wounds. McElroy's assertion of one to three deaths a night from the raiders' attacks simply cannot be substantiated by prison records.

Nor were the regulators the only attempt to quell the raiders, as McElroy implies. Diarists frequently mentioned raiders being captured and punished by the other prisoners. Robert Kellogg wrote in his 1865 memoir that, "It was not infrequent that one of the camp thieves or 'raiders' would be arrested in his prowling operations at night, carried to the brook, to endure the process of 'gagging' and 'bucking,' having one side of his head shaved, and this not being considered sufficient punishment, he would finally be thrown into the swamp, there to consider the propriety of discontinuing his 'raids' for a season."

Memoirist Warren Lee Goss reported the organization of an earlier attempt at formal prison justice under the auspices of a man he identified as "Big Pete," a nickname for Peter Aubrey of the 2nd Massachusetts Heavy Artillery. According to Goss, "Big Pete . . . became the terror of evildoers. Pete exhibited so much courage . . . and subsequently so much good sense and natural judgement that he gradually became the administrative power for punishment of offenses committed. He performed for us the services of shaving, and in a dignified, impartial manner gave the culprit a trial—hearing both sides before pronouncing judgement and inflicting punishment. . . . Peter was an uneducated Canadian—a man of gigantic stature and great physical strength, of an indomitable good will, great good nature, and with innate ideas of justice . . . I never knew him to make a wrong decision." Goss states that Big Pete reportedly established his own "strong police force" within the stockade with himself as chief of police. According to Goss's account, while investigating the disappearance of one of the prisoners, a murdered body was found buried beneath his empty tent, its throat cut. Big Pete's police force are the ones who "proceeded to the shelter of several notorious thieves and bad characters of the prison and arrested them . . . the supposed murderers, some fifteen in number were arrested. . . . Six of the men were pronounced guilty of murder." Goss stops short, however, of saying that Big Pete and his men conducted the execution, nor does he ever mention Leroy Key or the regulators. Although this description of a body being discovered differs from the version given in contemporary diaries, it should be remembered that Goss was writing four years after the prison closed.

McElroy identifies the six men who were executed by name and by regiment, but then goes on to say, "These names and regiments are of little consequence, however as I believe all the rascals were professional bounty-jumpers, and did not belong to any regiment longer than they could find an opportunity to desert and join another." This assertion does not stand up under scrutiny. William Collins served with the 88th Pennsylvania for two and a half years, fought, was wounded, and captured at the Second Battle of Manassas; paroled, he eventually rejoined his regiment and fought at Chancellorsville and Gettysburg where he was promoted to corporal. James Sarsfield, mistakenly assigned by McElroy to the 144th New York, was with the 140th New York for eight months, and was apparently a good enough soldier that his regiment never listed him as a deserter, but rather "missing in action" following the Battle of the Wilderness. Sarsfield was kept on the company roles after his capture, listed as being on Detached Service as a Prisoner of War. The real Charles Curtis of the 5th Rhode Island Heavy Artillery (not the man hung using his name) stayed with his regiment for seventeen months before deserting. Nor does McElroy's assertion of bounty jumping hold up for the two sailors, Ritson and Muir (a.k.a. Rickson and Munn). From the time William Ritson enlisted in the Navy in May 1861 until he was captured in September 1863, 27 months had passed. Andrew Muir had finished his year of enlistment and was waiting for transportation home when the USS *Water Witch* was captured in June 1864. It's unlikely that men would have joined the Navy with the intention of deserting because it's very hard to desert when you're on a ship at sea. Taken altogether, the six men executed had served an average of just over a year before being taken prisoner. In addition, Delaney and Sarsfield were drafted, which suggests that they did not enlist voluntarily and so no bounty would have been involved. John Sullivan (who came from the 76th New York rather than the 72nd as McElroy claimed) likely was a bounty jumper, but McElroy's assertion that all six names were fake and that the executed men were all bounty jumpers does not hold up under scrutiny.

To be fair, McElroy's assertions about the men he professed to have hung may have been an honest mistake; he may have been provided with inaccurate information or simply been repeating the rumors that had circulated around the camp, as rumors always did. But a closer reading of his account of the arrests and the executions of the raiders reveals more problems.

McElroy gives much of the credit for the formulation of the regulators and the prosecution of the raiders to Sergeant Leroy L. Key, of the 16th Illinois Cavalry, the same regiment McElroy himself belonged to, although they were assigned to different companies. In 1864, Key gave a statement to the Christian Commission, detailing the events that led up to the execution. This interview was given to the press by the Christian Commission and published in a variety of newspapers as early as November 1864. Although 15 years pass between Key's recounting of events and McElroy's, one would expect that the two versions would be essentially the same. The particulars, however, vary.

Both agree that Key was accosted by some of the raiders once his plans to organize an ad hoc police force became known. According to McElroy, "information as to [Key's] scheme reached the Raiders. It was debated at their headquarters and decided there that Key must be killed. Three men were selected to do this work. They called on Key, at dusk, on the evening of the second of July. In response to their inquiries, he came out of the blanket-covered hole on the hillside that he called his tent. They told him what they had heard and asked him if it was true. He said it was. One of them drew a knife, and the other two, 'billies' [i.e., clubs] to attack him. But, anticipating trouble, Key had procured a revolver which one of the Pilgrims had brought in his knapsack and drawing this, he drove them off without firing a shot."

McElroy's memory appears to be faulty with regards to the dates. According to the diaries kept by prisoners at the time, the roundup of the raiders began on June 29, and the following day, Eugene Forbes wrote that one of them had been tried and sentenced to death, with a wide-scale roundup of the raiders continuing for several days thereafter. Therefore, by July 2 the raiders would have been either arrested or in hiding. Nor does it seem likely that any raiders might have escaped the June 29 and 30 roundup and openly approached Key's tent if the incident truly occurred on the second of July.

Key's version of the same incident differs on several key points: "Before the organization [of the regulators] was complete, I was one day walking on the north side of the camp, when I saw ahead of me the chief of the raiders [Curtis], and in pursuit of me five men on the 'double quick,' with knives in their hands. The chief slapped me on the shoulder and turned me round, saying to me, 'I understand that you are getting up a band to clear out the Irish.' I replied, 'The report is false and you are mistaken.' 'Well, you are getting up a band for some purpose; what is it for, if not to clean out the Irish?' Meanwhile the five men closed around us, forming a ring around CURTIS and myself.

"He again demanded to know the object of the band. Said I to him, boldly, 'we are organizing a band to clean out the "raiders," and if you are one of them we intend to clean you out.' They did not proceed to violence, but the leader put his knife into his left hand and with his right hand offered to shake hands with me. They then let me go."

The intent of the raiders in each of these incidents is quite different; in McElroy's version, they are out to kill Key, who fends them off with showing a gun, whereas, according to Key, a small group of raiders led by Curtis threaten him with knives when they suppose he is after the Irish, but shake his hand and let him go when he tells them he was going after the raiders. Since Key's account was written much sooner after the event described, and Key was writing about his own, personal experiences rather than giving a secondhand account, Key's version is given more credibility than McElroy's. One gets the sense that, outnumbered six to one and surrounded by armed men while Key himself apparently held no weapon, if Curtis and his companions had wanted to murder Key, they easily could have. Therefore, McElroy's version, where the raiders wanted to murder Key to stop his prosecution of them, simply does not hold up.

Which raises the question of embellishment in other aspects of the story. McElroy writes about the day in which the regulators set out to arrest the raiders, describing it as a desperate battle between two organized lines of combatants. It reads like a turf war between two gangs:

> When all was ready we moved down upon the Big Tent. . . . The prison was as silent as a graveyard. As we approached, the Raiders massed themselves in a strong, heavy line, with the center, against which our advance was moving, held by the most redoubtable of their leaders. How many there were of them could not be told, as it was impossible to say where their line ended and the mass of spectators began. They could not themselves tell, as the attitude of a large portion of the spectators would be determined by which way the battle went.
>
> Not a blow was struck until the lines came close together. Then the Raider center launched itself forward against ours, and grappled savagely with the leading Regulators. For an instant—it seemed an hour—the struggle was desperate.

While this is a thrilling and dramatic account of the struggle between good and evil, by all earlier accounts, and according to the prison's own records, this isn't what happened. McElroy goes on to state that as the prison guards looked on "with loaded guns. The cannon in the works were slotted, the fuses thrust into the touch-holes and the men stood with lanyards in hand, ready to mow down everybody, at any instant. . . . There were at least fifteen thousand perhaps twenty thousand—men packed together on the back, and every eye was turned on us. . . . It was as if the whole broad hillside was paved or thatched with human countenances." Surprisingly, not a single diarist or early memoirist mentions such a battle, a startling omission if there were, indeed 15,000 to 20,000 witnesses as McElroy claims. Not only is there no contemporary record of such a battle, but the men who wrote about the arrests at the time or in memoirs written in the 1860s all reported that the raiders were actually captured by prisoners backed up by prison guards, although John McElroy vehemently denied that the Confederate prison officials played any role in the downfall of the raiders.

McElroy is adamant that the Confederates played no role in the seeking out and arresting of the troublemakers, writing, "The Rebels never made the slightest attempt to maintain order in the prison. . . . I doubt if they would have interfered had one-half of us killed and eaten the other half." He claims that Leroy Key was the one who called the shots in forming the regulators and exercising his own brand of prison justice. "[Key] informed Wirz what he proposed doing, so that any unusual commotion within the stockade might not be mistaken for an attempt upon the stockade, and made the excuse for opening with the artillery. Wirz, who happened to be in a complaisant humor, approved of the design, and allowed him the use of the enclosure of the North Gate to confine his prisoners in."

McElroy contradicts this idea that the Confederates were aware of this plan a few pages later, saying "The Rebels learned through their spies that something unusual was going on inside." In fact, many of the prisoners who wrote about the events when they occurred or within a year or two later stated that the prison officials not only knew about the attempt to prosecute the thieves and robbers, but actually initiated it and furnished the manpower to achieve it. Prisoner Eugene Forbes, who would die in another prison camp after leaving Andersonville wrote in his diary, "[Dowd, a prisoner who'd been robbed and assaulted by a pack of raiders] was badly cut up, but finally got away and reached the gate, and reported to Capt. Wurtz [*sic*], who came up behind him and demanded that the robbers should be given up, under penalty of no rations for a week; in a short time, a guard came in, and took eight men from a tent near the dead line of our side . . . Capt. Wurtz [*sic*] deserves credit for his prompt action in the matter, and will probably be successful in checking the operations of these thieving scoundrels." The following day, Forbes added, "(I) t is an act of justice on the part of the Confederate authorities which the men have not expected, they supposing that no notice would be taken of their com-plaints; but just the reverse has been the case, and we now feel secure from the attacks of daylight and midnight murderers; the issuing of rations was promptly commenced as soon as the men known as ring leaders were captured." Robert Kellogg, in his prison memoir published the following year wrote, "The Rebel Quartermaster, rebel sergeants and guard, went into the prison and, piloted by a notorious character known as 'Limber Jim' and his comrades, soon ferreted out the infamous scoundrels." Memoirist Henry Davidson wrote in 1866 that "at the request of [the prisoners], a force of Confederate soldiers was sent into the prison and eight-six men were arrested, taken out and placed under a strong guard." Prisoner Warren Lee Goss, in his 1866 prison memoir goes as far as to say, "I and many others of the prison were grateful to Henry Wirz for the privilege afforded us, to enable us to give the accused a fair, impartial trial."

Furthermore, McElroy totally omits the fact that the regulators were operating with not only the consent of Henry Wirz, but were supported by a general order issued by Wirz's superior, General John Winder. On June 30, the day after the arrests of the raiders began, Winder issued the following order:

> *General Orders No. 57, Camp Sumter, Andersonville, Georgia, June 30, 1864*
> *A gang of evil-disposed persons among the prisoners of war at this post have banded together for the purpose of assaulting, murdering, and robbing their fellow-prisoners, and having already committed all of these deeds, it becomes necessary to adopt measures to protect the lives and property of these men, and in order that this may be accomplished, the well-disposed prisoners may and they are hereby authorized to establish a court among themselves for the trial and punishment of such offenders. On such trials, the charges will be distinctly made with specifications setting for the time and place, copy of which will be furnished the accused. The whole proceedings will be properly kept in writing, all of the testimony will be fairly written out as nearly in the words of the witnesses as possible. The proceedings, findings, and sentence in each case will be sent to the commanding officer for record, and if found in order and proper, the sentence will be ordered for execution. By order of Brig. Gen. John H. Winder, W. S. Winder, Assistant Adjutant General.*

Again and again, McElroy's assertion that the Confederate authorities played no role in the downfall of the raiders is refuted, both by the other prisoners and historical records. He states that not only were the Rebels unhelpful, but he posits that the prison officials essentially punished the pris-oners for their efforts to quell the raiders. Once the regulators captured the raiders, McElroy writes. "We were very tired, and very hungry. The time for drawing rations had arrived. Wagons containing bread and mush had driven to the gates, but Wirz would not allow these to be opened, lest in the excited condition of the men an attempt might be made to carry them. Key ordered operations to cease, that Wirz might be re-assured and let the rations enter. It was in vain. Wirz was thoroughly scared. The wagons stood out in the hot sun until the mush fermented and soured, and had to be thrown away, while we went rationless to bed, and rose the next day with more than usually empty stomachs to goad us to our work."

Captain Wirz did, in fact, order rations to be withheld on June 29, the day that the arrests of the raiders began, but the order was not made out of fear that the excited prisoners might rush the gates when they were opened to let the food wagons in, but rather to pressure the prisoners into giving up the raiders. Leroy Key, the alleged organizer of the regulators, reported that, "The day after CURTIS stopped me in the street, word came that no more rations would be sent into camp until we delivered up the raiders into the hands of the rebel authorities." Prisoner Samuel Grosvenor, who would be killed on the way home from prison when the ship he was sailing on, the *Massachusetts*, collided with another ship in the Potomac River, wrote in his diary, "Capt. Wirtz ... orders no ... more rations til the raiders were brought out. The men went at it with a zest." Several other prisoners' accounts also confirm that Wirz stopped the issuing of rations only as a way of increasing the pressure on the prisoner to give up the raiders, and that the issuing of rations recommenced as soon as Wirz felt he had the men he wanted.

McElroy also fails to mention that, according to several sources, Henry Wirz assisted in the selection of the jurors. Leroy Key reported, "Capt. WERZ [*sic*] selected twenty-four Sergeants from those that knew most of the matters in dispute, and out of this number appointed twelve jurymen and a Judge-Advocate." This is confirmed by prisoner Henry Davidson, "Capt. Wirz summoned all the Sergeants of detachments and divisions, laid the matter before them, and proposed that they request each of their respective divisions to select one man to represent it. This was accordingly done, when these representatives chose twelve of the most unprejudiced from among the men in the stockade to act as a jury." In his June 29 entry, prisoner Samuel Grosvenor wrote in his diary, "Were called out in the forenoon to Capt. Wirtz's Quarters to choose a jury to the trial of the raiders at General Order from Gen. Winder set for the evil dispositions of such persons."

McElroy is so intent in excluding the prison officials from getting any credit in helping to stop the raiders' crime spree that he even goes so far as to add a line to the short speech given by Henry Wirz as he handed the condemned men over for execution. Almost all prior accounts to McElroy's were like the version related in Robert Kellogg's book: "These men have been tried and convicted by their own fellows, and I now return them to you in as good condition as I received them. You can now do with them as your reason, justice and mercy dictates. And may God protect both you and them."

McElroy takes the essence of this speech, but translates it into a sort of "pigeon English":

"Brizners, I return to you dose men so goot as I got dem. You haf tried dem yourselves, and found dem guilty. I haf had notting to do wit it. I vash my hands of eferyting connected wit dem. Do wit dem as you like, and may Gott haf mercy on you and on dem. Garts, about face! Vorywarts, march!"

No prior account of Wirz's speech as he hands over the raiders contains any statement similar to "I haf had notting to do wit it." McElroy appears to have inserted this line to support his assertion that the prison officials had nothing to do with the suppression of the raiders. Again and again, McElroy does everything he can to cast the Rebels and the raiders as villains, and the regulators and himself as the heroes.

McElroy's use of dialect is interesting as well. McElroy is only the second writer to relate Wirz's speech as a dialect, although many writers who followed copied his example. McElroy appears to be playing on the readers' prejudices and has a decided bias against both Wirz and the men he describes as "N'Yaarkers." Take, for example, his first description of Wirz:

He was an undersized, fidgety man, with an insignificant face, and a mouth that protruded like a rabbit's. His bright little eyes, like those of a squirrel or a rat, assisted in giving his countenance a look of kinship to the family of rodent animals—a genus which lives by stealth and cunning, subsisting on that which it can steal away from stronger and braver creatures. He was dressed in a pair of gray trousers, with the other part of his body covered in a calico garment, like that which small boys used to wear, called "waists." This was fastened to the pantaloons by buttons, precisely as was the custom with garments of boys struggling with the orthography of words in two syllables. Upon his head was perched a little gray cap. Sticking in his belt, and fastened to his wrist by strap two or three feet long, was one of those formidable looking, but harmless English revolvers that have ten barrels around the edge of the cylinder, and fire a musket ball from the center. The wearer of this composite costume, and bearer of this amateur arsenal, stepped nervously about and sputtered volubly in very broken English.

McElroy suffers from an intense xenophobia and appears to view anybody who is not a white Midwesterner with contempt. He emphasizes Wirz's foreignness through his speech patterns, and compares him to a rodent, a slow learner, a child, a dandy, and an "amateur"—and that's just in his introductory paragraph about Henry Wirz. Xenophobia may well have played a role in the prejudices that led to Wirz being the only Confederate officer to be executed for war crimes because he was an immigrant rather than a native-born American. This general prejudice against foreigners likely played a part in the execution of the raiders, since five of the six men hung as raiders were Roman Catholic, and likely, Irish, rather than Protestants of Anglo-Saxon descent. McElroy's apparent dislike of Wirz as a foreigner is rivaled only by his description of the men he refers to as "N'Yaakers."

We now formed an acquaintance with a species of human vermin that united with the Rebels, cold, hunger, lice, and the oppression of distraint, to leave nothing undone that could add to the miseries of our prison life.

There were the fledglings of the slums and dives of New York—graduates of that metropolitan sink of iniquity where the rogues and criminals of the whole world meet for mutual instruction in vice.

They were men who, as a rule, had never known a day of honesty and cleanliness in their misspent lives; whose fathers, brother, and constant companions were roughs, malefactors and felons; whose mothers, wives and sisters were prostitutes, procuresses and thieves; men who had from infancy lived in an atmosphere of sin, until it saturated every fiber of their being as a dweller in a jungle imbibes malaria every one of his, millions of pores, until his very marrow is surcharged with it. They included representatives from all nationalities, and their descendants, but the English and Irish elements predominated. They had as argot peculiar to themselves. It was partly made up on the "flash" language of the London thieves, amplified and enriched by the cant vocabulary and the jargon of crime of every European tongue. They spoke it with a peculiar accent and intonation that made them instantly recognizable from the roughs of other cities. They called themselves "N'Yaarkers"; we came to know them as Raiders.

Here, again, McElroy emphasizes the foreignness of the men he wishes to portray as the villains of his story, and just in case his readers had no prejudices against the residents of New York City, he carefully explains that they were sons of felons and whores who were sinful to the very marrow of their bones. Although he appears to be equating all six raiders with the slums of New York City, only Sarsfield and Muir were enlisted in that metropolis. Sarsfield enlisted in Brooklyn, and, having been born in Ireland was likely a recent immigrant, while Muir was a professional seaman who claimed to have been born in England, although his auburn hair and Catholic religion suggest that he may have been Irish. It's possible that Muir was not an American citizen, but a sailor who was lured to enlist in the US Navy by the promise of potential prize money and he happened to enlist in New York simply because it was the closest port of call when he decided to enlist.

Besides Muir and Sarsfield, only Sullivan enlisted in New York State, signing on in Rochester, approximately 300 miles away from New York City. Of the others, Patrick Delaney enlisted in Reading, Pennsylvania, while Collins and Ritson signed on in Philadelphia. Charles Curtis of the Fifth Rhode Island Heavy Artillery's records indicate that he was a Canadian and that he enlisted in Rhode Island. McElroy's generalization that all the raiders were from the crime-ridden slums of New York City appears to be an attempt to intentionally play on his readers' Midwestern stereotypes of the New York City hoodlums. Because he listed the regiments of the condemned, he had to have known that only two of the condemned men, Sarsfield and Sullivan, were from New York regiments.

McElroy's account of the actual execution is both detailed and thrilling, but as with the confrontation scene between Curtis and Key, McElroy's version differs significantly from the details Key himself reported.

Key portrays Curtis as a desperate man who pleads for mercy.

Most of the criminals were Roman Catholics, and a Priest came in to attend them. He requested us to have mercy upon the men, and earnestly plead for them; and after he had got through CURTIS asked me to spare him as he had never done me any harm. I told him it was not for me to pardon him, I was appointed to see that the men were hung; but if he had anything to say, I would hear his confession on the scaffold. Then he said he would not stand it, and made a break for the lines, and ran about the camp until he was recaptured. He was brought back perfectly exhausted.

While CURTIS was absent, the other criminals were taken on to the scaffold, and the ropes placed around their necks, the executioners standing behind them. Immediately after CURTIS was brought back, he was delivered to the executioner and taken on to the scaffold likewise. No confessions were made, but the men disposed of their property, and CURTIS gave his watch to the priest, Father WHALEN.

McElroy, on the other hand, describes a profane, unrepentant man who puts up a "superhuman effort" to escape his fate. He creates an extended account, portraying not only Curtis's actions, but also those of the key players around him, including Limber Jim, Patrick Delaney, Henry Wirz, and John McElroy himself:

Curtis turned from the crowd with desperation convulsing his features. Tearing off the broad-brimmed hat which he wore, he flung it on the ground with the exclamation:

"By God, I'll die this way first!" and, drawing his head down and folding his arms about it, he dashed forward for the center of my company, like a great stone hurled from a catapult.

"Egypt" and I saw where he was going to strike, and ran down the line to help stop him. As he came up we rained blows on his head with our clubs, but so many of us struck at him at once that we broke each other's clubs to pieces, and only knocked him on his knees. He rose with an almost superhuman effort, and plunged into the mass beyond.

The excitement almost became delirium. For an instant I feared that everything was gone to ruin. "Egypt" and I strained every energy to restore our lines,

before the break could be taken advantage of by the others. Our boys behaved
splendidly, standing firm, and in a few seconds the line was restored.

McElroy also uses the execution to create another example of Henry Wirz's supposed cowardice and callous disregard for the welfare of the prisoners. As he did with the great battle that was supposedly witnessed by 15,000 to 20,000 men, not one of whom ever mentioned it in their diaries, McElroy creates another scene that is remarkable not only for its lack of corroboration, but also its defiance of both the laws of physics and logic:

> *When Wirz saw the commotion* [surrounding Curtis's attempt to flee] *he was panic-stricken with fear that the long-dreaded assault on the Stockade had begun. He ran down from the headquarter steps to the Captain of the battery, shrieking:*
> *"Fire! fire! fire!"*
> *The Captain, not being a fool, could see that the rush was not towards the Stockade, but away from it, and he refrained from giving the order.*
> *But the spectators who had gotten before the guns, heard Wirz's excited yell, and remembering the consequences to themselves should the artillery be discharged, became frenzied with fear, and screamed, and fell down over and trampled upon each other in endeavoring to get away. The guards on that side of the Stockade ran down in a panic, and the ten thousand prisoners immediately around us, expecting no less than that the next instant we would be swept with grape and canister, stampeded tumultuously. There were quite a number of wells right around us, and all of these were filled full of men that fell into them as the crowd rushed away. Many had legs and arms broken, and I have no doubt that several were killed.*
> *It was the stormiest five minutes that I ever saw.*

Compare this to Warren Lee Goss's 1867 memoir, which states: "There was never a hanging conducted in a more orderly manner. There was no clamor of voices, but in silence and decorum befitting such a scene, thirty thousand men were its witness." Goss acknowledges the attempt to flee, but makes no mention of the confusion and danger, both to the prisoners and civilian onlookers, that McElroy describes. Nor does any writer, either in a diary or early memoir, mention limbs being broken or men being killed in the tumult surrounding Curtis's break for freedom, although there are two "unknown" men listed in the Register of Deaths who died that day with no cause of death given.

McElroy's assertion that Wirz ordered the guards to open fire on the prisoners is also suspect. Not only is such an occurrence missing from every contemporary or near-contemporary account of the execution, but it's logistically impossible given the circumstances that McElroy himself outlines. He claims that Wirz "Ran down from the headquarter steps" to order the captain of the battery to fire. This means that Wirz was not actually inside the 15-foot-tall walls of the stockade at the time, making it questionable as to how McElroy would have been able to see him, particularly if McElroy was struggling with Egypt to restore the perimeter around the gallows following Curtis's bolt. Furthermore, Wirz's headquarters was located inside the Star Fort, several dozen yards away from the southwest corner of the stockade. Given this distance and that "the din was so overpowering" that the men pursuing Curtis could not hear McElroy, then how could McElroy possibly pick out the voice of a single man shouting from outside the stockade? It also seems unlikely that McElroy could have heard Limber Jim "hiss" his threat to disembowel Patrick Delaney when Curtis bolted. There's just no way that McElroy could have picked out these two voices from the thousands of voices shouting all around him, which suggests that, like the attempted murder of Leroy Key and the purported battle between the raiders and the regulators, McElroy is making events up for the sake of his story.

Other details from McElroy's version of accounts also don't hold up under scrutiny. He writes that Limber Jim "[p]icked [Collins] up like a baby and carried him to the scaffold and handed him up" after the first, failed attempt at hanging him, which seems unlikely given that Collins was six feet tall, by some accounts weighed 200 pounds and was, in all probability, struggling. McElroy also apparently invents a palatable motive to explain Jim's single-minded determination to see Collins hung, writing about "Mosby, a large, powerful, raw-boned man, one of the worst in the lot . . . who, among other crimes, had killed Limber Jim's brother." Without knowing Limber Jim's last name, it's impossible to determine he even had a brother, but other sources attribute a different motive. Prisoner John L. Hoster wrote in his diary that, "[Collins] offered Lumber Jim $1000 to save his life. Lumber Jim replied, 'You followed me for my money, I'm now following you for your life.' He then took him up on the scaffold adjusted the rope and hood—then jerked the scaffold from under him." Hoster's account suggests that one of the regulators, at least, was motivated by vengeance.

McElroy ends his execution scene with two of the raiders, Dick Allen and Pete Donnelly, kneeling and wiping the froth off of Patrick Delaney's lips, and swearing "vengeance against those who had done him to death." It's another thrilling moment in an exciting read, but also a highly unlikely one. Soon after the raiders had been rounded up and captured on June 29, those not chosen to be tried were forced to run through a gauntlet of angry prisoners who beat them, reportedly, in some cases, to death. It would have been foolish in the extreme for any man in that place and time to openly align himself with the raiders, let alone openly swear vengeance while the gallows were a few feet away. Furthermore, there's some evidence that Dick Allen, at least, had already been tried, convicted, and punished. The article in the August 20, 1865, *Sunday Mercury* relates that one "Richard Allen" of the 83rd Pennsylvania—the same regiment which Patrick Delaney had belonged to—had been tried along with the other accused raiders, found guilty of robbery and assault, and sentenced to be handcuffed and shackled during the remainder of his imprisonment. McElroy makes no mention of these men being in chains. Although he does earlier state that he himself had arrested Pete Donnelly, he does not follow up with what happened to Donnelly's case after that. If the two had been arrested, tried, and barely escaped the same fate as their six executed comrades, it seems very unlikely, indeed, that they would have been foolish enough to draw further attention to themselves at the scene of the execution—particularly if they were already in chains and unable to flee or defend themselves and surrounded by 26,000 men who had been thirsting for the raiders' blood.

Much of the fame of Andersonville in the years following the Civil War is due to John McElroy's book. Because he was a prisoner at Andersonville, the reading public eagerly embraced his story and accepted it as true. Much of what he says about the careers, arrests, and execution of the men known as raiders, however, is contradicted by other prisoners' accounts, historical records, and in some cases, simple logic. He exaggerates the number of raiders in the camp, denies the role the Confederates played in their downfall, invents scenes that never happened, and refuses to let the facts get in the way of a good story. Although *A Story of Rebel Prisons* can be recommended as an interesting read, as far as the prosecution of the raiders is concerned, it should not be viewed as a reliable one. For that reliable picture, therefore, we need to look to other sources to answer the question, "Who were the Andersonville raiders?"

NOTES ON CHAPTER 3

Where he remained until the following October—After leaving Camp Sumter, McElroy was sent to Savannah and Camp Lawton in Millen, Georgia, before finally being paroled on March 1, 1865.

"Plymouth Pilgrims"—This humorous nickname was used by the POWs captured at Plymouth to describe themselves.

Spies and other accomplices—Robert Kellogg described the extreme difficulty in escaping by tunnel because "Our greatest source of trouble was the fact that there were so many contemptible traitors in our midst, who, for the sake of an extra ration, would betray any attempt to escape on the part of their comrades." Betraying one's comrades for the sake of a reward is not the same thing as robbing and assaulting them directly, although in the eyes of the prisoners, both were equally reprehensible.

In fact, it is more than twice as high as almost all other prisoners' estimates as to the number of raiders—Henry Davidson, in his 1865 memoir *Fourteen Months in Southern Prisons*, also puts the number of raiders at 500. In 1867, in his book *At Andersonville: A Narrative of Personal Adventure at Andersonville, Florence, and Charleston Rebel Prisons*, Josiah Brownell estimated the number of raiders to be "about seven hundred strong."

Sergeant Leroy L. Key, who McElroy identifies as the chief organizer of the arrests and executions, said in an 1864 interview, "'Raiders' numbered, about the 20th of June, 150 or 200"—This interview was reportedly recorded by Reverend J. M. Clark of the Christian Commission following Key's return to the North in November 1864. The Christian Commission then relayed the report to a correspondent from the *Boston Journal*, and it appeared on the front page of the *New York Times* at the end of a long article on various aspects of the war on December 11, 1864.

There were approximately 26,000 prisoners—According to the prison's Morning Report, on July 11, 1964, there were 26,464 prisoners within the prison stockade that day, with another 1,517 in the prison hospital, making an official total of 27.981 prisoners.

Nor were the regulators the only attempt—Several diarists, including Frederic James, Eugene Forbes, and Robert Kellogg, mention encounters in which raiders were punished by mob justice, often involving having their half of their heads and beards shaved and then being paraded around the camp as a warning to others.

"Big Pete"—Because Goss identifies this man as a Canadian-born corporal with the 2nd Massachusetts Heavy Artillery, he can be identified as Peter Aubrey, one of the "Plymouth Pilgrims" captured at Plymouth, North Carolina, on April 20, 1864. Father of at least ten children, his December 6, 1897, death certificate lists his profession as "blacksmith" and his cause of death as "Gangrene of foot resulting from disease and injury contracted and recurred in the War."

According to the diaries kept by prisoners at the time, the roundup of the raiders began on June 29, and the following day; Eugene Forbes wrote that one of them had been tried and sentenced to death—Prisoner John L. Hoster wrote that prison commandant Henry Wirz began the prosecution of the raiders on July 29 and a court-martial was convened "a day or two later." In his diary, reprinted by the Connecticut Historical Society, Charles Lee reported on the first of July that four or five of the raiders had already been sentenced to be hung. James Vance of the 5th US Cavalry, Company M, wrote in his diary on July 1 that three men had been sentenced to hang; transcripts of his diary are held in the National Prisoner of War Museum Archives at Andersonville and at the Ohio History Connection Library.

The Big Tent—No earlier reference indicates the raiders having one large tent, but McElroy describes a mammoth structure. "Their headquarters was a large, roomy tent, with a circular top, situated on the street leading to the South Gate, and capable of accommodating from seventy-five to one hundred men." The existence of such a tent is not supported by any contemporary source. Robert Kellogg, George Robbins, Charles Lee, William T. Peabody, and Harmon Anderson specifically refer to the raiders' "tents," plural, in their diaries.

McElroy is only the second writer to relate Wirz's speech as a dialect—Early memoirist William Pitt also used a dialect in his 1865 memoir when relating Wirz's gallows speech: "Now poys you have tried these men by a jury of your own men, and a schudge of your own choosing, now you do schust what you please mit dem."

Xenophobia may well have played a role in the prejudices that led to Wirz being the only Confederate officer to be executed for war crimes because he was an immigrant rather than a native-born American—Wirz's superior officer at the prison camp, General John Winder, had died on February 7, 1865, just two months prior to the end of the war, and thus could not be prosecuted.

This general prejudice against foreigners likely played a part in the execution of the raiders, since five of the six men hung as raiders were Roman Catholic, and in all likelihood, Irish, rather than Protestants of Anglo-Saxon descent—Father Peter Whelan, one of the Roman Catholic priests who visited the prison daily, testified at Wirz's trial that five of the six raiders were Roman Catholics. Collins, who had reportedly been born in England, was likely the lone non-Catholic in the group. Sarsfield, Sullivan, and Delaney listed "Ireland" as their place of birth.

Compare this to Warren Lee Goss's 1867 memoir—Goss's book was titled *The Soldier's Story of His Captivity*. Goss's book should also be viewed critically, as he places the date of execution as July 12, rather than July 11, and combines Collins's failed hanging with Curtis's escape attempt, saying that "five of the prisoners hung by their necks, swaying in the air; the sixth . . . broke the rope about his neck, gained his feet, and forced his way through the police and crows, ran swiftly, was pursued, beaten over the head and recaptured."

Although there are two "unknown" men listed in the Register of Deaths who died that day with no cause of death given—These two deaths are numbers 3,171 and 3,186, the deaths for July 11. Probably because the hanging happened late in the day, the register lists the raiders' deaths on July 12, and two more unknown dead, numbers 3221 and 3229, were listed in the register on July 12. No cause of death is listed for any of the unknown men.

Collins was six feet tall, by some accounts weighed two hundred pounds—Former POW T. H. Mann wrote in the July 1890 issue of *Century Magazine*, "The sixth man, who weighed nearly 200 lbs, broke his rope." Collins's compiled military service record variously records his height as being five foot eleven and three quarters to six and a half feet.

Dick Allen and Pete Donnelly—Although records can be found for a prisoner named Richard Allen, who apparently deserted from the 83rd Pennsylvania the same night as (and probably along with) raider Patrick Delaney, no records can be found for a prisoner by the name of Pete Donnelly. McElroy may have misremembered the man's name as he wrote his account 15 years after the event. According to the *Sunday Mercury* account of the trial, there was a prisoner named Thomas F. O'Connell, of the 9th Maryland, who was tried along with Richard Allen, and "The jury returned a verdict finding Richard Allen and Thomas F. O'Connell guilty of robbery and assault; and they were sentenced to be handcuffed and shackled during their imprisonment." Because of this association, and because, according to the clipping, they are the only two raiders to have received this sentence as a punishment, the possibility exists that the man John McElroy refers to as "Pete Donnelly" may have been Thomas O'Connell. Sergeant Thomas O'Connell of the Ninth Maryland, Company D, enlisted on June 22, 1863. He was captured at Charlestown, Virginia, on October 18, 1863, and was sent to Baltimore to be mustered out on November 29, 1864.

· 4 ·

Patrick Delaney

Known aliases: Patrick Delaney, J. Delaney, P. Delany, P. Delancy, Patrick
Delany, Patric Delana
Regiment: 83rd Pennsylvania Infantry, Company E
Rank: Private
Place of birth: Ireland
Approximate year of birth: 1841
Enrolled: September 10, 1863, Reading, Pennsylvania
How entered military: Drafted
Mustered in: September 16, 1863
Age at time of enlistment: 22
Deserted: October 14, 1863, near Bristoe Station, Virginia
Arrived at Andersonville: March 21, 1864
Assigned Mess at Andersonville: 5th Detachment, 2nd Mess
Approximate age at time of death: 23
Profession: Laborer
Term of enlistment: 3 years
Physical description: 5 feet 8 inches, blue eyes, brown hair, light complexion

WHAT HISTORY TELLS US

*A*ccording to the different sources that mention him, Patrick Delaney is a
man of contradictions.

Several sources for information relating to Patrick Delaney exist, but
some are known to be strongly biased. The best-known source is John
McElroy's book *Andersonville: A Story of Rebel Military Prisons*, which depicts

Delaney as a profane villain. Less commonly known is a book by another former Andersonville POW named James Madison Page, *The True Story of Andersonville Prison: A Defense of Major Henry Wirz*. Although Page wrote from the uncommon perspective of defending Wirz in his 1908 book, he also wrote that he knew Patrick Delaney personally, and had known him for several months, having first met him while both were prisoners at Belle Isle in Virginia. A third, seemingly more objective source of information on Delaney is the *Sunday Mercury* article, which recounts the crimes which led to Delaney's execution.

JOHN McELROY'S ACCOUNT

John McElroy's version of Patrick Delaney seems to be a bundle of contradictions. He is a reprehensible criminal, but shows a certain nobility when he urges one of the condemned men to "show yourself a man and die game." He spends his last few minutes talking over the priest who's praying for him, and yet he asks his fellow prisoners for forgiveness. He makes a move to follow Curtis and attempt to escape his fate, but at the same time "cheerfully" bids his friends good-bye just as he's about to have the noose placed around his neck.

Just as he claimed that each of the soldiers who were hanged were the "leaders" of a band of cutthroat thieves, McElroy assigns a band of ruffians to Delaney's charge, writing that, "Delaney's Raiders," was a group of robbers "about twenty-five strong." Patrick Delaney was accused of attacking a prisoner named Marion Friend, assisted by an unknown number of fellow raiders: "They knocked him down, cut him across the wrist and neck with a razor, and robbed him of his forty dollars." Friend survived and lived to see Delaney hanged.

McElroy tells us that Delaney made an aborted attempt to run when fellow raider Charles Curtis bolted away from the gallows. "Delaney, a brawny Irishman standing next to him, started to follow. He took one step. At the same instant Limber Jim's long legs took three great strides and placed him directly in front of Delaney. Jim's right hand held an enormous bowie-knife, and he raised it above Delaney as he hissed out "If you dare move another step, I'll open you—I'll open you from one end to the other. Delaney stopped."

Delaney is the one doomed man who seems to not be cowed by the situation he finds himself in. "When Curtis finally arrived, he sat back on the ground for a minute or so, to rest, and then, reeking with filth, slowly and painfully climbed the steps. Delaney seemed to think he was suffering as much from fright as anything else, and said to him, "Come on up, now, show yourself a man and die game.""

But McElroy also has Delaney spending his last minutes on earth thinking about his worldly goods instead of his spiritual disposition. "Again the priest resumed his reading, but it had no interest to Delaney, who kept calling out directions to Pete Donnelly, who was standing in the crowd, as to the dispositions to be made of certain bits of stolen property: to give a watch to this one, a ring to another, and so on. Once the priest stopped and said, 'My son, let the things of this earth go, and turn your attention toward those of heaven.' Delaney paid no attention to this admonition."

Yet McElroy also has Delaney, who was a Roman Catholic, seeking absolution, not from the priest, but from his victims.

> *Key pulled a watch from his pocket and said "Two more minutes to talk."*
> *Delaney said cheerfully, "Well, good by, b'ys; if I've hurted any of yez, I hope ye'll fogive me. Shpake up, now, any of yez that I've hurted, and say ye'll forgive me."*
> *We called on Marion Friend, whose throat Delaney had tried to cut three weeks before while robbing him of forty dollars, to come forward, but Friend was not in a forgiving mood, and refused with an oath.*

Delaney was hanged along with the other raiders, but after his body was cut down, it became a sort of relic on which his friends swear an oath. "Pete Donnelly and Dick Allen knelt down and wiped the froth off of Delaney's lips, and swore vengeance against those who had done him to death."

Although McElroy's Delaney is full of apparent contradictions, he seems to meet death calmly, and on his own terms, and that provides him with a sort of dignity that the other doomed men seem to be lacking.

JAMES MADISON PAGE'S ACCOUNT

James Madison Page claimed to have known Patrick Delaney both at Andersonville and at Belle Isle, where they were both held before being transferred to Andersonville. Page's bias is just as strong as McElroy's, but in the opposite direction. Page wrote a 1908 book titled *The True Story of Andersonville Prison: A Defense of Major Henry Wirz*. In it, Page attempts to refute the idea that Wirz was responsible for the prison conditions and blames the conditions on Wirz's superiors (particularly John Winder) and on the US government. It is as biased a document as those declaring Wirz to be "The Demon of Andersonville," however, it's also one of the few positive accounts of any of the raiders. Page writes:

> *One of the most startling developments to me in this trial was the conviction of Pat Delaney of murder. We had been neighbors in our prison life for many*

months, both at Belle Isle and at Andersonville. He was sent from Belle Isle with the same detachment that my comrades were. He was always ready to help others and appeared to take great pleasure in doing some kind act for my comrades and myself. He appeared always to have money and plenty to eat, and he was extremely generous with both. I was under many obligations to him, and I always regarded him as a brave, generous Irishman. A chapter could be written on the generous qualities of this unfortunate man. I sought to save him, but was confronted with overwhelming testimony of his guilt. To me, it looked like a case of "poor dog Tray." ["Poor Dog Tray" is an Irish song about a dog that was faithful to its owner to the point where it starves to death rather than leaving his friend.] *It was agreed beforehand among the regulators that the guilty would have to take their medicine.*

Page states that he managed to talk to Patrick Delaney after his sentence was handed down. According to Page, Delaney professed his innocence, blaming his fate on the others. "After Delaney was sentenced I had a talk with him. Said he, 'Jim, I am innocent. I'll admit that I associated with marauders; that I received money from them because I was hungry and starving. You know I had money but I never assaulted a man or stole a dollar; but here I am about to die. Ah, that is what comes of keeping bad company.'"

As McElroy has Delaney "cheerfully" calling out good-byes during the last few moments of his life, Page also describes an unexpected expression on Delaney's face, "I do not think that Delaney thought the Regulators would take extreme measures, for he smiled as the noose was placed around his neck."

It's difficult to find Page's account credible. His description of Delaney as "kind" and "generous" are at odds with the image of a man who's been tried and convicted of assault and robbery. It seems unlikely that Page would have had access to Delaney or any of the other men after the trial because the accused were held outside the stockade from the time of their arrests, and the condemned men were apparently all held in stocks outside the stockade from the time they were convicted until the time they were hanged. It also seems unlikely that the other raiders, who have stolen from some of the most vulnerable men in the prison, would have given Delaney money "because I was hungry and starving." There were thousands of starving men all around them, and it seems impossible to believe that the raiders would have shared their bounty with anyone unless they received some benefit in return.

SUNDAY MERCURY ACCOUNT

According to the *Sunday Mercury*, Patrick Delaney was tried on the second day of proceedings, "charged with assaulting with intent to murder (if necessary) and highway robbery." It goes on to say that Delaney worked in conjunction with Sullivan, Sarsfield, and Muir in committing assaults and robberies. The most damning testimony against Delaney was reportedly given by witness Ramiro E. Spicer, of the 76th New York, the same regiment Sullivan came from.

> *R. E. Spicer recalled: [I] saw Sullivan, Delaney and Gilmore rob a man the day before; he resisted, when Sarsfield came up and brandished a knife at him . . . saw Delaney in Sullivan's tent take hold of men, gag them; and take their money away. . . . The next night, between 11 and 12 o'clock, Delaney came to that tent, told one of the men in it to "come here"; the man hesitated. "Are you not coming?" said Delaney; the man was lying down in his tent at the time, he rose, when Delaney struck him on the head with a club having an iron knob in the end; he then struck another of the men in the same tent; Delaney then came to a boy fifteen years of age who was lying outside the same tent and beat him with the wooden end of the stick; saying that if he heard any more noise, he would knock their brains out and "let every man mind his own business"; knew Delaney to shove men into the tent, and rob them; knew him to draw men into the tent by telling them he had something to sell them.*

OTHER ACCOUNTS

Although McElroy and Page offer the most detailed accounts of Patrick Delaney, other prisoners mentioned him in some detail as well.

John Ransom, who didn't let the facts interfere with a good story, claimed that Delaney, standing on the gallows, announced "he would rather be hung than live here as the most of them lived, on their allowance of rations. If allowed to steal, then he would get enough to eat, but as that was stopped had rather hang. Bid all good-bye. Said his name was not Delaney and that no one knew who he really was, therefore his friends would never know his fate, his Andersonville history dying with him." While this is an interesting story, Ransom is so far off with his other stories (he claims Sarsfield was a lawyer when records show him to be a shoemaker, and he has Muir declaring himself a "poor Irish lad" when he was a 22-year-old seaman who gave "England" as his place of birth and who had at least three years of sailing experience when he enlisted) that he must be considered unreliable, and therefore it is doubtful that Delaney ever said this. Also, Delaney was drafted rather than enlisting voluntarily, which suggests that he was likely using his own name rather than an alias.

Prisoner Charles Hopkins kept a diary while in prison and later drew on that diary to write a private memoir at the request of one of his sons in

1890, filling in details missing from the diary with his memories of that awful summer almost a quarter of a century before. Hopkins is sympathetic to Delaney, whom he refers to briefly and calls him "the only manly one of the six." Hopkins goes on to say that Delaney was "not guilty of murder, but admitted he was willing and ready to do murder, were it necessary to their success." There is a sense, when taking all the different accounts of Delaney's last moments together, that there was a dignity about him that seems to be lacking in the others. Whether he really did tell Curtis to "show (him)self a man and die game" as McElroy claims or smiled as the noose was placed around his neck as Page reported, Delaney seems to have faced death calmly and *showed himself a man.*

WHAT THE RECORDS SHOW

Patrick Delaney was drafted on September 10, 1863, and mustered in for three years' service in Reading, Pennsylvania. He joined the 83rd Pennsylvania Infantry, Company E six days later. Although the 22-year-old, blue-eyed, brown-haired Delaney gave his profession as "laborer" when he enlisted in the army, a Prisoner of War Memorandum written after his death gives his profession as "shoemaker." This may have been because the Confederates, short of manpower, asked for volunteers from among the POWs to work making shoes for the Confederacy. The prisoners generally disdained such offers and likened it to working for the enemy, so it's interesting that that's the profession assigned to Delaney after his death.

As was the case with some of the other raiders who were hanged, there is some confusion regarding Delaney's first name. In the Confederate copy of the prison's Register of Deaths, the last name "Delaney" is clearly followed by the first initial "J" rather than "P." Delaney's compiled service record also lists the man executed "under the prison stockade" as "Delaney, J." on one of the three "Memorandum from the Prisoner of War Records" forms, although there's a handwritten note at the bottom: "See Delaney, P." Although the spelling of the last name and the given first initial vary, the information given on the forms (regiment and circumstances of his execution) indicate that these records are for the same individual.

It's possible that somewhere along the way, Delaney's first initial, J, was misread as a P. It's also worth mentioning that, in the case of all three of the raider's whose first name is in contention—Delaney, Sarsfield, and Sullivan—in every case, some of the sources suggest that either the man's name was John or that it began with the letter J. In nineteenth-century Irish culture, it was traditional to christen a baby "John" if it was a boy or "Mary" if it was a girl, if the child or one of the parents was in danger of dying. The belief was that Jesus would take a special interest in children who were named either for His Mother or the disciple whom He loved. Children christened with these names often went by the names their parents originally intended to name them in their day to day lives, but their formal name was still "John" or "Mary." It's also true that "John" is a very generic name, and one frequently assumed by men who are hiding their actual identities. Sullivan was almost certainly a bounty jumper and used a variety of first names in his military career, and it makes sense that he likely enlisted under a pseudonym. As far as Delaney and Sarsfield are concerned, either explanation of the confusion concerning their first names might be valid.

Patrick Delaney was assigned to the newly reformed Company E of the 83rd Pennsylvania, a regiment that had been formed early in the war, mustering into service on September 8, 1861. The 83rd is notable for participating in nearly every major battle in the East, including the Seven Days Battle, Antietam, Fredericksburg, Gettysburg, Petersburg, and Appomattox Courthouse. One of the 83rd's most famous battles was fought defending Little Round Top alongside the 20th Maine at the Battle of Gettysburg, where they lost their colonel, Strong Vincent. The 83rd is also noteworthy for having had the second highest number of battle deaths among Union infantry regiments, with 11 officers and 271 enlisted men killed or mortally wounded (plus another 2 officers and 151 enlisted men who died of disease during the war). By the time Patrick Delaney was drafted and joined the regiment, it was an efficient, battle-proven unit stationed on picket duty two miles beyond Culpeper, Virginia.

The military draft, or forced conscription, had never existed in the United States prior to the Civil War. Unable to entice the number of men they needed by offering volunteers a cash bounty for enlisting, the US Congress authorized a draft to increase the soldiers needed for the war effort. The draft, however, was not a popular idea, particularly with immigrants and those from lower socioeconomic classes. The Civil War Military Draft Act not only allowed immigrant men between the ages of 20 and 45 who indicated that they planned to become US citizens to be drafted, but it provided loopholes for those well-off to avoid military service, either by paying a $300 commutation fee to avoid military service or by hiring a substitute to serve in their place.

As one might expect, the draft was not only extremely controversial but also extremely unpopular with the lower classes, and resulted in violent protests in some places, most notably in New York City, where the Irish protests of the draft exploded into three days of violent, destructive rioting. Not surprisingly, men who were drafted frequently turned out to be less than dutiful soldiers. Desertions from the military increased, as well as discipline problems with the decline in the quality and commitment of soldiers. Captain

Amos Judson, of Delaney's Company E, recalled the poor quality of the men who had been sent against their will to be soldiers, "[This type of man] can no more withstand the temptation to steal than a hungry man can resist the temptation to eat. He is a regular bounty jumper and cares as much about the country as the devil is supposed to care about religion. He is also awaiting his chance to desert. He stole money from his comrades on the way to this army and had to be tied up by the thumbs before he would disgorge the stolen property. He stole after he got to the army and had to be tied up again before he would confess his guilt. He becomes sick just before every battle or falls out of the ranks and is nowhere to be found when his services are most needed."

Judson, who later wrote a history of the 83rd Pennsylvania, described the new recruits who arrived in August and September 1863, pointing out that their crimes began even before they reached their regiments. His description sounds remarkably like the later accounts of the raiders and their crimes:

> *(T)he majority of them were the grandest scoundrels that ever went unhung. These were the cream and flower, the very head and front of New York rioters, gamblers, thieves, pickpockets and blacklegs, many of whom, it is said, had fled to escape punishment for crimes of arson, robbery and homicide. . . . On board the boats that took them to Alexandria, they fought, gambled, and stole from each other. Some of them stole several hundred dollars at a time and, in justice to the plundered parties, the officers in charge had to tie their arms behind them and almost swing them from the yard arms for hours before they would disgorge the stolen money. They fought, gambled, and stole after they got to the regiment. The once peaceful Eighty-Third became uproarious at times with their midnight broils and battles. They were always spoiling for a fight except when in the presence of the enemy. One would have supposed that when men would wake up at midnight and fall to pummeling each other in bed, as they often did, they would have become transported at the prospect of battle; but it was at such times that they skulked and seized the opportunity to desert. They would get each other drunk and pick each other's pockets while asleep. They would decoy each other out of camp after dark on the pretense of going out to take something good to drink, and then knock their deluded victims down and rob them of money. In short, these men would have disgraced the regiment beyond all recovery had they remained three months in it, but thanks to a kind Providence, or to some other invisible power of redemption, they kept deserting, a dozen at a time, until they were nearly all gone. In a few weeks the morals of the Eighty-Third began to recover from the shock and return to its former normal and healthy condition.*

Judson also recorded the day that Patrick Delaney deserted. After several weeks of picket duty, the 83rd was moving rapidly back and forth across the Virginia countryside, trying to anticipate the enemy's movements, beginning on September 10. Four days later, the new soldiers had had enough. A dozen men, including Patrick Delaney, fell out during a two-mile jog, tossed aside their guns and simply walked away, never to return. Judson wrote: "October 14—We double-quicked about two miles, during which a great many fell out from fatigue and most of the substitutes took good care never to fall in again." All these men were subsequently captured by the Confederates, but Captain Judson viewed their capture as a relief, rather than a loss.

Delaney's compiled service record contains a muster roll that bears a notation about "stoppage [of pay] on acct. of ord[nance] thrown away." He had the misfortune to desert at approximately the same time as the Battle of Bristoe Station and was captured roughly five miles from the battlefield. The next record of Patrick Delaney is his arrival at one of the Richmond, Virginia prisons on October 23, 1863. He likely encountered the retreating Rebel forces as he attempted to head back North and was captured.

Delaney likely first encountered some of the men he was executed with shortly after his capture. William Collins and John Sullivan were also both captured near Culpeper, Virginia, within three days and 35 miles of Delaney's desertion and capture. All three were sent first to Richmond, Virginia, likely to Belle Isle, with Delaney reportedly arriving 3 to 10 days after the other two. Belle Isle is where the raiders are first known to have begun preying on their fellow prisoners. A prisoner named Jacob Osborne Coburn wrote about "raiders" stealing bread from him while he was at Belle Isle in 1863. Despite whatever criminal activities Delaney engaged in, life in the prison tents was not easy for him. He became sick and was admitted to the prison hospital on December 15 with a case a catarrh, a respiratory infection with much congestion. He remained in the hospital for five days before returning to his quarters.

Delaney was sent to Andersonville on March 21, 1864, 17 days after Collins and Sullivan. This core group of thieves continued operations once they reached Camp Sumter, adding more men as the prison population grew. Delaney was not the only raider to come from the 83rd Pennsylvania. Among the dozen men who deserted on the same night was Richard Allen, the same "Dick" Allen whom John McElroy depicts swearing vengeance over Delaney's dead body following his hanging. Another draftee from Reading, Pennsylvania, Allen reported for duty the day before Delaney did, and they would have traveled together under the supervision of two officers of the 83rd, moving from Reading, Pennsylvania, to Philadelphia, and from there were shipped via the Delaware and Chesapeake Canal and Chesapeake Bay to Alexandria, Virginia, and from there by railroad to Culpeper, Virginia, where the 83rd was on picket duty.

Neither Allen nor Delaney had wanted to be in the army, and they both tossed away their guns and deserted on the same day, along with ten other recent arrivals, less than a month after mustering in. They arrived at Richmond as prisoners of war on the same date, likely together. Dick Allen arrived at Andersonville on March 19, over three weeks after the prison camp received its first prisoners, and Patrick Delaney joined him there two days later, apparently reuniting with Collins and Sullivan and the other raiders. Not long after their arrival, they fell into their old pattern of robbing their fellow prisoners.

Both John McElroy and the *Sunday Mercury* article suggest that, like Patrick Delaney, Dick Allen belonged to the gang of thieves that preyed on their fellow prisoners. It also seems probable that the two of them may have raided together once they became prisoners. It's unlikely that Dick Allen really did openly swear vengeance over Delaney's dead body, but it does seem extremely likely that he would have witnessed his friend's execution, possibly while wearing a ball and chain as the *Mercury* article suggests. Patrick Delaney paid the ultimate price for his crimes, but it would seem, he was neither alone nor friendless at the end.

KNOWN TIMELINE

1841 Born in Ireland
1863 September 10 Drafted and enlisted in the army
1863 September 16 Mustered in with the 83rd Pennsylvania Infantry, Company E
1863 October 14 Captured at Bristoe Station
1863 October 23 or November 1 Confined at Richmond, Virginia (probably at Belle Isle)
1863 December 15 Admitted to prison hospital, suffering from catarrh
1863 December 20 Released from prison hospital and returned to quarters
1864 March 21 Sent to Andersonville
1864 July 11 Executed as a raider, Camp Sumter

NOTES ON CHAPTER 4

Patrick Delaney was accused of attacking a prisoner named Marion Friend—There is some evidence that Delaney and Curtis believed that Friend had stolen a blanket from them, and they were trying to get it back. See chapter 5, "Curtis."

James Madison Page—James Madison Page was a sergeant in the 6th Michigan Cavalry, Company A, when he was captured at either Liberty Mills or Fisher's Mill, Virginia, on September 22, 1863. Like Edward Wellington Boate, Page felt that the US government was more to blame for the suffering of the prisoners than the Confederates were, and in 1908 published a book titled *The True Story of Andersonville Prison*. He died in Long Beach, California, in 1924.

Delaney, who was a Roman Catholic—In his testimony at the Wirz trial, Father Peter Whelan, testified that all but one of the condemned men were Roman Catholic. The exception was most likely William Collins, who had been born in Nottingham-shire, England, which is a predominantly Protestant country. Sullivan, Delany, and Sarsfield all gave their place of birth as Ireland, where the population is predominantly Roman Catholic. Charles Curtis was reportedly born in New Brunswick, while William Ritson claimed to have been born in Philadelphia. At the time of his enlistment, Andrew Muir claimed to have been born in England, but is identified by John Ransom as being Irish.

"For he smiled as the noose was placed around his neck"—This seems to be unlikely, as several sources say that meal sacks were placed over the condemned men's heads in the place of hoods. These hoods would have been placed over the condemned men's heads before the nooses were fastened, prohibiting Page from seeing Delaney smile as the noose was placed around his neck.

The most damning testimony against Delaney was reportedly given by witness Ramiro E. Spicer—During the account of the first day's proceedings, a witness is referred to as "R. C. Spicer, Seventy-sixth New York, Company E"; on the following day, the witness is referred to as R. E. Spicer, with no regiment given. According to the muster rolls for the 76th New York, the man in question is Sergeant Ramiro Ernest Spicer, who was captured at the Battle of the Wilderness on May 28, 1864. His first name is also sometimes given as "Ramira." He survived the war and later returned to Andersonville for the 1914 dedication of the New York Monument at Andersonville, bringing a bottle of water from Providence Spring home with him. He died on May 4, 1926.

A prisoner named Marion Friend—Friend, whose actual name was James Marion Friend, was a member of the 16th Illinois Cavalry, the same regiment as John McElroy and Leroy Key.

Prisoner Charles Hopkins kept a diary while in prison and later drew on that diary to write a private memoir—Unfortunately, Hopkins recorded little more than the names of the men who were executed and their time of death in his July 11 entry. Most of the information he provides on the raiders comes in the form of memories, and it's very likely that he was influenced by John McElroy's book, which was published more than a decade earlier.

The 83rd is also noteworthy for having had the second highest number of battle deaths among Union infantry regiments—Only the 5th New Hampshire, with 295 men killed and 756 wounded, suffered heavier losses.

It provided loopholes for those well-off to avoid military service, either by paying a $300 commutation fee to avoid military service or by hiring a substitute to serve in their place—Setting the $300 commutation fee also had the effect of limiting the amount that a man might receive for substituting for someone else; no man would pay a substitute $300 or more when he could simply pay the government that amount to avoid military obligation.

Captain Amos Judson, of Delaney's Company E, later wrote a history of the 83rd Pennsylvania—Although Judson was a captain in Delaney's own company, he seems to have made a conscious decision not to include Patrick Delaney and other deserters like him in the story of the regiment, and he included a footnote that reads, "It is probable that a number of names are yet to be found in the rolls at the end of the volume, of men who are deserters but were not so accounted for on the Muster-Out Rolls. I shall endeavor to hunt them all up and expel them from the Roll of Honor before it goes to press."

"October 14—We double-quicked about two miles, during which a great many fell out from fatigue and most of the substitutes took good care never to fall in again"—Also listed as having been drafted and deserted from Company E on or about the same time as Patrick Delaney are Richard Allen, Peter Bradbury, John Briggs, William Barnes, Andrew Blakemore, James Caney, John Keaugh, James M'Carty, James O'Neil, William C. Williams, and John Williams. A total of 43 men eventually deserted from Company E (Judson, *History of the Eighty-Third Regiment Pennsylvania Volunteers*, page 125).

With Delaney reportedly arriving 3 to 10 days after the other two—John Sullivan's compiled military service record says that he arrived at Belle Isle between October 13 and 20.

A prisoner named Jacob Osborne Coburn wrote about "raiders" stealing bread from him—Coburn, a sergeant with the 6th Michigan Cavalry, Company I, kept a diary while a prisoner at Belle Isle. The diary was published under the title *Hell on Belle Isle: Diary of a Civil War POW* in 1997. Coburn died of chronic diarrhea at Belle Isle on March 8, 1864, at age 34, just as prisoners were beginning to be sent to Andersonville. He is buried at Richmond National Cemetery in Section 4A; O, MA 11.

This core group of thieves continued operations—Other prisoners also wrote that the raiders began their career in crime at Belle Isle and continued at Camp Sumter. Gilbert Sabre wrote, "The system of 'raiding,' which was carried on with so much annoyance at Belle Isle, was practiced, with even greater industry, at Camp Sumter." John L. Hoster reported in his diary, "a large band of raiders that began murdering and plundering at Belle Isle and went on unmolested until lately."

Another draftee from Reading, Pennsylvania, Allen reported for duty the day before Delaney did—Delaney mustered in on September 10; Allen on September 9. The actual date of desertion varies slightly from form to form within each man's compiled service record, but each form agrees with the form in the other man's record. According to Delaney's Memorandum from Prisoner of War Records, he was captured near Bristoe Station on September 14, and Allen's notes the same. Both men's muster out records state, "Deserted Oct 17/63 Stoppage on account of ord. thrown away." Given that both men were in the same place at the same time almost constantly from the day Patrick Delaney enlisted, it would have been impossible that the two did not know each other, and they deserted on the same night, in all likelihood, together.

They would have traveled together under the supervision of two officers of the 83rd—Amos Judson mentions the names Captain Stowe and Lieutenant Gifford as the officers escorting the newly drafted men, or their substitutes, to join the regiment. In his record for August 20, 1863, Judson refers to Captain George Stowe, Company G, and Lieutenant Martin V. Gifford of Company A. Both would later die in combat.

"Curtis"

Known aliases: Charles Curtis, Charles F. Curtis, Chas. Curtis
Regiment: Fifth Rhode Island Heavy Artillery
Rank: Private
Place of birth: New Brunswick, Canada
Approximate year of birth: 1842
Enrolled: Substitute for Frederick W. Perry of Providence, Rhode Island
Mustered in: July 27, 1863
Age at time of enlistment: 21
Deserted: October 19, 1864 (January 1, 1865, according to company muster
  roll)
Approximate age at time of hanging: 22
Profession: Carpenter
Term of enlistment: 3 years
Physical description: 5 feet 8 inches, hazel eyes, light brown hair, light com-
  plexion

WHAT HISTORY TELLS US

*H*istory books remember Charles Curtis as the man who tried to run away.
Although most contemporary sources identify William "Mosby" Collins
as the chief of the raiders, Leroy Key, the man who presided over Curtis's
execution, referred to Curtis as "the leader." Most sources agree that Curtis
finally seemed to realize the gravity of the situation as he was about to be
bound and made to mount the gallows, and so he suddenly bolted. He managed to break through the ring of regulators surrounding the execution site

and charged through the crowd of witnesses who were waiting to see the hanging. He made it across the fetid, filthy sink that served as both the prison water supply and its toilet, wading in and crossing it to escape his fate, but there is nowhere to hide when close to 25,000 men are watching. Curtis was quickly recaptured and sent to his doom.

JOHN McELROY'S ACCOUNT

By his own account, John McElroy was one of the men forming a perimeter around the gallows during the execution of the raiders. This would have provided him with an excellent view of the proceedings as they developed.

> At this the priest closed the book upon which he had kept his eyes bent since his entrance, and facing the multitude on the North Side began a plea for mercy.
>
> The condemned faced in the same direction, to read their fate in the countenances of those whom he was addressing. This movement brought Curtis—a low-statured, massively built man—on the right of their line and about ten or fifteen steps from my company. . . .
>
> Curtis turned from the crowd with desperation convulsing his features. Tearing off the broad-brimmed hat which he wore, he flung it on the ground with the exclamation!
>
> "By God, I'll die this way first!" and, drawing his head down and folding his arms about it, he dashed forward for the center of my company, like a great stone hurled from a catapult.
>
> "Egypt" and I saw where he was going to strike, and ran down the line to help stop him. As he came up we rained blows on his head with our clubs, but so many of us struck at him at once that we broke each other's clubs to pieces, and only knocked him on his knees. He rose with an almost superhuman effort, and plunged into the mass beyond. . . .
>
> While this was going on two of my company, belonging to the Fifth Iowa Cavalry, were in hot pursuit of Curtis. I had seen them start and shouted to them to come back, as I feared they would be set upon by the Raiders and murdered. But the din was so overpowering that they could not hear me, and doubtless would not have come back if they had heard.
>
> Curtis ran diagonally down the hill, jumping over the tents and knocking down the men who happened in his way. Arriving at the swamp he plunged in, sinking nearly to his hips in the fetid, filthy ooze. He forged his way through with terrible effort. His pursuers followed his example, and caught up to him just as he emerged on the other side. They struck him on the back of the head with their clubs, and knocked him down. . . .
>
> When Curtis finally arrived, he sat on the ground for a minute or so, to rest, and then, reeking with filth, slowly and painfully climbed the steps. Delaney

seemed to think he was suffering as much from fright as anything else, and said to him:

"Come on up, now, show yourself a man, and die game."

LEROY KEY'S ACCOUNT

Curtis is unique among the raiders because there is an account of an encounter with him that takes place before the arrests and trial, written by a man who would ultimately take part in the execution. In late 1864, Leroy Key, the acknowledged organizer of the regulators who played a lead role in the executions, gave an interview with a member of the Christian Commission, an organization which helped serve prisoners of war following their release. This interview was then published by the *Boston Journal* and picked up by other newspapers. Key's account paid attention to Curtis, who, he said, had accosted him shortly after learning about the formation of the regulators. According to Key, Curtis, "the chief of the raiders," got wind of Key's efforts to organize the regulators and accosted Key:

> *I spoke to a few of my friends to organize a band of protectors against these raiders. We began to organize, and had proceeded to the formation of thirteen companies, with thirty men and a captain in each. Before the organization was complete, I was one day walking on the north side of the camp, when I saw ahead of me the chief of the raiders, and in pursuit of me five men on the "double quick," with knives in their hands. The chief slapped me on the shoulder and turned me round, saying to me, "I understand that you are getting up a band to clear out the Irish." I replied, "The report is false and you are mistaken." "Well, you are getting up a band for some purpose; what is it for, if not to clean out the Irish?" Meanwhile the five men closed around us, forming a ring around CURTIS and myself.*
>
> *He again demanded to know the object of the band. Said I to him, boldly, "we are organizing a band to clean out the 'raiders,' and if you are one of them we intend to clean you out." They did not proceed to violence, but the leader put his knife into his left hand and with his right hand offered to shake hands with me. They then let me go.*

Although Curtis let him go once he'd ascertained that Key wasn't raising a group to "clean out" the Irish, Key did not extend the same courtesy once he had Curtis at the foot of the gallows: "CURTIS asked me to spare him as he had never done me any harm. I told him it was not for me to pardon him, I was appointed to see that the men were hung; but if he had anything to say, I would hear his confession on the scaffold. Then he said he would not stand it, and made a break for the lines, and ran about the camp until he was recaptured."

Thus defeated, Curtis's final act is to hand over his watch to Father Peter Whelan, the Catholic priest who had accompanied the men to the gallows. "Immediately after CURTIS was brought back, he was delivered to the executioner and taken on to the scaffold likewise. No confessions were made, but the men disposed of their property, and CURTIS gave his watch to the priest, Father WHALEN."

JOHN L. HOSTER'S ACCOUNT

Like Key, prisoner John L. Hoster reported that Curtis was one of the leaders of the raiders. Hoster focuses on Curtis in his July 11 diary entry. Many details in Hoster's account match John McElroy's, such as a man being knocked into a well during the scuffle, and Confederate witnesses scrambling out of the way of the artillery when Curtis makes a run for it, but, as usual, McElroy magnifies these incidents. McElroy claims, "There were quite a number of wells right around us, and all of these were filled full of men that fell into them as the crowd rushed away. Many had legs and arms broken, and I have no doubt that several were killed"; and goes on to say that "between one and two thousand" Confederate witnesses scrambled out of the way of the Rebel guns as Wirz screamed for his captain of the battery to fire. Hoster's account, written in his diary, is slightly out of sequence—he writes about Curtis being retrieved before he writes about Curtis running away—but is much more moderate in tone than McElroy's telling. In Hoster's version, only one man falls into a well, and Hoster does not attempt to quantify the number of civilians gathered to witness the execution, writing that "The rebels outside that had assembled to witness the scene ran back from in front of the artillery" when Curtis attempted to run. It's worth noting that, unlike McElroy, Hoster does not claim that the civilians are scrambling out of the way because Henry Wirz was screaming an order for the guards to open fire, an incident that almost certainly never happened.

It's easier to be sympathetic to Curtis in Hoster's version, as he stands bleeding from the ear and asking for friends to come forward but finding none.

> *The priest then went through with the ceremony and the prisoners' hands were tied behind them. During this operation Curtis, the ringleader, made a break through the crowd and tried to escape. He succeeded in getting across the creek, but was there surrounded and brought back. He also made several attempts to escape on his return to the scaffold. When retaken the blood was running out*

of his ear on account of the knocks received from the regulators. He threw his hands in the air and remarked that he would die there sooner than be taken on the other side and hung. As he made the break the crowd began to rush from the scaffold, thinking an attempt would be made to rescue the prisoners. During the excitement, one man fell into a well and remained there during the execution despite his yells. The rebels outside that had assembled to witness the scene ran back from in front of the artillery. When Curtis came back the other five were standing on the scaffold with a rope around their necks. Curtis was soon in his place. He confessed that he was easily led astray, but he never thought it would come to this. He requested some of his friends to come forward as he wished to see them but his friends, if he had any, did not make their appearance. He then requested his watch be left with his friends or with Father Martin, N.Y.C. At precisely 5 P.M. the drop fell, Mosby's rope broke and he fell to the ground. Curtis fell farther than the rest and died very soon.

SUNDAY MERCURY ACCOUNT

The *Sunday Mercury*'s account of the raiders' trial stated that Curtis was tried on the third and final day of the raiders' trials, along with two other men, Richard Allen of the 83rd Pennsylvania Regiment and Thomas F. O'Connell of the 9th Maryland, Company D. Richard Allen is apparently the same "Dick" Allen whom McElroy refers to in his book. William Collins was tried separately the same day. The *Mercury* reports:

Daniel Hayes, United States, Company L, swore that one day last week, Allen and his party, including Curtis, came to his tent and took a watch belonging to the witness, which was hanging up in his tent. He then forced out of the tent a man named Prentiss, threw him down on the ground and threatened his life unless he told where witness's other watch was. Allen and Curtis did this. They then forced Prentiss to accompany them, Prentiss promising that he would tell where the other watch was deposited if they would spare his life. Prentiss pointed out where the other watch was—in the custody of a friend. Prentiss got the watch from this friend, came out, and handed it to Allen and Curtis.

William Prentiss [William S. Prentice], *16th Illinois Cavalry, Company I, the man referred to in the evidence of the last witness, confirmed the statement of Hays* [sic]*; adding [Th]at when Allen & Curtis demanded the second watch, he tried to escape from the tent, but was taken hold of, jerked down, four of five of the gang having hold of him and threatening that if he did not give information where the other watch was they would cut his throat.*

At the beginning of the section on the third day of the trial the *Sunday Mercury* makes a very surprising claim—that the name "Curtis" was an alias, identifying the man as "William Wrixon, alias Curtis, United States steam ship *Powhattan* [*sic*]." During Prentice's testimony, the article refers to "Curtis, alias Wrixon," but given that the accused is known as Curtis to nearly all of the prisoners who recorded the hanged raiders' names, it is more likely that "Curtis" is the alias, and "Wrixon" is the name the *Mercury* writer believed to be the correct one. This is confirmed with the article referring to "Curtis, alias Wrixon" only once, however, during Prentice's testimony, it refers to "Wrixon, alias Curtis" four times during the course of the article, including at the official reading of the charges which he is accused.

> *Curtis, alias Wrixon, said he would cut out his (Prentiss's) heart. They had their knives out ready to do so, and he expected to be murdered every moment. They had him by the throat and their hands on his mouth. While accompanying them to where the second watch was deposited, they said if witness "went down there and got them into a mess, they would not give two cents for his life."*

The testimony continues, this time with another member of McElroy's 16th Illinois regiment testifying, although this time there is a suggestion that the actions of Curtis and Delaney may have been retaliatory, rather than predatory. Curtis and Delaney accused the witness of stealing from them before beginning to assault him, although, by the witness's account, the assault ends with the two defendants taking over $300 dollars from him—a massive sum for the place and time.

> *James M. Friend, of the 16th Illinois Cavalry, Company I, stated that, last Saturday night, while he was lying in his tent, Curtis and a man named Delany [sic] came and woke him up. They asked him who was lying in the back of his tent? Witness replied "No person." Curtis then charged the witness with having been down to their quarters and robbed them of a blanket. Having denied this, Curtis struck him in the face with a razor and cut him. The wound was a ghastly one, across the side of the cheek. Witness put up his hand, and received a gash between the thumb and first finger. They then made several passes of the razor at him, but he succeeded in creeping away from them on his all fours, and tried to throw his pocketbook into the "dead line," but did not succeed in throwing it far enough, and so he picked it up again, when one of them grasped it from him, saying, as he did so, "God d—n you, that is all we wanted." There were four hundred and forty nine dollars in the pocketbook. He had been trading a little.*
>
> *J. P. Erwin, 103rd Pennsylvania Regiment, Company B, swore that Wrixon, alias Curtis, had some weeks previously choked him down, when he was robbed of a watch and seventy dollars. While buying some beans he had a ten-dollar bill in his hand, which was snatched from him; Curtis, is at that moment come up [sic], and he took him to his (Curtis's) tent; and while there, Curtis choked him down and somebody else came up and robbed him.*

The *Sunday Mercury* account goes on to say that Curtis had taken the Oath of Allegiance to the Confederacy and that, after his conviction by the prison jurors, he demanded to be tried by a Confederate jury as a Confederate citizen. He reportedly took his case to prison commander, General John Winder, who responded by giving him a choice between being hung like a Yankee or killed by a firing squad as a Confederate. There is no evidence that supports this story, however, and if Curtis had taken the Oath of Allegiance, it seems unlikely that he would have remained in the prison stockade, given the Confederacy's need of manpower. No record of a man named Charles F. Curtis—or Wrixon—taking the Oath of Allegiance can be found.

WHAT THE RECORDS SHOW

The most intriguing aspect of Curtis's story, besides his failed, last-minute escape attempt, is the suggestion in the *Sunday Mercury* that he may have been using an alias. Although John McElroy insinuated that he believed that all the names of the raiders were aliases ("These names and regiments are of little consequence, however, as I believe all the rascals were professional bounty jumpers"), it seems unlikely that the two raiders who were drafted— Delaney and Sarsfield—would have enlisted under aliases, and William Collins, who enlisted for a three-year term six month after the war began was almost certainly using his own name. John Sullivan—the Irish equivalent of "John Smith"—*was* an alias, and "Andrew Muir" may or may not have been.

The records for the 5th Rhode Island Heavy Artillery confirm that Charles F. Curtis was indeed a member of that regiment. He enlisted as a substitute in Providence, Rhode Island, and was assigned to Company A. Charles F. Curtis's compiled service record suggests that, like many substitutes, he was not an outstanding soldier and that he spent prolonged periods "Absent in hospital at Morehead, N.C." before his eventual desertion, which, according to the company's muster roll, occurred while he was on furlough, New Year's Day, 1865.

This official date of desertion is problematic. The raider known as Charles F. Curtis of the Fifth Rhode Island Heavy Artillery was executed on July 11, 1864—four and a half months *before* his reported desertion. An explanation can found by digging into this man's medical records. Charles Curtis mustered in with the Fifth Rhode Island Heavy Artillery on July 27, 1863. On November 13, he was admitted to Mansfield General Hospital in Morehead City, North Carolina, with an intermittent tertian fever—likely malaria. He remained in the hospital for two and a half weeks and was discharged on the first of December. On April 14 of the following year, he was again admitted to the hospital at Morehead, this time suffering from "Convulsions." Three weeks later, on the morning of May 5, Curtis's entire company, Company A of the 5th Rhode Island Heavy Artillery, was captured at Croatan, North Carolina. The enlisted men in his regiment went on to Andersonville, while Curtis himself remained in the hospital in North Carolina until his discharge on August 12, one month and one day after his supposed death.

It seems likely that, since his entire company was captured, it was initially assumed by Washington that Charles Curtis had been captured with them, and so he was listed as having been captured at Croatan, even though he was not there at the time. He went back into the hospital, this time at Beaufort, North Carolina, on September 2, and he remained there until he was furloughed on September 19. He was due back from furlough on October 19, 1864, but he never returned. With his company still imprisoned, he was not officially listed as a deserter in the company's muster roll until January 1, 1865, but by then he had vanished, and nothing more is known of him.

A further examination of Charles Curtis's compiled military service record reveals a complete lack of any reference to his having been captured or a prisoner of war, and the Memorandum from Prisoner of War Records, which is present in the other hanged soldiers' files, is completely missing from Charles Curtis's. This suggests that Charles Curtis—the *real* Charles Curtis, from the 5th Rhode Island Heavy Artillery—was *not* the man who was hanged as a thief at Andersonville Prison.

The obvious explanation, if Charles Curtis was never captured, is that someone was using his identity as an alias while a prisoner of war. This would explain the strange inclusion of the name "Pvt Charles F. Curtis 5th Reg Art" appearing as one of the "honored dead" on the Rhode Island Monument at Andersonville Historic Site. The six executed raiders were buried away from the other prisoners in the prison graveyard because of the contempt the other prisoners felt for them. The inclusion of Curtis's name as one of the "honored dead" would make sense if that name appeared on the rolls of prisoners held at Andersonville, but none of the other fifty-eight Andersonville prisoners from the 5th Rhode Island—all captured May 5, 1864, at Croatan, North Carolina—recognized the raider as the man from their regiment. No diaries from the 5th Rhode Island prisoners are known to survive, and it's impossible to know if the men of the 5th believed the man hanged with the name Charles Curtis and the man they served with were the same person. It seems highly improbable that the other Rhode Island prisoners would have allowed the listing of Charles F. Curtis of the 5th Rhode Island Heavy Artillery, as one of their "honored dead," had they believed him to be a raider.

The practice of using aliases was not uncommon in the Civil War. There were several reasons for this, including, as McElroy pointed out, if one enlisted with the intention of collecting the enlistment bounty and then deserting, because an alias would make it easier to "disappear" and repeat the scam in a different location. Others used aliases if they were hiding from someone or something; if they were too young to legally enlist; or if they were beginning a new life and distancing themselves from their past. Soldiers from the South who fought for the Union would sometimes give false names when they were captured, for fear of the treatment they might receive at Rebel hands should their actual identities and origins become known. Other prisoners would maintain double identities while within the stockade in order to draw rations twice. Many veterans would reveal their aliases when they applied for pensions after the war, and the 1890 US government's census of the surviving Civil War widows and Veterans revealed still more aliases 35 years after the war ended.

Since Charles Curtis was never at Andersonville with his regiment this must mean that his identity was used as an alias by another prisoner of war, as the *Sunday Mercury* article suggests. Surprisingly, there is also evidence in the prison records that this may well have been the case. As each prisoner died, his death was recorded in a Register of Deaths. This register was kept by Union prisoners who worked outside the stockade, a group of clerks that notably included Dorence Atwater, who would later smuggle a copy of the list of the dead out of the prison. He would eventually return to Andersonville with this list after the war as part of the expedition sent to establish the National Cemetery there. Atwater's original list was reportedly destroyed in the 1906 San Francisco Earthquake, but a microfilm of the original, Confederate copy of the Register of Deaths is still in existence at the National Archives in Washington, DC. The surviving register is in rough condition in places, but it has an entry for each corpse that was brought to the prison's "dead house" outside the stockade to await burial. The register's pages are divided into columns, reading from left to right, the chronological number of the dead prisoner, name, rank, regiment, company, date of death, number in the prison's register, the cause of death, and a place for remarks.

Unfortunately, the page in the register that lists the deaths of the six raiders is in rough shape, missing the bottom corners of the page, including most of the section that gives the names of the deceased. The center section of the bottom of the page survives intact, however, and it's possible to distinguish each raider by the regiment he fought for.

"Muir, A." is the only raider listing that survives intact. Given the nature of the cursive writing in the register, it is possible to see how "Muir" might have been misread as "Munn." His entry goes on to list him as in the US Navy and dying of "asphyxia." The only other name that can be read in its entirety is "Delaney, J." whose regiment is given as "83," which is mostly consistent with Patrick Delaney, although the initial of his first name is different. This may be a mistake, a misreading, an intentional deception on Delaney's part, or it may have been that Delaney was one of many Irish who were given the baptismal name of "John" if it appeared that he might not survive as an infant, but who went by his middle name or a nickname in his daily life.

The other raiders' names in the Register of Deaths must be pieced together according to the regiments listed. "ivan, J, Priv. 140 NY, Co. F" is consistent with John Sullivan, whose name does not appear on any of the grave markers, but who is mentioned in several prisoners' diaries. The man with the first initial J. served with the "140 [N]Y, Co. C" is J. Sarsfield of the 140th New York. The listing that shows the first initial W, the rank of corporal, and the 88th Regiment is consistent with William Collins of the 88th Pennsylvania, the only corporal in the group.

This accounts for five of the six raiders. This means that the remaining listing *should* be for Charles Curtis of the 5th Rhode Island, but it's not. The name is completely missing, but for rank it appears to say "seaman" and under regiment, instead of a number, there is a "U" at the tattered edge of the page, similar to the one that begins the words "US Navy" in Muir's listing.

This unexpected listing is supported by a second document from Andersonville, the "Register of Prisoners Admitted to the Prison Hospital." This ledger, possibly the one kept in part by hospital clerk Dorence Atwater, differs in several ways from the Register of Deaths. For example, it lists both the dead and soldiers who were deemed well enough to be returned to the stockade, but it omits all the unfortunates whose identities were not known when they died. The pages of the register are written in neat, methodical handwriting, and the pages are intact, but the dates are slightly off. It lists the six raiders as having died from "asphyxia" on July 12 rather than July 11, and deaths from other days are often recorded a day after the Register of Deaths reports them. Because we know that the raiders were executed on July 11, it seems logical to assume that the Admissions Register may have drawn on the information taken from the Register of Deaths, since the Admissions Register recorded the deaths of identified prisoners, even if they had never been admitted and treated at the prison hospital, as was the case with the six raiders. Furthermore, the raiders are listed in the Admissions Register in the same order as the Register of Deaths, and this time, all names are legible. Top to bottom, the men "tried by court martial and executed inside the prison" are Muir, A.; Sullivan, J.; Sarsfield, J.; Collins, Wm; Rickson, W. R.; and Delaney, J.

Charles Curtis is not listed in the prison's hospital and death registers, but a seaman by the name of Rickson is.

The obvious question then becomes if Charles Curtis did not desert his regiment until months after his reported death, how did his name end up on one of the grave markers at Andersonville National Cemetery? And who was W. Rickson?

For the past century and a half, historians have assumed that the name Rickson was an error made by the postwar expeditionary group that tried to identify and mark the graves of the prisoners who died at Camp Sumter. There is no record of a man named W. Rickson ever having served in the Union Navy, and most historians, knowing that the prisoners referred to one of the men hanged as "Sullivan" in their diaries and memoirs, assumed that Sullivan was misidentified as W. Rickson and that perhaps Sullivan used the alias "Rickson." The National Park Service's policy is to leave the graves as the expeditionary force identified them, even if information comes to light that the names on the grave markers are incorrect. Even though it's now generally accepted that Sullivan of the 76th New York was hanged, no effort will be made to correct the grave marker. Clearly, at least one of the grave markers for the raiders is wrong, but whether the sixth man executed was Curtis, or Sullivan or Rickson, the grave markers in the National Cemetery at Andersonville will not be changed.

The key to who "Curtis" may have been lies in the *Sunday Mercury* article. In the introduction to the events of the third day of the raiders' trial, it refers to one of the accused as "William Wrixon, alias Curtis, United States steamship *Powhattan* [*sic*]." This assertion is supported by a neatly lettered list of the raiders that's tucked into a file on Dorence Atwater at the National Archives. The final entry on the list reads "Wm Wrixon alias Curtis" and lists his vessel as the "USS *Powhatton* [*sic*]."

The USS *Powhatan* was a sidewheel, steam frigate that was stationed off Charleston Harbor for most of the war as part of the South Atlantic Blockading Squadron. While there is no sailor named W. Rickson stationed on the *Powhatan*—or on any other ship in the Union Navy—there was a sailor on the *Powhatan* whose name is remarkably close, and that man was a prisoner of war.

William Ritson was a quartermaster on the USS *Powhatan*. He was already an experienced sailor when he signed on with the US Navy a month after the war began. When he enlisted in Philadelphia on May 13, 1861, he stated that he was 30 years old, had been born in Philadelphia, and gave his profession as "mariner." Ritson was assigned the rank of "seaman," which meant that he had at least three years sailing experience prior to enlisting. The dark-haired, dark-eyed, dark-skinned man with the compact build (he stood five feet, three and half inches), and a scar on his left wrist signed on for three years' service. Ritson spent under a month training on the receiving ship the USS *Princeton*, leaving her to serve as a seaman on the USS *Jamestown* from June 9 to September 30, 1861. He was then promoted to coxswain on October 1, 1861, and served in that position on the *Jamestown* until August 22, 1863. He was then transferred to the *Powhatan* on August 23, 1863, and was promoted to quartermaster the next day. He remained in that position until he was captured the night of September 8, 1863.

On September 8, 1863, under the cover of darkness, approximately 400 men set forth from Union ships in Charleston Harbor as part of an amphibious nighttime assault intended to take back Fort Sumter from the Confederates. The plan was that several small boats would be towed close to Fort Sumter by a tugboat in the dark of night. Once they were in proximity to the fort, the line towing the boats would be cut, turning them loose to row in silently on their own for a surprise amphibious attack on the fort. The attack was an unqualified failure; the hastily arranged attack was announced to the officers the same morning the attack was to happen, and some of the attacking boats did not contain anyone who was familiar with the plan. Problems began when the tug, with a line of approximately 25 boats in tow, turned back because of navigational concerns. The tug took on a new pilot, and approached a second time, but this time the line of boats being towed ran afoul of a buoy, and they were cut loose in disarray. Much to the attackers' surprise, the Confederates were expecting the attack and had brought in reinforcements. Less than one-fifth of the boats made landfall, and after a battle that lasted less than 20 minutes, the sailors and marines who had managed to land reluctantly surrendered.

Among the hundred plus casualties of the Second Battle of Fort Sumter were 31 men from the *Powhatan*: all 2 officers, 19 sailors, and 10 marines. Quarter master William Ritson was among those taken by the enemy. Of these 31 men, one promptly deserted upon being captured and subsequently joined the Confederacy; another managed to escape not long after; and one was exchanged when his crewmates were sent to Andersonville. The two officers from the *Powhatan*, Master's Mate Christopher Hovey and Acting Master E. L. Hines were separated from their crew at Libby Prison and remained there when the rest of the *Powhatan* prisoners were sent to Camp Sumter.

Although it can't be conclusively proven that all the remaining sailors and marines were sent to Andersonville, it seems likely. At least 18 of the 29 can be placed at Andersonville either through pension applications; references to them by other *Powhatan* men held at Andersonville; because they signed a November 1, 1864, letter to Secretary of the Navy Gideon Welles concerning their treatment in Rebel prisons after they were paroled; or because they remain in Andersonville at the National Cemetery. A list of prisoners exchanged at Cox Landing on October 16, 1864, believed to be the sailors and marines from Andersonville along with a few dozen Navy officers held elsewhere, lists all but three or four of the marines (one of the names may have been misspelled on the list), and all but one sailor from the *Powhatan*. Although this list cannot possibly be accurate because it includes the five *Powhatan* sailors and marines who died at Andersonville, it's interesting to note that the only *Powhatan* sailor missing from the list of sailors leaving Andersonville is quartermaster William Ritson.

The sailors and marines from the *Powhatan* who were captured at the Second Battle of Fort Sumter remained together for their first three months of captivity, transferring from Fort Sumter to Charleston Jail, to Richland Jail in Columbia, South Carolina, and to the Pemberton/Crewes building on the campus of Libby Prison in Richmond, Virginia. At the end of December 1863, however, a small group of Fort Sumter captives was separated from the other sailors and marines that were held in Richmond. A Confederate guerilla by the name of John Yates Beall was captured along with his crew after burning ships along the Rappahannock River. The US government charged Beall and his crew with piracy and threatened to hang them. The Confederate government asserted that Beall was working for the Confederacy, and therefore should have been treated as a prisoner of war rather than a criminal. To assure that the federal government did not follow through with their threat to hang Beall and his crew, the Confederate government designated two captive naval officers and fifteen sailors as hostages for the lives of Beall and his crew. The terms were simple, if the federal government went through with the execution, the Confederates would hang the seventeen prisoners of war in retaliation.

The two officers selected as hostages remained at Libby Prison, but the fifteen sailors were separated from the other prisoners and sent to Salisbury Prison in North Carolina. At that time, Salisbury was primarily a political prison, holding deserters, those suspected of crimes against the Confederacy, Southern citizens who actively opposed the Confederacy, and Union hostages. The fifteen sailors left Richmond on December 30, 1863, and arrived at Salisbury shortly afterward. No list of the men named as hostages is known to exist; most of Salisbury Prison's records were destroyed when the prison camp was leveled by General George Stoneman at the end of the war. Frederic Augustus James, one of the hostages, mentioned the names of five of the hostages, including himself, in his diary. Three more can be discovered by reading the pension records of the men captured at Second Sumter; these included two *Powhatan* sailors, John Friedline and Daniel Quigley. The identities of the other seven hostages is unknown, but some evidence exists that Ritson, already using the name Curtis, may have been one of them.

In early 1863, a prisoner of war from the 2nd Tennessee Infantry named Paul Grogger was recaptured after jumping off a train bound for Andersonville near Raleigh, North Carolina. He was sent to Salisbury Prison, where he was held on the top floor of an old mill building with the hostages from the Second Battle of Fort Sumter. Four decades later, Grogger wrote about his experiences in an article that was published in the *National Tribune*: "The Sergeant of the third floor was one of the six raiders that later were hung in Andersonville. His name was Curtiss [*sic*], and he is the one that broke away and ran, causing such a panic after they marched them inside the big gate at Andersonville. I was standing below the gate where he ran down towards the creek. I at once recognized him as the same man."

Grogger's assertion that he was held at Salisbury prison along with the fifteen hostages from the Second Battle of Fort Sumter seems to be confirmed by Frederic James. According to James, the only people held on the top floor of the mill building in February 1864 were the fifteen sailors, two Union army captains who were sent to Salisbury by Jefferson Davis in retaliation for the Union's sentencing of two Kentucky men to hard labor for trying to recruit members of their home state to fight for the Confederacy, and "Four prisoners who managed to escape from the cars while being conveyed from Richmond to Americus, Ga."

Grogger was not the only Salisbury prisoner to associate the raiders with Salisbury. New York journalist and Salisbury prisoner Junius Browne incorrectly reported in his 1865 prison memoir, *Four Years in Secessia*, that "The better class of prisoners (at Salisbury) talked seriously of instituting a 'Vigilance Committee,' and hanging some of the principal Muggers, as had been done at Andersonville, Georgia, a few months before—by the by, four of the individuals executed there had gone from Salisbury, where they had been held as deserters." Although there is no evidence that any of the executed men other than Curtis were held at Salisbury, Browne may have been either misinformed or was thinking of some of the other men who were tried, but not executed.

The idea that Curtis was one of the sailors held at Salisbury is also suggested by the date of his apparent arrival at Andersonville. We know from Frederic James's diary that the Salisbury hostages arrived at Andersonville on June 1, 1864. When prisoners arrived at Andersonville, they were immediately divided into detachments of 270, which were then further split into three messes of ninety men, who would draw their rations together. Detachments were numbered consecutively, and men who arrived together would be assigned to the same detachment, and possibly the same mess. In his one and only letter home from Andersonville, James wrote that he had been assigned to Detachment 69, Mess number 2. The Register of Prisoners Admitted to the Prison Hospital records the detachments and messes of the patients who passed through there, including those of the six raiders. According to the register, W. R. Rickson, who died of asphyxiation with the other raiders, belonged to Detachment 69, Mess 2, the same mess that Frederic James and the other hostage sailors from Salisbury Prison were assigned to, indicating that "Charles Curtis" arrived at Andersonville with the small group of sailors that were captured at the Second Battle of Fort Sumter and then held as hostages at Salisbury Prison.

If the raider identified as Charles Curtis was already using his alias before he arrived at Andersonville, this would explain why there are no records for William Ritson as a prisoner of war at Andersonville. Because many of the witnesses identified William Collins as "Collins, alias Mosby," it seems probable that they would have done the same for Curtis if they had known he was using an alias. The obvious conclusion would be that they were not aware that it was an alias. If "Curtis" really did arrive at Andersonville on June 1, 1864, then only 28 days would pass between his arrival and his arrest as one of the raiders, not a lot of time for the masses held there to discover his "real" identity. But if the other prisoners only knew him as "Curtis," how did he come to be identified as seaman "Rickson" on the prison's Register of Deaths?

As it happens, the only sailor known to have kept a diary while at Andersonville was Frederic Augustus James, who, as mentioned before, was also one of the fifteen sailors captured at the Second Battle of Fort Sumter and held as one of the hostages at Salisbury. A sailor on the USS *Housatonic*, James began keeping a diary in February 1864 while a prisoner at Salisbury and made daily entries in it until August 23 of that same year, just three weeks before he died in Andersonville. Although James was in the stockade during the executions, he opted not to watch "having no relish for such scenes." James began to record the names of the raiders in his diary, but, frustratingly, he did not finish, writing, "Six of the raiders who have been on trial for their lives by a jury of our own men were hung at about five P.M. today. Their names were ———." It's the only time in the entire six months James kept a diary that he left a blank. Could it have been because he couldn't find out the names, because he had seven different names for the six men hanged, or because he knew one of the men who was condemned and did not wish to record his name? There is no way of knowing.

James does, however, provide a possible explanation as to how a sailor ended up in the Register of Deaths instead of the name Charles Curtis. In his diary, James mentions seven different sailors, all of whom were captured along with himself and Ritson, leaving the stockade and working in the prison hospital. Although none of these men were from the *Powhatan*, all had been kept together from the time of their capture in early September until the hostages left Richmond at the end of December, therefore the roughly 100 men in the group would have known each other. And of the seven sailors who went out to work at the prison hospital, at least one, James's close friend and the former ship's nurse on the *Housatonic*, Richard Tinker, had also been one of the group of hostages held at Salisbury Prison. It stands to reason, then, that any one of these seven men who worked at the prison hospital could have provided the name "Ritson," which easily could have been incorrectly transcribed as "Rickson" in the Register of Deaths and "Wrixon" in the raiders' trial transcript.

What is known about William Ritson is consistent with the possibility that he many have been "Curtis." The names on the Andersonville grave marker (W. Rickson), in the *Sunday Mercury* article (Wrixon), and of the sailor from the *Powhatan* (Ritson) are undeniably similar. The fact that all three names have a first name beginning with the letter W (and, in the case of both Wrixon and Ritson, the first name is given as "William") also supports the idea that they might, in fact, be the same man. There is no known enlistment record for a sailor named Rickson, nor one for a William Wrixon even though later sources indicate that they were both sailors in the Navy. Only a small number of the sailors at Andersonville would have held the rank of seaman; most naval prisoners held at Andersonville held the rank of landsmen because they were men who joined the Navy with limited or no prior sailing experience.

When the sailors left Andersonville, many of them left the prison stockade on September 27, 1864, slowly making their way north until they were finally exchanged at Cox Landing on the James River on October 16, 1864. A list of the sailors, 190 strong, was compiled and remains among the holdings of the National Archives in Washington, DC. The list is not entirely accurate, however. The sailors conspired to rescue as many soldiers as they could by assigning them the identities of sailors who had died during their imprisonment, such as Frederic James, who had died on September 15, and then packing the soldiers in the middle of their ranks when they left the stockade so that they could march out unrecognized and escape the hell that was Camp Sumter.

Wilbur Hale, a private with the 120th New York, was one beneficiary of this plot. Prisoner Hale was spending the night of September 20 at the prison hospital, sitting with a dying comrade. As night wore on, Hale fell asleep only to be awoken late at night by one of the nurses, a man who identified himself as Richard Lamphier Tinker, one of the sailors captured at the Second Battle of Fort Sumter. "He then said Wirz had sent for him in the early evening and told him to notify and enroll all sailors preparatory to being sent north to Charleston for parole, and thinking of a comrade that had succumbed to the cruel treatment of his captors he had entered me on the roll as Frederick A. James, carpenter's mate of the gunboat *Housatonic*."

This plan was confirmed by one of Ritson's *Powhatan* shipmates, marine Robert Scanlin, in Scanlin's pension application: "Of the 118 men who were captured on the night of September 8, 1863, 110 died of starvation while in prison. The survivors were paroled by a special act and managed to release 110 soldiers for those who had died with them."

Although Scanlin's numbers are off—considerably more than eight of the sailors captured at the Second Battle of Fort Sumter survived—the sailors' use of their comrades' identities to save soldiers is borne out by a Roll of Federal Naval Prisoners Exchanged at Cox Landing on the James River October 16, 1864. On that list are the names of many "exchanged" sailors and marines who never left Andersonville and are laid to rest in the cemetery. Of the 19 *Powhatan* sailors captured at the Second Battle of Fort Sumter and who were likely subsequently held at Andersonville, 18 are included on the list of sailors being exchanged. Only William Ritson is unaccounted for.

It may be that Ritson was held in such contempt by his fellow sailors that they would not assign his name to a soldier, even if it meant one man less was freed. Or perhaps his hanging was so notorious that the sailors thought that they may have been caught if they used his identity. We can only conjecture, but Andrew Muir's name is also missing from the sailors from the *Water Witch* who were exchanged at the same time as the other sailors.

It's not known how a sailor would have come across the name of a soldier with the 5th Rhode Island or if Charles Curtis and William Ritson ever met, but the Andersonville registers, the *Sunday Mercury* article, and the list of raiders contained in Dorence Atwater's National Archive's file, taken altogether, raise the very real possibility that the man buried under the name "Charles Curtis" may in fact have been the sailor variously identified as "William Ritson," "William Wrixon," or "W. Rickson." An 1889 letter from the War Department states William Ritson's "final disposition not reported."

A century and a half after the event, it is impossible to ferret out the entire truth behind the man that the diarists and memoirists of Andersonville called "Curtis." Given the evidence that Charles Curtis of the 5th Rhode Island was never a prisoner of war, it is entirely possible that "W. Rickson" did exist, and he was a sailor called William Ritson, from the USS *Powhatan*.

TIMELINE

1830 Born, reportedly in Philadelphia
1861 May 13 Enlists in Navy in Philadelphia, Pennsylvania
1861 May 13 to June 8 Serves on the receiving ship USS *Princeton*

1861 June 9 to September 30 Serves as seaman on the USS *Jamestown*
1861 October 1 Promoted to coxswain on the *Jamestown*
1862 August 23 Transferred to USS *Powhatan*
1862 August 24 Promoted to quartermaster on the *Powhatan*
1863 September 8 Captured at the Second Battle of Fort Sumter

WILLIAM RITSON

Known aliases: William Ritson, W. Rickson, W. Wrixon, W. Rixon, W. R. Rickson, William Riekson, Charles F. Curtis
Vessels: USS *Princeton*, USS *Jamestown*, USS *Powhatan*
Rank: Seaman; coxswain
Place of birth: Philadelphia, Pennsylvania
Approximate year of birth: 1830
Enrolled: May 13, 1861, Philadelphia, Pennsylvania
Mustered in: May 1861
Age at time of enlistment: 31
Approximate arrival at Andersonville: June 1, 1864
Assigned Mess at Andersonville: 69th Detachment, 2nd Mess
Approximate age at time of hanging: 34
Profession: Seaman
Term of Enlistment: 3 years
Physical description: 5 feet 3½ inches, dark hair, dark eyes, dark complexion, scar on left wrist

NOTES ON CHAPTER 5

Leroy Key, the man who presided over Curtis's execution, referred to Curtis as "the leader"—Diarist John L. Hoster, of the 148th New York, also described Curtis as the "ringleader."

A low-statured, massively built man—Although McElroy describes Curtis as "low-statured," records indicate that Charles F. Curtis was five feet, eight inches tall.

This interview was then published by the *Boston Journal* and picked up by other newspapers—Key's interview appears at the end of a long article on general happenings in the war in the December 11, 1864, issue of the *New York Times*.

"I understand that you are getting up a band to clear out the Irish"—This is a somewhat surprising statement because Curtis is not a particularly Irish name and Curtis's records indicate that he was born in Canada. However, according to Father

Peter Whelan's testimony at the trial of Henry Wirz, five of the six men hanged were Roman Catholic, a religious majority in Ireland and among Irish descendants.

He then requested his watch be left with his friends or with Father Martin, N.Y.C.—According to New York City Archdiocese records, there were no priests with the surname "Martin" during the Civil War, although there were two priests by that name prior to the start of the war.

Thomas F. O'Connell of the Ninth Maryland, Company D—Thomas F. O'Connell, a sergeant with the Ninth Maryland, Company D, was captured at Charleston, West Virginia, on October 18, 1863, and survived his interment at Camp Sumter. According to the regimental history of the Ninth Maryland, Sergeant O'Connell was sent to Baltimore on November 29, 1864, and there are no further records of him.

Daniel Hayes, United States, Company L—No records can be found for a prisoner by this name.

William Prentiss—Actually William S. Prentice, a private in the 16th Illinois Cavalry, Company I, the same regiment that John McElroy and Leroy Key belonged to. He was captured in January 1864 and survived his incarceration at Andersonville.

James M. Friend—James Marion Friend, referred to by John McElroy as "Marion Friend" of the 16th Illinois Cavalry, Company I, survived his imprisonment at Camp Sumter. Like William Prentice, he was a member of the same regiment but a different company than John McElroy and Leroy Key. He was captured near Jonesville, Virginia, in January 1864.

The wound was a ghastly one, across the side of the cheek. Witness put up his hand, and received a gash between the thumb and first finger—Compare this account with McElroy's statement that "Marion Friend, of Company I of our battalion, was one of the small traders, and had accumulated forty dollars by his bartering. One evening at dusk Delaney's Raiders, about twenty-five strong, took advantage of the absence of most of us drawing rations, to make a rush for Marion. They knocked him down, cut him across the wrist and neck with a razor, and robbed him of forty dollars."

There were $449 dollars in the pocketbook—This is a huge sum of money and suggests that Friend had been doing more than trading "a little." Union privates made $16 per month beginning in June 1864.

J. P. Erwin, 103rd Pennsylvania Regiment, Company B—No record can be found for a prisoner by this name and that regiment, however, there are three prisoners from Pennsylvania with similar names. John P. Erwin was a private with the Fourth Pennsylvania Cavalry, Company M, who was exchanged on April 5, 1865. Hiram Irwin was from the 103rd Pennsylvania, Company H, and was one of the "Plymouth Pilgrims" captured on April 20, 1864, who would have come into the stockade possessing a large sum of money. Irwin survived his time at Camp Sumter and was reportedly still living in 1902. Another possibility is J. C. Irwin of the 78th Pennsylvania, Company D, who died July 8, 1864, and is buried in grave 3038.

The records for the Fifth Rhode Island Heavy Artillery confirms that Charles F. Curtis was indeed a member of that regiment—There is also a Charles S. Curtis who fought with the Fourth Rhode Island, but that man was never a prisoner of war, and census records indicate that he returned to his family in Providence after the war was over.

Charles F. Curtis's compiled service record suggests that, like many substitutes, he was not an outstanding soldier and that he spent prolonged periods "Absent in hospital at Morehead, N.C." before his eventual desertion, which, according to the company's muster roll, occurred while he was on furlough, New Year's Day 1865.

Before his eventual desertion while on furlough, New Year's Day 1865— Although Curtis avoided being captured, Company A was particularly hard hit by captivity: of the 51 men captured, 32 died in prison, and 7 others died elsewhere, with one additional man shot while escaping, leaving 11 members of Curtis's Company A to survive Andersonville. Curtis himself was furloughed on September 19, but never returned, and he was listed as a deserter on October 19, 1864, two and a half months before the company muster rolls reported that he deserted, but still more than three months after his alleged execution in the prison stockade at Andersonville. Record Group 94: Records of the Adjutant General's Office, 1762–1984, Carded Medical Records, Volunteers: Mexican and Civil Wars, 1846–65 (RG94, Entry 534).

It seems highly improbable that the other Rhode Island prisoners would have allowed the listing of Charles F. Curtis of the 5th Rhode Island Heavy Artillery, as one of their "honored dead," had they believed him to be a raider—Of the 38 members of the Rhode Island delegation who traveled to Georgia to dedicate the Rhode Island monument, only three of them, Sergeant (later Captain) Emmons D. Guild, 1st Rhode Island Cavalry; Captain James C. Hubbard; and Sidney S. Williams were former prisoners, and only one of these, Emmons D. Guild was from a Rhode Island regiment. Williams fought with the 10th Massachusetts, and Hubbard with the 99th New York, although both were Rhode Island natives. Given that the monument was commissioned and erected by politicians rather than former prisoners, it seems likely that whoever created the monument saw the name "Charles Curtis" on the list of names of soldiers buried in the prison cemetery and simply included it on the monument, unaware of either the fact that the real Charles Curtis was never at Andersonville or that the man using his name was hanged as a criminal. No one from the 5th Rhode Island Heavy Artillery appears to have been involved in the making of the Rhode Island Monument.

Ritson spent under a month training on the receiving ship the USS *Princeton*, leaving her to serve as a seaman on the USS *Jamestown* from June 9 to September 30, 1861—Surprisingly, a man named "William Ritterson" served on board the *Jamestown*, and some records on William Ritson were accidently added to William Ritterson's pension file. They were not the same person, however, since William Ritterson enlisted on August 2, 1862, and served on the *Princeton* from August 4–17, 1862, then for the rest of the war on the *Jamestown* from August 28, 1862, to September 30, 1865; he then transferred to the USS *Vermont* October 1, 1865, and was discharged on October 25, 1865. Because of the similarity between their names and that they both served on the *Jamestown*, some of William Ritson's records appear in William Ritterson's widow's pension file. One of the two men apparently caused some discipline problems while on the *Jamestown*. A summary medical records in Ritterson's file states that while on the *Jamestown*, William Ritson, the seaman, was treated for "oedema" (now spelled "edema") on February 12, 1863: "Has oedema of both feet, also complains of numbness in them, caused by wearing double irons 15 days in sweat box." However, William Ritson had transferred to the *Powhatan* on August 23, 1862, which suggests that it was Ritterson and not Ritson who had been punished.

The summary continues to say that on November 9, 1863, "William Ritson" was diagnosed with "syphilis," but since William Ritson, the suspected raider, had been captured on September 8, 1863, this also likely refers to William Ritterson.

On September 8, 1863, under the cover of darkness, approximately 400 men set forth from Navy ships in Charleston Harbor as part of an amphibious nighttime assault intended to take back Fort Sumter from the Confederates—For a detailed account of this battle, see the introduction of *Frederick Augustus James's Civil War Diary*, written by Jefferson J. Hammer.

Among the hundred plus casualties of the Second Battle of Fort Sumter were 31 men from the *Powhatan*, 2 officers, 19 sailors, and 10 marines—The names of the men who were captured can be pieced together through the reports made by the captains of the various ships the morning following the battle. These reports can be found in the Official Records of the War of Rebellion and include a report from Captain Charles Steedman of the USS *Powhatan*, which includes the name of the ship's quartermaster, William Ritson. According to captured sailor Frederic Augustus James, "ninty three men and twelve officers" were captured at the Second Battle of Fort Sumter.

One of these men promptly deserted upon being captured and subsequently joined the Confederacy; another managed to escape not long after; and one was exchanged when his crewmates were sent to Andersonville—Seaman William Hill deserted upon capture and ultimately took the Oath of Allegiance and joined the Confederacy. Landsman John Nagel reportedly managed to escape, although the circumstances of his escape are not clear. Seaman Francis Birnbaum was paroled at City Point, Virginia, on March 23, 1864, and his pension application states that his "Name does not appear upon the records of Andersonville, Ga."

They signed a November 1, 1864, letter to Secretary of the Navy Gideon Welles—This letter appears in the Annual Report of the Secretary of the Navy, Washington: United States Government Printing Office, 1864, page 689.

A list of prisoners exchanged at Cox Landing on October 16, 1864—Roll of Federal Naval Prisoners of War, Exchanged at Cox Landing, on the James River, October 16, 1864, available at the National Archives and on Fold 3.

No list of the men named as hostages is known to exist—Most of the Salisbury Prison records were destroyed along with the rest of the prison by Union General George Stoneman at the end of the war. The sailors known to have been held as hostages for the lives of Beall's crew include Frederic A. James, Victor Bartlett, Richard L. Tinker, and Joseph Conneton of the *Housatonic*; John Friedline and Daniel Quigley of the *Powhatan*; and William O'Connor of the *Wissahickon*, all of whom had been captured at Fort Sumter; and Thomas Reynolds of the *T. A. Ward*, who had been captured at Murrell's Inlet on October 20, 1863.

Four decades later, Grogger wrote about his experiences in an article that was published in the *National Tribune*—This quotation is from the March 3, 1910, issue. Grogger wrote about having known "Curtis," the raider, in the *National Tribune* several times, including in the August 5, 1897, and February 8, 1906, issues. Grogger's use of the word "sergeant" in describing Curtis at Salisbury is curious, since he was listed as a private at Andersonville. It may refer to simply having had specific duties rather than a rank, although at Andersonville, most of the "Sergeants of the mess" were actual sergeants.

According to Frederic James—Frederic August James, acting carpenter's mate on the USS *Housatonic* at the time of his capture, is buried at Andersonville National Cemetery in grave number 8858. It is believed that either Richard Tinker or fellow prisoner and shipmate Joseph Conneton brought James's diary home to his widow after their exchange. James's diary is currently at the Massachusetts Historical Society.

Two Union army captains who were sent to Salisbury by Jefferson Davis in retaliation for the Union's sentencing of two Kentucky men to hard labor for trying to recruit members of their home state to fight for the Confederacy—Although not all sailors who were designated as hostages can be identified, the two army captains who were held on the same floor as the sailors were Captain Benjamin C. G. Reed of the 3rd Ohio Cavalry and Ralph O. Ives of the 10th Massachusetts, who were held as hostages for the safety of Kentuckians William Waller and Shulte Leach.

"Four prisoners who managed to escape from the cars while being conveyed from Richmond to Americus, Ga"—Frederic James's diary entry for February 20, 1864.

Junius Browne—The book in question is *Four Years in Sessesia*, published in 1865 by O D Case and Company.

James wrote that he had been assigned to Detachment 69, Mess number 2—This is from James's only letter sent from Andersonville, dated June 6, 1864, and is currently in the Frederic A. James Collection of the Massachusetts Historical Society.

In his diary, James mentions seven different sailors—In his entry for June 16, James identifies three sailors and one marine from the USS *Housatonic*, ship's nurse Richard Lamphier Tinker; coxswain Thomas McCart(h)y; ordinary seaman John Angier Hyde; and Private Martin Bannon; as well as USS *Wissahickon* landsman John S. White; USS *Ladona* seaman Nathaniel K. Suydam; and carpenter's mate Alexander Clark from the USS *Dan Smith* as working outside the stockade at the prison hospital.

Wilbur Hale, a private with the 120th New York, was one beneficiary of this plot—The story of Hale's rescue by assuming Frederic James's identity is detailed in Cornelius Van Santvoord's book *The One Hundred and Twentieth Regiment New York State Volunteers*, chapter 10, pages 102–103.

Richard Lamphier Tinker—Richard Lamphier Tinker was the ship's nurse on the *Housatonic*, and also one of Frederic James's closest friends. He survived the war, married, and had three children.

This plan was confirmed by one of Ritson's *Powhatan* shipmates—the plan was also confirmed by a nonparticipant, with the curiously titled and anonymously published book, *The Story of a Strange Career, Being the Autobiography of a Convict: An Authentic Document*. In it, author George Anderson, Acting Ensign of the USS *Perry*, who had been captured at Murrell's Inlet, South Carolina, encountered a group of sailors at Libby Prison while en route to being released. When he inquired after the members of his crew, he was told that only three of the 16 men captured with him still survived, and that approximately 75 percent of the sailors had died as prisoners. When he inquired why there were so many men present if the mortality rate was so high, the men returning from Andersonville told him a remarkable story. "Information was received at the different prisons that the sailors were to be exchanged. They originated a plan to free all the soldiers possible. Sailors gave their most intimate friends names of their deceased shipmates, the names of ships, where and when captured, the names of the officers, and, in fact, all information that would be useful. The scheme had been successful, so far."

Robert Scanlin—Scanlin's name is also given as "Scanlan," however, it is spelled Scanlin on his pension application, and therefore it is most likely the correct spelling. Scanlin's account of the plan is contained in his pension application.

It's not known how a sailor would have come across the name of a soldier—One possibility is geographical. Charles Curtis spent most of the spring of 1863 in the hospital at Morehead, North Carolina, near the Atlantic coast, while William Ritson and the *Powhatan* were patrolling the blockade just off the coast of South Carolina.

An 1889 letter from the War Department states William Ritson's "final disposition not reported"—This letter is in the pension file on William Ritterson and was sent in error when the Commissioner of Pensions asked for Ritterson's service record. It states that William Ritson, seaman on the USS *Powhatan*'s service records ends on "Sept 9," 1863, when marked, "Missing. No Further Record." There is no record of Ritson ever being discharged from the Navy, and the letter concludes with the words: "Final disposition not reported."

· 6 ·

William Collins

Known aliases: Mosby, Moseby, Jack Mosby, Samuel Collins
Regiment: 88th Pennsylvania Infantry, Company E (October 1861–January 1, 1862); Company K (January 1, 1862); Company D (January 1–July 11, 1864)
Rank: Mustered in as Private; Promoted to Corporal, July/August 1863
Place of birth: Nottingham, England
Approximate year of birth: 1835
Enrolled: October 3, 1861, Philadelphia, Pennsylvania
Mustered in: October 3, 1861
Age at time of enlistment: 26
Captured: October 12, 1864, near Rapidan River, Virginia
Assigned Mess at Andersonville: 9th Detachment, 3rd Mess
Approximate age at time of death: 29
Profession: Knitter
Term of enlistment: 3 years
Physical description: The Descriptive Books for Companies D and K differ slightly. According to Company D's description: 5 feet 11¾ inches, gray eyes, sandy hair, light complexion. According to Company K's description: 6 feet ½ inch, gray eyes, red hair, florid complexion.

WHAT HISTORY TELLS US

*W*illiam Collins is the man who was hanged twice.

William Collins is perhaps the most notorious of the six men hanged at Andersonville. In diaries where only one of the raiders is identified by name, the name given is almost invariably Collins's alias "Mosby," after the Confederate, Colonel John S. Mosby. It seems likely that the term "raiders" was inspired by Mosby's technique of attacking in small, highly effective bands and that Collins's band of thieves often copied. These Confederate raiders' attacks generally involved between 30 to 60 men, who would meet at a designated rendezvous point, strike at the enemy in a short, concentrated assault, and then disperse before the enemy could gather itself together to mount a defense. These lightning strikes of small groups of soldiers were highly effective, and the raiders at Andersonville employed similar tactics—a small group of men would select a victim, make a fast, concentrated attack in order to rob him, and quickly retreat, hopefully before reinforcements could be summoned by the victim. This style of "raiding" was successfully employed by bands of thieves at Belle Isle and Andersonville, both prisons where William Collins was held.

Corporal William Collins of the 88th Pennsylvania was the highest-ranking raider to be executed; the other five men hanged were all privates. There is little doubt that many of the prisoners perceived Collins as a leader of the men who preyed on their fellow soldiers. Warren Goss wrote that the raiders, "under the leadership of Mosby, became exceedingly bold, attacked new comers in open daylight, robbing them of blankets, watches, money, and other property of value." Charles Hopkins recalled "Mosby, or Collins, the leader of the gang, a slim, redheaded, sandy-featured, ill-looking specimen of mankind" and reported that anyone who displayed material wealth within the stockade "was noted by the sneaking spies of Mosby whose job it was to locate swag and spot where the 'prey' settled." Robert Kellogg wrote: "To add to our sorrow, and indignation, we found a large gang of desperadoes among our own men in camp, whom we called 'Mosby's Raiders' and who lived by robbing and beating, sometimes almost murdering their comrades in misfortune."

William Collins is famous not only because he was the reputed leader of the raiders, but also because his execution was botched. He mounted the gallows with the others, but the rope holding him broke during the hanging and he fell back to the ground. The executioners hastily examined him and found, to their dismay, that he was not yet dead. They hastily revived him, and, ignoring his "piteous" pleas for mercy and insistence that his fall was a sign that he was not meant to be hanged, they procured another rope, forced him back up onto the gallows, and "strung him up" a second time, this time fatally.

Unlike Delaney, Curtis, and Sullivan, there aren't any firsthand accounts written by people who claim to have known or spoken with Collins. He appears to have been universally reviled by most of the prisoners, and no one seems to have anything good to say about him. The two best accounts reputed to be about him are the *Sunday Mercury* article and John McElroy's book. The *Mercury* discusses the crimes he was responsible for, and McElroy describes his execution.

SUNDAY MERCURY ACCOUNT

According to the *Sunday Mercury*, William Collins was supposed to have been the first raider tried, but "as was understood more evidence could be had then was brought against him the first day, his case was postponed." After the others were tried, "William Collins, alias Mosby, of the Eighty-eighth Penn., Company D, was again put on his trial on charge of robbing, assaulting, and with being the leader of a gang of thieves." The testimony related against him seems less brutal than that of some of the other accused, but the reader gets the sense that something is missing from the account, because at the end of the testimony, it reports that "Mr. Higginson [the man who reportedly served as the raiders' defense attorney] said that after he had heard of Mosby's character, he declined to address the jury in his defense." But the article never relates exactly what was said about "Mosby's character."

According to the article, William Collins was finally put on trial the third day of the proceedings, after Sarsfield, Delaney, Sullivan, Muir, and Curtis had already been tried, convicted, and sentenced. The testimony against Collins is given as follows:

> *William Curtis* [sic], *alias Mosby of the 88th Penn. Company D. was again put on his trial on charge of robbing, assaulting, and with being the leader of a gang of thieves.*
>
> *George Ogleby, of the 4th Kentucky Cavalry, Company A.—I know the prisoner at the bar as "Mosby." Saw Mosby come up to a German who was buying some onions, asking the person from whom he sought them could change the bill. He said no; but said that this man (pointing to Mosby) could, the onion seller passing the bill to Mosby, who carried it off and lay down in his tent. The German demanded his change. The onion seller said he knew nothing about it. Mosby came back from his tent, and the German asked him for his bill. "Get along," Mosby said, "I know nothing of your bill." A crowd gathered around them. Mosby told the German to clear out, or he would give him a thrashing. The German went away and did not get the bill. It appeared to me that the onion seller and Mosby were acting in concert. Both their tents adjoined on another [sic].*
>
> *Joseph Ackers, of the 14th Connecticut, Company I, testified that he knew the prisoner. Knew a man to be robbed one night in his tent. It was midnight. Heard the man cry out in his tent. Just before the cry he saw Mosby creep along the tent*

and then go inside. I know Mosby did not take part in the robberies himself, but I know him to be a planner of robberies for others. I know it because I heard him lay the plans to rob persons. When any person came along who had things for sale, Mosby's gang would go along, he leading the way, and take the articles from the owners by force and violence sometimes. Saw the gang attack parties selling articles, when a fight ensued, Mosby taking part in the fight. Heard Mosby tell his men to be ready to go round at night, and take boots or shoes or any other articles they could find.

James Keating, of the 42nd New York, Company [?], was called for the defense. Said: I heard Mosby say he would not go hungry, while he could steal anything. He was called a raider, a name which he deserved.

Mr. Higginson said that after he had heard of Mosby's character, he declined to address the jury in his defense.

The jury found Mosby guilty of robbing and assaulting his fellow prisoners, and with being a leader of an organized band of thieves, robber, and garrotters, and he was sentenced to be hanged.

JOHN McELROY'S ACCOUNT

John McElroy describes the horrific incident where Collins's hanging was botched with the following words:

Five of the bodies swung around dizzily in the air. The sixth—that of "Mosby," a large, powerful, raw-boned man, one of the worst in the lot, and who, among other crimes, had killed Limber Jim's brother—broke the rope, and fell with a thud to the ground. Some of the men ran forward, examined the body, and decided that he still lived. The rope was cut off his neck, the meal sack removed, and water thrown in his face until consciousness returned. At the first instant he thought he was in eternity. He gasped out:

"Where am I? Am I in the other world?"

Limber Jim muttered that they would soon show him where he was, and went on grimly fixing up the scaffold anew. "Mosby" soon realized what had happened, and the unrelenting purpose of the Regulator Chiefs. Then he began to beg piteously for his life, saying:

"O for God's sake, do not put me up there again! God has spared my life once. He meant that you should be merciful to me."

Limber Jim deigned him no reply. When the scaffold was rearranged, and a stout rope had replaced the broken one, he pulled the meal sack once more over "Mosby's" head, who never ceased his pleadings. Then picking up the large man as if he were a baby, he carried him to the scaffold and handed him up to Tom Larkin, who fitted the noose around his neck and sprang down. The supports had not been set with the same delicacy as at first, and Limber Jim had to set his

heel and wrench desperately at them before he could force them out. Then "Mosby"
passed away without a struggle.

Although McElroy embellished several details of the events concerning
the arrest, trial, and execution of the raiders, he did not fabricate the botched
hanging. The breaking rope features prominently in many of the witness's diaries. For example, Eugene Forbes wrote: "Shortly after five o'clock, the whole
six were swung off, but Moseby's rope broke, bringing him to the ground,
but he was soon strung up again." John L. Hoster reported in his diary that,
"Mosby's rope broke and he fell to the ground." And Robert Kellogg wrote in
his 1865 memoir that "as the drop fell, the rope around the neck of the leader
of the gang broke."

OTHER ACCOUNTS

John L. Hoster recorded: "At precisely 5 P.M. the drop fell, Mosby's rope
broke and he fell to the ground. Curtis fell farther than the rest and died very
soon. Mosby when he fell begged for some of his friends to come forward
and rescue him. He offered Lumber Jim $1000 to save his life. Lumber Jim
replied, "You followed me for my money, I'm now following you for your
life." He then took him up on the scaffold adjusted the rope and hood—then
jerked the scaffold from under him."

And Edwin T. Marsh of the 140th NY said in his diary that: "The rope
broke and the sixth man fell to his knees. . . . He begged hard to be let off.
Said he had been hung once and it was not 'lawful' to hang him again. The
executioner showed him the same kind of mercy he had accorded his victims.
He was walked up the little ladder where he stood on the stringer until a
noose was adjusted, then 'Slim Jim' pushed him off with his hands."

WHAT THE RECORDS SHOW

William Collins has the longest compiled service record of any of the six men
who were executed. Some aspects of it are consistent with what might be
expected of a rogue and a thief, while other parts are surprising.

Collins enlisted in the army early in the war, mustering in October 3,
1861, less than six months after the war began. He was not drafted and did
not serve as a substitute for another man, but enlisted, apparently, under his

own volition. He gave his name as William Collins, and his age as 26 years old. He said that he'd been born in Nottingham, England, and gave his profession as "knitter"—a rather surprising occupation for a man in his prime who, at close to six feet tall, towered over most men.

Although John McElroy claimed that all the hanged men were bounty jumpers and used aliases, William Collins was not a bounty jumper. He may have been exactly who he claimed he was. At the time of his enlistment in Philadelphia, Pennsylvania, William Collins stated that he was 26 years old and had been born in Nottingham, England. Births were not registered in England until 1837, roughly two years after William Collins's military records say that he was born. Although William Collins is such a common name it's impossible to say if this is the right man, an 1849 manifest for a ship called the *America*, lists 13-year-old W. Collins, his 11-year-old sister Charlotte, and a 55-year-old woman named Louisa Smallwood, possibly their grandmother, as sailing from England to New York Harbor on a ship called the *America*. The 1850 US census shows the family of John Collins, a cordwainer, his wife Anne, 16-year-old William, and 14-year-old Charlotte living with Louisa Smallwood in the South Ward of Philadelphia, the same city where William Collins, the raider, enlisted in the army. Although some boys in the 1850s would have held a job by the age of 16, William has no profession listed. By the 1860 census, the family has moved to Philadelphia's 8th Ward; Charlotte is no longer with them, but Louisa Smallwood still is. Curiously, although he's now 26 years old, William Collins still has no listed profession. Louisa Smallwood died May 25, 1861, and a William Collins of Philadelphia enlisted in the army five months later. There's no way to prove whether this William is the same William who joined the 88th Pennsylvania—the household seems to have broken up by the 1870 census and there are no William Collinses living in Philadelphia after the war. The William Collins who came to America with the same name in 1849 might be the man known to history as a raider, or he might not be.

Whoever he was before joining the army, William Collins of the 88th Pennsylvania was not a great soldier. When he enlisted on October 3, 1861, probably at the newly established recruiting center at 527 Chestnut Street in Philadelphia, the 88th was still in the process of being formed and outfitted. Collins was originally assigned to Company E, but he was transferred to Company K by order of the regiment's commanding officer, Colonel George McLean, on January 1, 1862, and then transferred again to Company D on the same day. This may suggest that Collins had already proven himself to be a discipline problem, because Company D was notorious for its discipline problems within its ranks; "hard cases," who had a reputation for hard drinking, flouting of regulations, and general insubordination. Collins may have demonstrated discipline issues even before he left Company E; the muster rolls for his time there say "not stated" on the line that asks "present or absent," suggesting that he may have spent at least some of his first three months in service away from his regiment. Collins is listed as "present" with Company D for January and February, but AWOL for March and April 1862.

Somehow, the army managed to get him back by the muster roll for May and June 1862, more than half a year after he'd originally signed on. By the end of June, there is a notation in the muster roll saying that Collins owed the sutler $7.00, although there is no designation as to what he owed it for. He apparently managed to stay with his regiment (or perhaps more accurately, the regiment managed to keep him) for almost all of July and August, but it didn't last long.

Collins took part in the Second Battle of Bull Run, where he was wounded in the thigh and captured by the Confederates on August 30, 1862, the last day of the battle. He was paroled back to the Union at Groveton Battlefield three days later. Collins was sent to the hospital for his wound to be treated, remaining there while his regiment went on to fight at Antietam and Fredericksburg. He returned to duty December 4, 1862, but only stayed with his company for 10 days before returning to the army hospital set up at Steuart's Mansion on the outskirts of Baltimore on December 14.

Collins apparently preferred the hospital to active duty. He was supposed to return to his regiment on January 21, 1863, but apparently left the hospital grounds and stayed in town while the other hospitalized members of the 88th were escorted to rejoin their regiment. He was spotted, quite possibly in an inebriated condition, by an assistant surgeon at the hospital, who summoned assistance and had Collins placed in the guardhouse. The assistant surgeon, DeWitt Peters, had had quite enough of the hard-drinking, injury-faking Collins and wrote to the provost marshals office in Baltimore the following day, requesting a special escort to return him to his regiment at the first opportunity, writing:

U.S. Army General Hospital
Steuart's Mansion
Baltimore, Md, Jan 22, 1863

Major:
  Private Wm Collins Co D 88th Regt Penn Vols, was down on the list (of yesterday) to go to his regiment, but escaped & went into the City. I saw him on the street today & caused him to be arrested & brought to our Guard House. He had an old wound of the thigh, which causes him to limp when under inspection but today I saw him walking as well as any person could. He is a hard drinker & has been in our Guard House before. Can you not take him under charge & send

him to his regiment by the first opportunity? We may not have convalescents to send for some time to come & this man is better off in the field than confined here, where he is a source of annoyance.

Hon Sir
Very Respectfully—
DeWitt C. Peters
Assistant Surgeon
USA

Collins rejoined the 88th on February 25, 1863, and was marked "present" on the Company Muster Roll in March and April. Except for his 10-day stint with the 88th in December, it was the first time Collins was back with his company since the Second Battle of Bull Run, six months before.

At the beginning of May, Collins was apparently present and took part in the Battle of Chancellorsville, a six-day major battle that ended with a Confederate victory. Two months later, he took part in the Battle of Gettysburg. On the opening day of the Battle of Gettysburg, Baxter's Brigade (of which the 88th was a part) fought fiercely on Oak Ridge and bloodied three Confederate brigades, destroying Iverson's Brigade. The 88th captured two regimental colors (23rd North Carolina's and 26th Alabama's). After the initial killing volley, the 88th charged over the stone wall to capture the survivors of the 23rd North Carolina, which had suffered over 80 percent casualties. It was noted that the "hard cases" of Company D were the first over the wall. Apparently, the large soldier from Philadelphia must have performed well enough to merit a promotion, because he was promoted to corporal on the first day of battle, and his name appears on the plaque dedicated to the 88th on the Pennsylvania Monument at Gettysburg.

Collins was with his company three months later when the 88th Pennsylvania made a series of night maneuvers in Northern Virginia, getting ahead of Confederate forces that had been spotted in the area. According to the regimental history, on October 9

at ten o'clock at night, marching orders were received, and the column moved off silently at two o'clock the next morning, keeping under cover, and going in a northeasterly direction for some four or five miles before halting . . . at nightfall numerous campfires were kindled at the edge of the woods for the purpose of deceiving the enemy, then the road was taken, the troops halting near Pony Mountain in the 'wee sma' hours.' Before day-dawn orders were again given, but the march was delayed until nine o'clock . . . fording the chilly waters of the Rappannock at Kelly's Ford in the afternoon. Here the tired soldiers bivouacked for the night. . . . The brigade remained at the ford until the 12th, but at midnight the men were aroused, and, proceeding to Warrenton Junction, formed line of battle to protect the immense wagon-train parked there. The position had hardly been taken when the bugle sounded 'Forward, march,' the head of the column pulling out at once for Bristoe, which was reached by nightfall, the command having marched not less than thirty miles by the sinuous route taken.

Collins's compiled service record contains three different Memorandum from Prisoner of War Records, each with a different date of desertion on it. He deserted on either October 11 or 12, or possibly during the night of October 11 and 12, most likely going missing in the wee hours of October 12 because records indicate that the regiment was on the move when Collins went missing, and because when he did, he was carrying equipment intended for the garrison. Records indicate that Collins may have arrived at Belle Isle in Richmond as soon as October 13, although Sullivan's records say that he arrived at Belle Isle between October 13 and 20. It may be that Collins arrived at Belle Isle during the week of October 13 rather than on the day itself.

At any rate, somewhere along all the stops and starts the 88th Pennsylvania was making, the large, hard-drinking Corporal Collins went missing. The Descriptive List of Deserters states that William Collins left the regiment on October 12, "Deserted on the retreat from the Rapidan River." It seems odd that a man who had fought at the Second Battle of Bull Run, at Chancellorsville and at Gettysburg with almost two and a half years of military service would suddenly desert while on maneuvers with just seven months left to his period of enlistment. There were Confederates in the area, and their presence would culminate in the Battle of Bristoe Station on October 14, although the 88th Pennsylvania did not fight in that battle. Also worth noting is that the night William Collins allegedly went missing was moonless; on the night of October 12, the moon was in its new phase, so seeing would have been very difficult that moonless night. Nor did Collins throw away his gun, as Delaney did. The Company Muster Roll for September/October 1863 bears the notation, "To be deducted from his pay $26 75/100 for loss of arms accoutrements, Camp & Garrison Equipage."

Given the circumstances, Collins may have deserted, or he may have simply gotten separated from his company while they were on night maneuvers (for example, if he left them to relieve himself) and then not been able to find them again. Regardless, he was roaming the woods in the dark and stumbled into enemy soldiers while in uniform and carrying a gun and full pack of equipment.

Either way, William Collins ended up a prisoner of war. Collins arrived at Belle Isle Prison Camp in Richmond, Virginia, soon after his capture. Not long after, he reportedly began a career of organizing a band of thieves and henchmen within the prison. He adopted the nickname "Mosby" and continued leading his band of thieves until he was transferred to Camp Sumter, more commonly known as Andersonville Prison, on March 4, 1864, making him one of the earliest prisoners to be held at the prison, which had only received its first prisoners on February 24, 1864, eight days earlier. It didn't take long for him to renew his thieving ways.

Despite his reputation as a "leader" or "chief," Collins seemed to have been more of an orchestrator than a perpetrator. Perhaps the earliest mention of him at Andersonville was in the diary of Robert Kellogg, who wrote on May 5 that "the Moseby gang" had made an unsuccessful attempt to stage a raid on Kellogg and his companions. It was Kellogg's third day in camp.

One thing that is surprising is that the testimony against him that was related in the *Sunday Mercury* article appears to be relatively mild when compared to the vicious attack on Dowd, and that one witness even states, "I know Mosby did not take part in the robberies himself, but I know him to be a planner of robberies for others." On the other hand, the article continues, "Mr. Higginson said that after he had heard of Mosby's character, he declined to address the jury in his defense." There is a definite sense that something is missing in the telling, but there's no way of knowing what.

Although John McElroy assigned a band of raiders for each of the six executed men ("They formed themselves into bands numbering five to twenty-five, each led by a bold, unscrupulous, energetic scoundrel. We now called them 'Raiders,' and the most prominent and best known of the bands were called by the names of their ruffian leaders, as 'Mosby's Raiders,' 'Curtis's Raiders,' 'Delaney's Raiders,' 'Sarsfield's Raiders,' 'Collins's Raiders,' etc."), none of the prisoners who wrote about the raiders in their diaries or in memoirs within the first couple of years following the war confirm this, although several cite Collins, a.k.a. Mosby, as the chief of the raiders. It's also interesting that McElroy lists two different bands as being led by the same man, one as "Mosby's Raiders" and the other as "Collins's Raiders," even though he acknowledges elsewhere that Collins used the alias Mosby. According to the *Sunday Mercury*, it appears as if Delaney, Sullivan, Sarsfield, and Muir worked together, along with several others rather than being the leaders of competing gangs.

Which is not to say that the gang Collins led was the only one in the prison. Leroy Key also describes Curtis as the "chief of the raiders" while John Hoster calls Curtis "the ringleader." Just as it's hard to get an accurate estimate of the number of raiders, it's impossible to tell how many bands of raiders there were and how many men acted as leaders within the groups. It is certain, however, that the big, six-foot-tall redhead from Philadelphia stood out in the minds of the witnesses, both because of his notoriety and because of his botched hanging.

TIMELINE

1835-ish Born, Nottingham, England

1861 October 3 Enrolled in Philadelphia, Pennsylvania, for a three-year enlistment, assigned to Company E, and mustered in the same day. Enlistment papers state that Collins was born in Nottingham, England, and lists his occupation as "knitter." Collins's physical description is "eyes gray; hair: sandy, age: 26, Height 5' 11 ¾," assigned to Co. E.

1861 November/December "Not stated"; sometime in this period, Collins was transferred to Company K

1862 January 1 Transferred to Company K, and then to Company D on the same day by order of the colonel commanding the regiment

1862 March/April AWOL, April 16 Co. D

1862 May/June Present, owes sutler $7

1862 July/August Absent, wounded, in hospital

1862 August 28–30 Took part in the Second Battle of Bull run; wounded in thigh

1862 September 2 Paroled at Groveton Battlefield

1862 September/October Absent, sick, and wounded at Bull Run. Missed the Battle of Antietam September 17, 1862, because he was still on parole after being captured and exchanged at Bull Run.

1862 November Still absent, but parole is met so Collins can now officially rejoin his regiment

1862 December 4 Returned to duty following his injury at Bull Run

1862 December 16 Sent to hospital as being "sick," but it may also have been for a reported aggravation of his injured thigh

1863 January/February Absent, sick

1863 January 22 "Source of annoyance" at hospital letter, locked in guardhouse ("He is a hard drinker and has been in our guard house before"). An escort is requested to return him to his regiment.

1863 February 25 or March 24 Rejoined his regiment

1863 March/April Present

1863 April 10 Present on Special Muster Roll

1863 May/June Present; Present at the Battle of Chancellorsville, May 1–6, 1863

1863 July 1 Promoted to corporal

1863 July 1–3 Took part in the Battle of Gettysburg

1863 July/August Present

1863 October 12 Deserted/was captured while on retreat from the Rapidan River

1863 October 13 (or later that week) Arrived Belle Isle

1864 March 4 Arrived at Andersonville
1864 July 11 Executed

NOTES ON CHAPTER 6

Corporal William Collins—Collins came into the army as a private, but was promoted to corporal on July 1, 1863, the first day of the Battle of Gettysburg.

"and with being the leader of a gang of thieves"—This charge is unique among the accused, according to the *Mercury*'s account of the trial. The other defendants were charged with robbery and assault, but only Collins is charged with leading a gang.

George Ogleby, of the 4th Kentucky Cavalry, Company A—No record can be found for a soldier by this name; this probably refers to William Oglesby, Fourth Kentucky Cavalry, Company A, who was captured at Somerville, Georgia, on September 13, 1863. He arrived at Richmond September 26, 1863, transferred to Andersonville March 19, 1864, and was paroled at Savannah, Georgia, November 19, 1864.

Joseph Ackers, of the 14th Connecticut, Company I—According to the *History of the Fourteenth Regiment, Connecticut Volunteer Infantry,* Joseph Acker of the 14th Connecticut, Company I, was an alias for Private George Fennel, who enlisted on September 11, 1863, and deserted a month later, on October 16, 1863.

James Keating, of the 42nd New York, Company [?]—James F. Keating of the 42nd New York, Company K, enlisted on August 26, 1863, and reportedly deserted on October 12, 1863. The *Sunday Mercury* leaves a blank where the letter indicating his company should go.

Mr. Higginson—Henry C. Higginson, a private from the 19th Illinois, Company K, enlisted June 16, 1861 (he is also sometimes reported to have belonged to the 31st Illinois Infantry, but there's no record of him in their muster roll). He was captured at Chickamauga on September 20, 1863, and was sent first to Richmond, then to Andersonville. Although Higginson is reported to have acted as the raiders' defense attorney, his only legal "experience" appears to have been the fact that his father was elected sheriff of Pekin, Illinois, in 1855, when Higginson was 11 years old. Following the raiders' trial, he was one of a delegation of prisoners sent from Andersonville in August to bring a petition asking the federal government for a resumption of prisoner exchanges and supplies for the prisoners. Higginson mustered out September 28, 1864, because his term of service had expired while he was a prisoner. He later testified at the inquiry into the assassination of Abraham Lincoln, saying that one of his guards showed him a letter from someone in the North who was sympathetic to the Southern cause, and that that letter was signed "J. Wilkes." Following the war, Higginson worked as a life insurance salesman and later as a decorator.

"And who, among other crimes, had killed Limber Jim's brother"—McElroy is the first to charge Collins with murder, however, "Limber Jim" has never been positively identified, and consequently, there is no proof that he actually had a brother.

Then picking up the large man as if he were a baby, he carried him to the scaffold and handed him up to Tom Larkin—Thomas Larkin was a private in the 16th Illinois, Company H. Given that William Collins was a strapping six-footer, it is doubtful that Limber Jim could have carried him "like a baby."

The supports had not been set with the same delicacy as at first, and Limber Jim had to set his heel and wrench desperately at them before he could force them out—Earlier in the chapter, McElroy states that two men, "Wat" Payne and "Stag" Harris "were appointed to pull the stays from under the platform at the signal," and when Leroy Key gives the signal "Payne and Harris snatched the supports out with a single jerk." In McElroy's version, Jim appears to be one of the men guarding the perimeter of the gallows. Prisoner Edwin Marsh, however, wrote in his diary that, "the trap was sprung by 'Slim Jim' the executioner with an axe, knocking the prop out from under a swing door on which the murderers stood. By this act, five were launched into eternity. The rope broke and the sixth man fell to his knees. . . . The executioner showed him the same kind of mercy he had accorded his victims. He was walked up the little ladder where he stood on the stringer until a noose was adjusted, then 'Slim Jim' pushed him off with his hands." Most accounts of the hanging don't indicate who actually sprang the trap on the gallows.

A rather surprising occupation for a man in his prime who, at close to six feet tall, towered over most men—Collins's compiled service records list his height at five feet eleven and three quarters, and six feet and one-half inch, making him much taller than the other raiders. Delaney and Charles Curtis both stood five feet eight inches; Muir was five feet five inches; and Sullivan, Sarsfield, and William Ritson are all listed as being five feet three and half inches.

An 1849 manifest—"New York Passenger Lists, 1820–1891," database with images, *FamilySearch* (https://familysearch.org/ark:/61903/1:1:27P4-ZS1, April 15, 2015), Smallwood, 1849; citing NARA microfilm publication M237 (Washington, DC: National Archives and Records Administration, n.d.); FHL microfilm.

There are no William Collinses living in Philadelphia after the war—There are several William Collinses living in Pennsylvania in 1870, none of them gave England as their birthplace and date of birth in the mid-1830s.

Company D was notorious for its discipline problems within its ranks; "hard cases," who had a reputation for hard drinking, flouting of regulations, and general insubordination—Correspondence with Major Michael N. Ayoub, author of *Campfire Chronicles: The Words and Deeds of the 88th Pennsylvania, 1861–1865.*

The assistant surgeon, DeWitt Peters, had had quite enough of the hard-drinking, injury-faking Collins—This letter is enclosed in William Collins's compiled service record at the National Archives in Washington, DC.

Steuart's Mansion—Located in Baltimore, Maryland, this mansion was built in 1795 and belonged to the Steuart family. When owner George H. Steuart resigned his commission in the US Army to join the Army of Northern Virginia as a brigadier general and fight for the Confederacy, the US government confiscated the property. Jarvis Military Hospital was set up on the grounds, and the Steuarts' mansion served as the hospital's headquarters.

Two months later, he took part in the Battle of Gettysburg—Collins's name is included on the Pennsylvania Monument at Gettysburg, which is considered to be solid proof that he took part in the battle. According to 83rd Pennsylvania Regiment historian, Major Michael Ayoub, author of *The Campfire Chronicles; The Words and Deeds of the 88th Pennsylvania 1861–1865*, the men of the 88th were so zealous about only the names of men who actually took part in the fighting being included on the monument, that they personally chiseled away names of men who were not present at the battle. This apparently happened to the name that was originally listed below Collins's. Since Collins's name is included, the other members of the 88th must have known him to have been present.

According to the regimental history—*History of the 88th Pennsylvania Volunteers in the War for the Union, 1861–1865*, by John D. Yautier.

· 7 ·

J. Sarsfield

Aliases: James Sarsfield, John Sarsfield, Patrick Sarsfield, Jack Sarsfield
Regiment: 140C New York
Rank: Private
Place of birth: Ireland
Approximate year of birth: 1841; Riker's Island Depot, New York City
Mustered in: Joined Regiment at Culpeper, Virginia, September 23, 1863
Enrolled in: Riker's Island Depot, New York City
Age at time of enlistment: 22
Captured: May 5, 1864 at Battle of the Wilderness
Arrived at Andersonville: Late May 1864
Assigned Mess at Andersonville: 52nd Detachment, 1st Mess
Approximate age at time of death: 23
Profession: Shoemaker
Term of Enlistment: 3 years
Physical description: 5 feet 3½ inches, gray eyes, brown hair, light complexion

WHAT HISTORY TELLS US

*P*rivate Sarsfield is one of the more challenging of the six raiders to discover, in part because of inconsistencies involving his first name and his regiment. Although his first name is recorded as "JNO"—an abbreviation of "John"—on his grave marker and by most of the diarists of the day and subsequent memoirists, there are no John Sarsfields on the rosters of either the 140th or 144th New York, the two regiments generally assigned to the raider Sarsfield. Most of the men who were present at the execution reported

84

his regiment as the 140th New York, with the exception of Gilbert E. Sabre's 1865 memoir, which reported that Sarsfield belonged to the 144th New York. Fourteen years later, John McElroy would also erroneously list Sarsfield as belonging to the 144th New York, a mistake that was repeated by subsequent authors, many of whom likely used McElroy as their source of information. While there are no soldiers named "Sarsfield" in the 144th New York, there is a James Sarsfield who fought with the 140th New York.

Two separate prisoners from the 140th New York confirm that one of the raiders was a man from their regiment. Edwin Marsh from the 140th New York witnessed the deaths of the six men while a prisoner, and wrote in his diary that, "One of them Sarfield [*sic*] was a member of Company 'C,' our regiment, a bounty jumper assigned to it from New York City." Another prisoner, Corporal Leonard Chester Colt of the 140th New York, Company D, also wrote in his diary that one of the hanged men was from his own regiment. The compiled service record for James Sarsfield states that he was assigned to the 140th New York Infantry, Company C, that he enlisted in New York City, and that he was "Tried by court martial, and executed inside the prison" at Andersonville, dying of "asphyxia."

Beyond the two diaries that confirm Sarsfield's regiment, there are four main sources of information on the man besides his compiled service record. Of these, two are unreliable, one is the article in the *Sunday Mercury*, and the fourth is the diary of a prisoner who witnessed Sarsfield's execution, but who died himself as a prisoner of war seven months later.

JOHN RANSOM'S ACCOUNT

The only account of the hanging that takes any particular notice of Sarsfield on the gallows is John Ransom, who claimed to have kept a prison diary, then copied the entire thing out by hand before the original was supposedly lost in a fire. His accounts are so overblown, however, that it's questionable whether such a diary ever existed. Of everything that he wrote about "John Sarsfield 144th New York," the only fact that stands up to scrutiny is that the man's last name was Sarsfield. All the other details existed only in Ransom's fertile imagination:

> *Sarsfield made quite a speech; he had studied for a lawyer; at the outbreak of the rebellion he had enlisted and served three years in the army, been wounded in battle, furloughed home, wound healed up, promoted to first sergeant and also commissioned; his commission as a lieutenant had arrived but had not been mustered in when he was taken prisoner; began by stealing parts of rations,*

gradually becoming hardened as he became familiar with crimes practiced; evil associates helped him to go down hill and here he was.

Ransom also describes Sarsfield's hanging with a bloodthirsty, self-righteous zeal: "Munn died easily, as also did Delaney, all the rest died hard, and particularly Sarsfield who drew his knees to his chin then straightened them out with a jerk, the veins in his neck swelling out as if they would burst. It was awful to see, but also a necessity." Ransom errs in stating that Sarsfield was a lawyer and that he'd served for three years as a soldier. There is no record of Sarsfield having been wounded in battle, his rank was private, and he never served as either a first sergeant or a lieutenant. Since Ransom referred to the executed sailors as "A. Munn" and "W. R. Rickson," this suggests that this is an account made up long after the fact, since the names "Munn" and "Rickson" do not appear until the organization of the National Cemetery at Andersonville after the war had ended.

"HONEST" JACK COTTER'S ACCOUNT

Interestingly, another long-after-the-fact account of Sarsfield survives, this one as fraught with errors as Ransom's book. It is an 1883 newspaper account by a man who claimed to have known Sarsfield and spoken with him on the morning of his execution. Under the exaggerated heading "How a Band of Union Raiders Successfully Robbed the Entire Camp at Andersonville," a man who identified himself as "Honest" Jack Cotter, a Hartford, Connecticut, police officer recalled "pushing his way to the front" of the newly formed prison police and taking over as chief. Although his version of events doesn't stand up to scrutiny, his account is repeated here simply because it is one of so few that refer specifically to Sarsfield.

> *"Yes," said honest "Jack" Cotter of the Hartford police force last night, "I remember the day as though it were but yesterday, when the half dozen "raiders" were executed at Andersonville. I knew one of the men well. He was Jack Sarsfield on the One Hundred and Fifty-fifth New York. The morning he was executed I had a talk with him and asked him if the raiders had ever murdered anyone. He said to me: 'Cotter, I'll tell you squarely. We have never killed a man here, but we have taken all the money we could get hold of.'"*

In addition to not knowing "Jack" Sarsfield's regiment, it is extremely unlikely that prisoners would have been allowed outside the stockade to speak with the condemned men, who were being guarded by prison guards. Nor is there any mention in prison documents of a prisoner named Cotter ascending to be the chief of police. "Honest Jack," therefore, cannot be taken seriously.

SUNDAY MERCURY ACCOUNT

The *Sunday Mercury* places Sarsfield as part of a particularly vicious attack on a prisoner identified as "Dowd," a supposition affirmed by prisoner Eugene Forbes who wrote in his diary on June 30 that "towards night news came in that Sarsfield, one of the principles, who said he 'would cut Dowd's heart out and throw it in his face' had been convicted and sentenced to be hung."

The attack on Dowd was, by many accounts, the catalyst that prompted the Confederate prison officials to take action. The story goes that Dowd heard Sarsfield calling out, "Who wants to buy this watch?" This was a frequent raider ploy to discover who in the prison had cash on them. Dowd asked to see the watch in question—a sign that he possessed enough money to make such a purchase—then declined to buy it, at which point Sarsfield departed. He returned a short while later with reinforcements, and demanded Dowd's money. When Dowd refused, they attacked him, beating him savagely before finally relieving him of his watch and a large sum of cash. Bleeding and bruised, Dowd made his way to the prison gate where he managed to gain the attention of Captain Henry Wirz. Dowd made such an impression on Wirz that the commandant immediately ordered the arrest of the guilty parties, saying that no rations would be issued until those responsible for the attack were given up. This incident, according to many accounts, led to the arrest, trial, and execution of the raiders.

The *Sunday Mercury* account identifies Sarsfield as both the prisoner who initially offered to sell the watch, and as one of the main assailants, using "brass knuckles" as he attempted to subdue Dowd through physical violence. This account links Sarsfield with Delaney and Sullivan, which suggests that the three men may have been part of a band of raiders, rather than each one leading a band of their own.

> *Patrick Murphy, Fifty-Second N.Y., Company B, and John Sarsfield, One Hundred and Fortieth N.Y., Company C, were charged with assaulting with intent to murder (if necessary) and highway robbery. They pleaded not guilty.*
>
> *John G. Dowd, Ninety-seventh N.Y., Company D, was the first witness. The appearance of this man excited the horror and pity of everyone present. His head and face, arms, legs, and body generally bore marks of the most brutal*

violence. He testified as follows—On the 28th [sic] of June, about one o'clock, I was sitting in my tent, when Sarsfield came along, crying out "Who wants to buy a watch?" (Sarsfield's object was to find out who had money.) I asked him what his watch was worth, and he replied, twenty dollars. Sarsfield left, and soon after returned with prisoner Murphy. Sarsfield renewed the offer to sell the watch, and while doing so, the other prisoner grabbed at my pantaloons, which I had in my hand, cleaning. In the scuffle, I was struck with "brass knuckles" in the face, by Sarsfield, as I believe. I then took my knife out of my pocket to defend myself. Several others then attacked me and one of them snatched the knife out of my hand, and, in doing so, cut me across the hand. Sarsfield had a dagger in his hand, and threatened if I resisted he would cut my heart out and throw it in my face. I was frequently struck with the "brass knuckles," I saw one of the men (not on trial) take hold of the chain of my watch and draw it out. I was then knocked down and turned over. They took hold of my watch pocket and turned it out. It contained a pocket book containing $136, which the raiders carried off.

Sergeant Joseph Rivers, Twenty-second N.Y., Co. M, swore that on the 26th inst., while looking for some of his boys, he was met by a man who brought him to his tent to sell him a blanket. Outside the tent they met Sarsfield, opposite his tent, who said he had a better blanket to see; called witness a s—n of a b—h, and dragged him back into the tent and assaulted witness with a screw. Sarsfield took witness by the pocket, and took of it $50.04, together with some small articles, a spoon, a comb, etc. He also took his haversack and blouse, in which there was tobacco. They then tried to knock him down, tried to pull him down by his hair. He made a struggle and got away.

R. E. Spicer, Seventy-sixth New York, Company E, swore that he was present at the attack on Dowd. Murphy was not there, but he recognized Sarsfield as one of the men who a tacked [sic] Dowd with a knife, with which he struck him on the head; Sarsfield's character is that of a thief and a robber; he goes about choking and robbing men and threatening to cut their throats if they say a word or make any resistance.

N. Baldwin, Seventy-sixth New York, Company C, while proving that Murphy did not take part in the riot, swore that Sarsfield was one of the men who attacked Dowd; witness stated that he knew Sarsfield to be a robber; the day before he decoyed five men into his tent, and, with others, swore he would kill those five men if they made any noise, and then robbed them. . . .

Joseph Terril, One Hundred and First Ohio, Company B, swore that he knew Sarsfield, who was generally seen in company with two men, one of then named Delany; witness saw as many as twenty or thirty men a day come out of Sarsfield's tent, their pants nearly torn off; the first that would be heard, after these men entered the tent, would be the men gasping for breath; Sarsfield and his gang raided on witness one night.

The result of the examination into this case was the acquittal of Murphy and the conviction of Sarsfield, who was sentenced to be hanged.

EUGENE FORBES'S ACCOUNT

Eugene Forbes was a 31-year-old sergeant with the Fourth New Jersey Infantry when he was captured, the day after James Sarsfield, at the Battle of
the Wilderness. His diary, beginning just before his capture, was written in
daily until just two days before his death on February 7, 1865. Although he
survived Andersonville, his frail body could not last long enough to see him
home, and he died at Florence Stockade in Florence, South Carolina, where
he was buried in an unmarked trench grave. One of the other prisoners, Peter J. Edmonds, who was with him when he died, brought the diary back to
Forbes's hometown of Trenton. Because Forbes was an orphan with no family, Edmonds gave the diary to Forbes's former employer, printers Murphy
and Bechtel, who published it as a 68-page pamphlet in 1865. Forbes's diary
is particularly detailed with regard to the attack on prisoner Dowd, which
precipitated the downfall of the raiders. Forbes makes particular mention of
the raider Sarsfield and reports that one of his tent mates, Samuel Oakley
Bellerjeau, went out to testify at the raiders' trial on the day Sarsfield was tried.

> *Thursday, June 30—... The crusade against the raiders continues, and several
> were taken today; three of those who robbed Dowd are reported to be among the
> number; the fourth and worse one has been caught since the above writing; they
> are now pretty well cleared out; ... Oak. went out as a witness; towards night
> news came in that Sarsfield, one of the principals, who said he would "Cut out
> Dowd's heart and throw it in his face," had been convicted and sentenced to be
> hung; the trial of the others will come off tomorrow.*

WHAT THE RECORDS SHOW

On March 23, 1863, a 22-year-old Irish immigrant named James Sarsfield
arrived at Castle Garden, which served as the immigration station for New
York City in the decades before Ellis Island was built. Young Sarsfield arrived
on a ship called *The City of Baltimore* and gave his profession as "laborer," an
all-purpose description for a man who would take any job, whether it be farm
work, digging ditches, or other kinds of physical labor that was suited for an
uneducated, needy man. It can't be proven for certain that this man was the
same person who would enlist in the army just under six months later, but
it seems likely. Arriving when he did, this young man would not have been
in New York City long enough to appear on any census records, and there
are no James Sarsfields in New York City in either the 1860 or the 1870 US

censuses, nor does he appear in the 1865 New York State census, or in the city directories in 1863 or 1864.

A curious thing happened on September 1, 1863, the day James Sarsfield enlisted in the army. A man named James Sarsfield, a 22-year-old, five foot three and half inches tall, gray-eyed, brown-haired shoemaker walked into the army recruiting station in Brooklyn, New York, and enlisted. He had been drafted and was reporting for duty, and he was assigned to the 140th New York Infantry. That same day, at that same recruiting station, a man named John Sarsfield, a 23-year-old, five feet three inches tall, gray-eyed, brown-haired shoemaker, walked into that same Brooklyn recruiting station and enlisted in the army. John Sarsfield was signing up to serve as a substitute for another man, not identified, who was paying him to take his place in the service. John Sarsfield was assigned to the 52nd New York Infantry, a regiment made up almost entirely of German immigrants. James Sarsfield reported to Riker's Island Depot, a training camp for incoming soldiers, and eventually joined his regiment, which was already fighting in Virginia. John Sarsfield did not report for duty, apparently deserted, and was never heard from again.

There is a notation on one of the returns filed by the 140th New York that states, "Name also appears as John." Given the uncommon last name and the confusion at Andersonville as to whether the doomed Sarsfield was named James or John, and that both appeared in the same recruiting office on the same day, the question has to be asked: Were these the same man?

The short answer is, we don't know. If, as was commonly claimed, Sarsfield and the other raiders were bounty jumpers, who would enlist, collect the bounty money paid to new recruits, and then desert and go on to repeat the process at different locations and using different names, then the idea that he might go to join the army twice under slightly different names would be a distinct possibility. However, the idea that a man might go into the same recruiting office twice, on the same day, would be a case of almost unbelievable hubris.

Which doesn't mean it couldn't have happened.

It's also possible that the two Sarsfields were related, which would explain the similar names, and proximity to the same recruiting station. It was not unusual for brothers or cousins to enlist together. This is not impossible, either.

Confusion at the time of enlistment aside, there is evidence that Sarsfield's voyage to join his regiment may have been as dangerous and disorderly as Patrick Delaney's had been. Another soldier from the 140th New York, John McGraw, reported that crime had been rampant on the boat trip to Alexandria, Virginia. In a letter to his wife, he reported that, during his ocean voyage south to join his new regiment, there was a "gang" of thugs on board the ship, some of whom ended up in the 140th New York along with him. In a September 1863 letter to his wife, McGraw wrote about the voyage, saying, "thank god we got out of it with our lives safe the hard is [hardest] place that I was ere in in my life thare was two got murdered and six stabbed three died and two shot by gard we had about four thousand soulds [souls] on board besides two hundred and fifty prisoners which some of them will be shot for Deserters." In a letter written on October 2, McGraw went on to admit that he himself had been the victim of theft somewhere between Elmyra and Alexandria, Virginia. "I received 25 dollars in Elmyra . . . but it was picket out of my poket when I was asleep it was well that I was so for if I had awoke up and cethed [catched?] them at it I would have piched [pitched] into them and got knifed like some of the rest but let it go dam them they got 18 dollars out of me. Thair is some of the gans [gang] in this regt . . . but I reported them to the corpole [corporal] and he had them arrested."

Without the name of the ship or the exact dates of the troop transport, there is no way to tell if Delaney and Sarsfield sailed on the same troop ship, but both men traveled by way of Alexandria, Virginia, mid-September on a transport ship that was fraught with robberies and assaults. If they did travel on the same ship after mustering in, then it is entirely possible that Sullivan and Delaney met en route to their regiments. This might explain why Sarsfield fell in with the raiders so quickly after his arrival at Andersonville. Delaney, Collins, and Sullivan were all captured in approximately the same place and time and began their combined crime spree at Belle Isle before continuing at Andersonville. Sarsfield arrived at Camp Sumter in May 1864, and if he reconnected with his old pal Delaney, this may be how he became one of the notorious raiders.

Once he joined the 140th, Sarsfield may have been the best soldier of the six men executed. Once enlisted, he went through training at Riker's Island in New York City, then joined his regiment in Culpeper, Virginia, on September 26. He fought in the Battles of Bristoe Station and Rappahannock Station, and took part in the Mine Run campaign. On paper, he appears to have been a good soldier; there are no absences recorded on the company's muster rolls, and he collected the $25 advance bounty for serving three months in January 1864. The only two items that appear out of the ordinary are that he owed two cents for "ord." (short for ordnance, which at this amount, would likely mean ammunition), and in November or December of 1863, he was fined $5 by a field officer, although there are no specific details about what led to the fine. It could have been for lost or damaged equipment, or it could have been a fine for some unknown misconduct.

Sarsfield was captured on May 5, 1864, on the first day of fighting in what would become known as the Battle of the Wilderness. On that date, Union forces were attempting to move through a heavily wooded area known as "the Wilderness," when they encountered a large Confederate force. The forward movement of the Union troops was halted as the Union forces squared off against the newly arrived Rebel forces instead. The 140th New York was in the front line of the first attack that charged across Saunders field, along the Orange Turnpike at about 1:00 in the afternoon, marking the beginning of the battle. They ran straight into Steuart's Brigade, a Confederate brigade led by the Maryland secessionist whose house had served as the army hospital where William Collins had stayed. The Union troops reached Confederate lines and held their position for about 30 minutes before being forced back across the field. Many of the men of the 140th were unable to return to their former line and were captured. It seems likely that James Sarsfield was one of the 55 men from the 140th captured on that May afternoon.

Prior to his capture, James Sarsfield had been counted as "present" on every muster roll for a solid eight months with no notation of absences. He was apparently a good enough soldier that when he went missing during the battle, his regiment considered him missing in action rather than as a deserter, and later, when they learned that he was in enemy hands, they crossed out "missing in action" and wrote in "May 5/64 D.S. Prisoner of War." "D.S." stands for detached service and indicates that Sarsfield was still considered a member of the regiment. They continued to carry him on the company muster roll until they received word of his death in April 1865.

It's difficult to know how long after his arrival at Camp Sumter James Sarsfield joined forces with the camp's criminal element, but if he did struggle against becoming one of them, he didn't struggle for long. Robert Kellogg's diary mentions 500 to 600 prisoners arriving at Andersonville on May 22, saying that they had been captured at the Wilderness. Eugene Forbes, who was captured the day after Sarsfield, also at the Battle of the Wilderness, recorded in his diary that he arrived at Andersonville prison pen around noon on May 24. This suggests that it likely took over two weeks for Sarsfield to arrive at Andersonville after his capture. If he did indeed arrive during the third week of May, then he would have been a prisoner at Andersonville for just five weeks when he was arrested and condemned, and seven weeks would have passed between his capture and his execution. Clearly, it did not take him long to become what Forbes described as a "principal" raider.

The arrests of the raiders began on June 29, 1864, and by the following evening, James Sarsfield had been convicted and sentenced to hang. He had taken part in the daylight robbery of a prisoner identified as Dowd. The consequent robbery and beating of Dowd was so vicious and brazen, happening in broad daylight in the early afternoon of June 29, that it served as the catalyst for ending the raider's reign. Dowd's own account of the attack was reprinted in the *Sunday Mercury*, and his testimony is supported by the diaries of other prisoners. Dowd named Sarsfield as the initial instigator and chief assailant during the attack.

But the attack on Dowd may not have been the most heinous of Sarsfield's crimes. The day after the attack on Dowd, several prisoners wrote in their diaries that bodies had been discovered buried underneath one of the raider's tents. As always, the prison rumor mill was imprecise—some men wrote that one body had been discovered while others wrote that there were two. Perhaps both are correct. The next day's listing in the prison's Register of Deaths reveals three "unknown" men with unprecedented blanks in the column labeled cause of death. Earlier entries always provided a cause of death, even if it was "unknown" as it was in separate deaths of two black soldiers. This raises the possibility that the bodies were so decomposed that no specific cause of death could be discovered, even though there would be little doubt that the men found buried under raider tents were likely murdered, even if the exact method of their deaths could not be determined. Although the deaths were not listed in the prison's Register of Deaths until July 1, it is quite possible that the men under the clay soil were found on June 30 as the diaries claim, but if they were discovered late in the day, their deaths might not have been recorded until the following day. The three unfortunates, who were buried in graves 2719, 2721, and 2722, may very well have been the victims of homicide. Curiously, the markers for grave numbers 2721 and 2722 are much closer than the other graves in that section of the cemetery, practically touching, which suggests that, perhaps the two bodies were so decomposed that the bones of one could not be told from the bones of the other, and so they were buried in the cemetery intermingled. It is also possible that the unfortunate in grave number 2719 is an indirect victim of the raiders—the unidentified man who was killed while being forced to "run the gauntlet" after the arrests of the suspected raiders. Killed late on June 29, his body may not have been retrieved until June 30 or July 1 because Henry Wirz had ordered that no rations be provided on June 29, and the same wagon that brought food to the prisoners was also used to remove the dead from the stockade. This man may or may not have been a raider—according to the *Sunday Mercury*, several of those accused and tried were found not guilty, raising the horrifying possibility that this man may have been forced back into the prison because there was insufficient evidence that he was a raider. This turned out to be a fatal accusation.

Several of the witnesses whose testimony is reported in the *Sunday Mercury* stated that victims were often lured into Sullivan's tent in order to be assaulted and robbed, and two of the men murdered may or may not have been buried there, but at least one diarist suggests that at least one of the dead men was found buried underneath Sarsfield's tent. George Robbins of the 16th Connecticut Infantry wrote about the trial in his diary on June 30: "One man was tried by a jury composed of 12 of the Sergts. and found guilty of Murder and the murdered man found buried in his Tent, they are all to be tried by the jury and whatever their decision is, Genl Winder sayes [*sic*] he will have executed." The *Sunday Mercury* states that the man tried and found guilty on the first day of the trial was James Sarsfield. Although the court transcript does not say he was convicted of murder (the bodies may have been discovered either while he was being tried or after he was convicted), it didn't really matter, he was going to hang either way.

Although judgment was swift for Sarsfield, it would be another 11 days before justice was served. He spent his remaining days in stocks outside the prison stockade, and none of the diarists at the time appear to have taken any special notice of him as he and the others were forced to mount the gallows and "launched into eternity."

TIMELINE

1841-ish Born in Ireland
1863 May 26 Arrives in the United States
1863 September 1 Enlisted
1863 September 26 Joined 140th New York at Culpeper, Virginia
1863 September/October Present "Drafted and MI in Sept, 1, 63 at Brooklyn, 3 Dist. For 3 years" "Due US for Ord $.02"
1863 October 14 Battle of Bristoe Station, Virginia
1863 November 7 Rappahannock Station, Virginia
1863 November 26 to December 2 Mine Run Campaign, Virginia
1863 November/December Present; "Due US by Sentence of Field Officer $5.00."
1864 January/February "Present; Due Soldier Advance Bounty $25.00"
1864 March/April Present
1864 May 5 Captured at Battle of the Wilderness; Originally listed as MIA; Listed as "Absent/D.S. (Detached Service) Prisoner of War" on subsequent Muster Rolls
1864 May/June Absent
July 11, 1864 Executed at Andersonville

NOTES ON CHAPTER 7

There are no John Sarsfields on the rosters of either the 140th or 144th New York—There was also a man named John Sarsfield who fought with the 105th New York Regiment. The John Sarsfield with the 105th New York, a corporal, was injured at the Battle of Bull Run and consequently discharged for disability in October 1862. He survived the war and later applied for a pension.

It is an 1883 newspaper account—Memphis, Tennessee's *Public Ledger*, June 12, 1883, page 2.

"Honest" Jack Cotter—There are two men named either J. Cotter or John Cotter at Andersonville. J. Cotter was a member of the 14th Illinois Infantry, while John Cotter was with the 82nd New York Infantry. Both survived the prison, but it's not clear if either of these men are the person who gave the interview, which reportedly first appeared in the *Hartford Post*.

This incident, according to many accounts, led to the arrest, trial, and execution of the raiders—Prisoners who stated that the attack on Dowd was the catalyst for the raiders' downfall include Eugene Forbes, Robert Kellogg, and John Duff, who described the beating victim as "an old man," although in reality, John Doud was in his early forties when he was drafted.

Patrick Murphy, 52nd New York, Company B—See notes for chapter 10.

John G. Dowd, 97th New York, Company D—See chapter 8, "Dowd."

I saw one of the men (not on trial)—Dowd may be referring to one of the attackers who was being tried on a different day than Sarsfield. Delaney, Sullivan, and Muir were all tried the following day.

N. Baldwin, 76th New York, Company C—Private Newton Baldwin of the 76th New York, Company C, was captured at the Battle of the Wilderness on May 5, 1864, and consequently sent to Andersonville. He survived the prison and returned home at the end of the war.

Joseph Terril, 101st Ohio, Company B—Joseph Terril, 101st Ohio, was captured on September 20, 1863, at Chickamauga. Although he survived Andersonville, he died on April 1, 1865, at Annapolis, Maryland.

Peter J. Edmonds—Peter Joseph Edmonds was a landsman in the Union Navy from Trenton, New Jersey. Curiously, he did not enlist until August 20, 1864, and there is no record of him ever having been held at Andersonville. Because of this, he likely acquired the diary from an acquaintance of Forbes and returned the diary to his and Forbes's hometown of Trenton, New Jersey.

Edmonds gave the diary to Forbes's former employer, printers Murphy and Bechtel, who published it—Forbes's former employers sold his diary under the title, *Diary of a Soldier and Prisoner of War in Rebel Prisons*.

Samuel Oakley Bellerjeau—Samuel Oakey Bellerjeau, of the 11th New Jersey, Company D, was a close friend of Eugene Forbes while he was a prisoner. Bellerjeau survived Andersonville and was released.

Three of those who robbed Dowd are reported to be among the number; the fourth and worse one has been caught since the above writing—Forbes probably refers to Delaney, Sullivan, and Muir, with Sarsfield possibly being the man he considered to be the "worst" assailant.

Oak went out as a witness—Forbes referred to his comrade Bellerjeau as "Oak."

In a letter to his wife—The contents of McGraw's letter were relayed to the author via correspondence with Brian Bennet, author of *Sons of Old Monroe: A Regimental History of Patrick O'Rorke's 140th New York Volunteer Infantry.* McGraw's letters to his wife describing his voyage are quoted in Bennet's book. The original letters have since been donated by McGraw's descendants to the University of Rochester.

Steuart's Brigade—Steuart's Brigade was headed by Brigadier General George H. Steuart, a pro-secessionist from Maryland. Ironically, after he joined the Confederacy, Union forces turned his Baltimore mansion into a hospital for injured Union soldiers, and it was here that raider William Collins faked a prolonged injury to avoid rejoining his regiment.

Robert Kellogg's diary—Robert Kellogg's unpublished diary is currently located at the Connecticut Historical Society in Hartford, Connecticut.

The day after the attack on Dowd, several prisoners wrote in their diaries that bodies had been discovered buried underneath one of the raider's tents—Among the prisoners who reported in their diaries that bodies had been found were Robert Kellogg ("Beneathe their tents were found knives, pistols, many watches &c.,&c. and it is said, the body of a murdered man was found beneath one tent, but I don't know it to be true."); George Robbins, also of the 16th Connecticut; possibly James Vance of the 5th Ohio ("One man dug out and $15,000 besides Watches and jewelry"); Harmon Anderson of the 110th Ohio ("There was 2 or 3 men found buried under some of their tents"). Memoirist Warren Lee Goss, writing a few years later, reported that "a dead man was unearthed, whose throat had been cut in a shocking manner, and his head bruised by a terrible blow. In the same space, beneath him, was found another victim, with his throat cut."

· 8 ·

"Rickson"

Known aliases: John Sullivan, Terry, Terrence Sullivan, Cary
Regiment: 76th New York, Company F
Rank: Private
Place of birth: Ireland
Approximate year of birth: 1837
Drafted and mustered in: August 5, 1863 (Substitute), Rochester, New York
Age at time of enlistment: 26
Deserted: Night of October 10 or 11, 1863, near Stevensburg, Virginia
Assigned Mess at Andersonville: 9th Detachment, 3rd Mess
Approximate age at time of death: 27
Profession: Laborer
Term of enlistment: 3 years
Physical description: 5 feet 3½ inches, blue eyes, dark hair, light complexion

WHAT HISTORY TELLS US

In many ways, Sullivan is the forgotten raider.

Although the fifth raider's grave marker says "W. Rickson, U.S.N.," not a single diarist mentions a raider by the name of Rickson, but several include a man named "Sullivan" among the names of those executed. This, coupled with the fact that there was no man by the name of "Rickson" enlisted in the Union Navy during the Civil War suggest that the name on the grave marker is in error, and that the man buried under the name "Rickson" may actually have been a soldier named "Sullivan." This identification is further confirmed by the original Confederate Register of Deaths which, although missing the corners of the page, reveals a listing for one of the raiders that clearly shows a last name ending in "ivan." This man is listed as having served in the 76th New York, Company F, Sullivan's Company.

Although many diarists mention the raider named Sullivan, the man's first name is not consistent. G. E. Sabre mentions Terrence Sullivan of the 72nd New York, an identification repeated by John McElroy. Eugene Forbes refers to the man in question simply as "Terry" in his prison diary. The 1865 *Sunday Mercury* referred to him as "John Sullivan" of the 76th New York, Company F. And in his 1904 memoir, a former prisoner named John Worrell Northrop identified the man in question as "Cary Sullivan" of the 76th New York, Company F. Ordinarily a book that was published 40 years after an event would be considered a less than reliable source of information, but Northrop's book has to be considered because he was a soldier in the 76th New York, Company F, and he makes a credible claim that he knew the prisoner called Sullivan, both before Sullivan deserted and while they were prisoners in Andersonville.

Although McElroy and Sabre both suggest that Sullivan was in the 72nd New York, rather than in the 76th, this doesn't hold up. There were only two men named Sullivan in the 72nd, neither of whom was ever captured. The muster rolls for the 76th New York, on the other hand, contain five men named Sullivan, including two John Sullivans, one of whom is listed as a deserter from Company F who ultimately died at Andersonville in July 1864.

The two major sources of information on Sullivan, the raider, are the *Sunday Mercury* article and a prison memoir written 40 years later by another Andersonville prisoner of war from the 76th New York.

THE *SUNDAY MERCURY* ARTICLE

According to the *Sunday Mercury*, John Sullivan was tried along with several others on the second day of trials. At this point, James Sarsfield, Sullivan's alleged partner in crime, had already been convicted and sentenced to hang. Among those testifying against Sullivan was a man named Newton Baldwin, who, like Sullivan, had been a member of the 76th New York, although in a different company. Baldwin had also testified against Sarsfield the day before. Like Sarsfield, several witnesses named Sullivan as a participant in the attack on John Dowd.

Second Day's Proceedings
   William John Kennedy, 52nd New York, Company C; Patrick Delany, 83rd Pennsylvania, Company E; John Sullivan, 76th New York, Company F; Peter

Gilmore, 145th Pennsylvania, Company J.; Owen Farley, news agent of the Calvary Corps, Army of the Potomac; William Holdings, 145th Pennsylvania, Company G; John Connolly, 52nd New York, Company C (Frank Connelly, 52 NY); Andrew Muir, United States steamer Waterwitch, [sic] were next put on trial.

The charges were similar to those in the previous case.

The prisoners pleaded not guilty.

N. Baldwin (Newton Baldwin), of the 76th New York, Company C, swore that Sullivan's business was that of robbing the prisoners and that he was one of those who attacked Dowd. He struck Dowd, who had his pants off [sic], and with his tent torn down, Dowd was imploring Sullivan to let him put on his pants. Witnesses saw Sullivan rob an orderly-sergeant who had come in that evening, and was induced to go to Sullivan's tent. Witness tented within a dozen yards of Sullivan. Next day five more men were taken at different times to Sullivan's tent, when they were robbed by Sullivan, Delany, and Sarsfield. These men (so robbed) had only just come into the camp. Witness saw one man stretched in the tent. Sullivan and another of the prisoners were holding him down, and they threatened to cut his throat unless he lay still. This was of daily occurrence. Delaney was generally present at these robberies. Sarsfield generally did the cutting out business, while the others held down the victims.

Sergeant Carpenter—Why did not the men in the neighborhood clear out that gang?

A. Well, there were so many of them, and they were all so armed with clubs, that people were afraid of them. Sullivan carried a club with an iron nut at the end of it. . . . The prisoner, Mullings acted as a runner for the gang. He went out, picked up, and brought to the tent the man intended to be robbed. Mullings picked up two of the five men robbed in Sullivan's tent. Whenever a lot of prisoners came into the prison Mullings would go among them, asking if they wanted to buy blankets or rations. By this means he decoyed them into Sullivan's tent, where they could be robbed. (The newcomers were those among whom the robbers plied their infamous trade, as they were ignorant of the robberies carried on by the band of scoundrels.) The general conversation of these men was about robbing, and how much they took from such and such a man. Heard one of the fellows say, "I got $20 out of that fellow; I got nothing out of that other son of a b—h."

R. E. Spicer recalled: saw Sullivan, Delaney and Gilmore rob a man the day before; he resisted, when Sarsfield came up and brandished a knife at him; Sullivan was also engaged in the attack on Dowd; saw Delaney in Sullivan's tent take hold of men, gag them; and take their money away. By "gagging" he meant putting something in their mouth, so that they could not cry out. While robbing on those occasions, heard them threaten men that if they made any noise they would cut their throat; one day last week, while they were robbing a man in Sullivan's tent, witness heard one of the gang say two or three times "Here is a razor, cut his throat." Sullivan, Delaney, and Gilmore were present at the time; Sullivan carried a club with a knob of iron at the end; a few nights previously,

*Delaney went to rob a man who had a watch; some of the persons in the next
tent made noise, and his purpose was defeated.*

*Joseph Farrel, 101st Ohio, Co. B, swore that some night ago a gang came to
mug him; but he could not identify any of them among the prisoners. A few days
ago he saw a man go into Sullivan's tent with a watch in his pocket, and saw
him leave without the watch. While the man was in the tent, he heard a scuffle,
and soon after he saw the man's feet sticking out from under the tent, and heard
him gasping for breath.*

This closed the prosecution.

*The jury, after an hour's deliberation, returned the following verdict: Ken-
nedy and Farley, not guilty; Connolly and Mullings, guilty of robbery; sentenced
each to wear a ball and chain 25 lbs weight, for four months; Gilmore's case
suspended; Sullivan, Delaney, and Muir guilty of all the charges, sentenced to be
hanged by the neck until dead.*

JOHN WORRELL NORTHROP'S ACCOUNT

Like Sullivan, John Worrell Northrop was a member of the 76th New York,
Company F. As such, he knew Sullivan during his brief sojourn with the 76th
and would likely have recognized him after Northrop's capture at the Battle of
the Wilderness on May 5, 1864. Forty years later, in 1904, apparently inspired
by the success of other Andersonville memoirs, Northrop published his own
book, titled *Chronicles from the Diary of a War Prisoner in Andersonville and
Other Military Prisons in the South in 1864.* His account is a product of the
Victorian era; interspersed with effusive poetry of Northrop's own competi-
tion; frequently laced with melodrama, and, in all likelihood, influenced by the
writings of other prisoners before him.

*Friday, June 17—. . . Soon after coming in, we learned that one of the dealers,
or "raiders" bore the name of Cary. He was at Belle Isle and is charged with being
the cause of several deaths. Today he was pointed out to us and we recognized
Sullivan of our company who deserted October 10, 1863, near the Rapidan
River, south of Mitchell, Va. He was a substitute from Buffalo, a "gambling,
fighting, bad tempered fellow, feared in the company." He thinks we suspect him,
and tonight sends word by Mooney, who knew him in Canada, that if we do not
expose him, Company F shall never be disturbed by raiders.*

*Tuesday, June 18th—. . . Sullivan has denied, to Mattison, having any con-
nection with the raiders, but knowing that we know he lies, he tells Mooney that
he controls the gang, being a chief we need not fear. It was by accident Mattison
met him as he evades us. But the wicked shall not go unpunished. He will find
the truth of this text.*

A few nights since Mooney's blanket was stolen. He appealed to Sullivan with threats and promises. Sullivan brought him the identical blanket. A man was attacked this afternoon, but the raiders were beaten. Prisoners come in so fast that we are terribly crowded. At night we lay down every passage, every space is covered, thousands sleeping without the least covering or shelter.

Wednesday, June 29th—More brutality and robbery. Half asleep I heard blows, groans of distress, and voices that combine the savage tones of ruffianism. One man badly injured; two reported missing. Steps are taken to organize police force. We are doing the little we can to assist. The safety of the camp requires it; our lives are every day in jeopardy. We are in greater immediate peril from these villains than from the atrocities of our keepers. At 3 p.m. a man was violently assailed in the street, while asleep, and robbed, he said, of $85 and a watch. He had arrived that day among others of Sherman's soldiers. With blood streaming down his face from a gash on his forehead, I saw him hasten to the gate where he reported the affair. A number went forward, among them several sergeants of detachments, and an earnest, but respectful appeal was made for assistance, or that we might be allowed to protect ourselves

Thursday, June 30—Men lay down last night feeling more secure of their lives. Hunting raiders continued, this time without assistance from Rebel guards, except a lieutenant a guard at the gate. The formidable resistance of yesterday was not repeated; the combined efforts of the raiders having so signally [sic] failed yesterday. Our men are armed with clubs; when one is found he is hustled to the gates, often with a kick or a punch in the back, amid the sneering and shouting from lookers on, and goes sneaking out. Lieutenant Davis gave me permission to go out with witnesses to take evidence when the trial proceeds, which is to be conducted by thirteen men recently in from the western army, as it is the design of Sergeant Keys that the hearing shall be before intelligent and impartial men with a view of giving them a fair trial; but feeling so badly, having been sick several days, I was obliged to return, Baldwin of my regiment goes out against Sullivan . . . .

July 10 . . . . It was announced tonight that six raiders have been convicted and condemned to death and are to be hanged tomorrow in the prison shortly after noon. The names of the convicted are Cary Sullivan, 76th N.Y. regiment; William Collins, alias Moseby, 88th Pennsylvania; Charles Curtis, 5th Rhode Island artillery; John Sarsfield, 144th N.Y.; Patrick Delaney, 83rd Pennsylvania; A. Muir, alias Jack the Sailor, U.S. navy. Sullivan's given name, announced by the regulators as Terrence, was carried on the company roll as Cary. It is understood that these men were professional bounty jumpers, going out for the money they could get, and were captured outside the line of duty. We know Sullivan deserted our regiment while it was forming for battle, on the night of October 10, 1863, and was captured by Rebel cavalry that was flanking our infantry a few hours prior to the beginning of Meade's great retreat to Centerville, VA. To carry out this grim project, Sergeant Keys and immediate assistants have got the use of timbers and tools and secured a few carpenters to build a scaffold.

Monday, July 11—Building the scaffold for executing the principal raiders, began at 9 a.m. a few yards within the dead line near the south gate. By 1 p.m. it was finished and the crowd assembled everywhere a footing could be had in view of the scaffold. Looking from my position near the scaffold to the north on the sloping ground I beheld the most densely packed crowd I had ever seen. They came from every extreme portion of the stockade until they could get no further. Evidently every man that could be was on his taps. A multitude of probably 30,000, all astir on so small an area is seldom if ever seen. The regulator squads, armed with clubs, formed a square around the scaffold to keep back the crowds. It was feared by leaders that an attempt would be made by associates of the doomed, to destroy the scaffold and release them Sometime was employed in attaching the halters to the beam and adjusting the nooses, then all was ready. Shortly after, the gate opened and Capt. Wirz, dressed in a white duck suit, upon his gray horse, accompanied by a Catholic priest, followed by the guard with the doubly doomed war prisoners. They were six dressed only in undershirts and drawers with heads uncovered. Capt. Wirz addressed us in broken Swiss nearly as follows:

"Prisoners, I deliver these men to you in as good condition as I found them. I have had nothing to do in convicting them of crime of which they are accused, except to lend my assistance for their and your protection; nor do I charge them or believe them guilty, and shall have nothing to do with the execution of your sentence. You have tried them; I have permitted it. You have convicted and sentenced them, if they are hung, you, not I, will be responsible for it. I deliver them to you, do with them as you please, and may God be with them and you. Guards, about face; forward march."

. . . (The priest) prays but Collins breaks in vehemently. "I am guilty, but not of this; I have been an awful man! I have not had a fair trial," and many other sentences, and all shout together, "Yes, yes!" Sullivan broke in:

"Neither am I guilty, but"—and he groaned. "I did not expect ever to come to this." "Nor I," all shouted in concert."

Northrop's account continues on until the executioners are about to perform their gruesome task. At the last minute, Sullivan and Muir both cried out, "May God bless our souls!" The execution proceeds, and that is the last mention that Northrop makes of Sullivan.

WHAT THE RECORDS SHOW

Of the six men hanged as raiders, John Sullivan is the one who was most certainly the bounty jumper and deserter that he's been accused of being. He joined his regiment on September 6, 1863, and deserted it just five weeks later. Furthermore, he enlisted as a substitute, for a man named William Oliver, of

Rochester, New York, meaning that he would have collected as much as $300 for taking the place of a wealthier man than himself.

Very little is known about John Sullivan prior to his enlistment in the army. Northrop claims that one of his colleagues recognized Sullivan from Canada, and while nothing in his service record suggests that he was Canadian, he did enlist in Rochester, New York, just across Lake Ontario from Canada. It also seems likely that Sullivan was a pseudonym, given all the confusion regarding his first name. Although his compiled service record clearly lists his name as "John Sullivan," Northrop doesn't appear to have ever known the man he briefly served with by that name: "Sullivan's given name, announced by the regulators as Terrence, was carried on the company roll as Cary." Eugene Forbes refers to the raider in question as "Terry," suggesting that he went by that forename while a prisoner, rather than John. There is no suggestion of any name other than "John Sullivan" in the compiled service record, nor was there a Terrence, Terry, or Cary among the five Sullivans who were in the 76th New York. This suggests that the man himself was cagy about telling people who he really was, which would be a logical thing to do if he was, in fact, a bounty jumper or feared that his transgressions against his fellow prisoners might follow him into his post-prison life. It would be easier to disappear if the military officials were searching for a man named "Terry Sullivan," and no one back in Rochester—or possibly anywhere else—would have known him by that name.

Sullivan deserted as the 76th New York was cracking down on the problem of bounty jumpers. Three weeks after Sullivan joined the regiment, a man named "Newton" had joined the 76th New York. In an almost unbelievable turn of bad luck, "Newton" was assigned to Company H, a company he had deserted from the year before. He was almost immediately recognized by his once-and-present comrades as the man they knew the year before as Winslow Allen. Allen was arrested, court-martialed, and sentenced to be executed by firing squad. The sentence was carried out in December 1863, just three months after he joined the 76th New York for a second time. It seems likely that Sullivan may have been aware of Allen's arrest, but even so, he wouldn't have considered it as a great deterrent to his own desertion two weeks later. Executions for desertion were unusual at that point, and even Allen himself was reportedly startled to realize, the day before he was to be killed, that they really intended to carry out his execution. Allen's ultimate fate, however, came too late to serve as a cautionary tale for the man called Sullivan, who deserted during the second week of October, after being with Company F for a month.

It seems likely that even though Northrop and Sullivan served in the same company, Northrop would have had very little memory of the man who had stayed with Company F for 35 days, 40 years before the memoir was written. It also seems apparent from his attributing the sentence "I have had nothing to do with it" to Henry Wirz that Northrop was relying at least in part on John McElroy's book to help with his "recollections." (Although Northrop correctly identifies Sullivan as having belonged to the 76th New York, he repeats McElroy's erroneous assertion that Sarsfield served with the 144th New York and also identifies Key as having been the organizer of the raiders, something no writer had done prior to John McElroy 24 years before, suggesting that he may have read and been influenced by McElroy's account when writing his own "diary.") Northrop also tends toward Victorian melodrama in his account, "Who has seen the soul's anguish pouring out in tears? This was the agony of guilt. It fired in the wild eye, flashed on the cowering cheek, darkened on the crazed brow and poured in frenzied tones from quivering lips. If the executioners were moved by these appeals, they knew their duty and performed it. The firm answer was, 'No you must die.'"

According to Sullivan's compiled service record, he was captured on October 10, 1863, near Bristoe Station. This is noteworthy because only a few days and a few miles separate the capture of Sullivan, Delaney, and Collins, and it is likely that Sullivan and Collins may have traveled to Belle Isle prison in Richmond, Virginia, together. The three of them definitely arrived at Belle Isle at approximately the same time, and presumably were among those who were soon stealing from their fellow prisoners.

But the prison at Belle Isle was a particularly harsh place in the winter of 1863. Sullivan was admitted to the prison hospital on the last day of November for pneumonia but returned to quarters the following day. Two weeks later, in December, it would be Patrick Delaney's turn to be admitted to the prison hospital, suffering from catarrh. It would be five days before Delaney would rejoin his friends in the general prison population.

Sullivan was one of the earliest prisoners sent from Belle Isle in Richmond to the remote stockade at Andersonville, arriving March 4, 1864, less than a week after the stockade received its first prisoners. John Worrell Northrop and others from the 76th New York would not join Sullivan at Camp Sumter until May 1864, following their capture at the Battle of the Wilderness. The arrival of men who would recognize him explains why Northrop says that Sullivan apparently tried to hide, and why he promised them special treatment if they would keep his official identity to themselves. If the newcomers from the 76th New York recognized Sullivan and shared his identity with the other prisoners at large, they might pass along his real identity to the Union officials upon being released, leaving him open to execution as a deserter as well as for any charges connected to his activities as a raider. By the time the others from the 76th New York were captured, their regiment had executed Winslow Allen. Given that Sullivan was both a predator and a deserter, he had to have known that the Union Army might have done the same to him, if they'd only been able to get hold of him.

TIMELINE

1863 August 5 Drafted and Mustered in as a substitute, Rochester, New York ($25 advance bounty paid)
1863 September 6 Received into his regiment in the field
1863 October 10/11 "Deserted while on the march" near Rapidan River/ Culpeper/Stevensburg, Virginia
1863 October 13–20 Arrived at Belle Isle Prison Camp, Richmond, Virginia
1863 November 30 to December 1 Hospitalized at Belle Isle Prison Camp for pneumonia
1864 March 4 Arrived at Andersonville
1864 July 11 Executed by hanging

NOTES ON CHAPTER 8

G. E. Sabre mentions Terrence Sullivan—Gilbert E. Sabre was a sergeant with the 2nd Rhode Island Cavalry when he was captured near Port Hudson, Louisiana. Originally named "Sabreville," he claimed to have changed his last name the day he was captured. Sabre survived Andersonville and wrote one of the earliest published memoirs of Andersonville, *Nineteen Months a Prisoner of War*, which was published in 1865. Because Sabre's errors in reporting the regiments of Sarsfield and Sullivan are repeated by John McElroy, it is possible that Sabre was the source of some of McElroy's information.

And in his 1904 memoir, a former prisoner named John Worrell Northrop— Northrop's book was titled *Chronicles from the Diary of a War Prisoner in Andersonville and Other Military Prisons in the South*. Although it purports to be a diary, Northrop likely drew on previously published material.

William John Kennedy, 52nd New York, Company C—The service record of this man in the 52nd New York's regimental history does not suggest that he may have been a raider. Kennedy enlisted as a private for three years of service on September 1, 1863. He was captured in action three months and one day later, at the Battle of Mine Run. No date is given for his parole, but he is transferred to Company G in August, back to Company C in September, and promoted to corporal and transferred to Company B in March 1865. He was promoted to sergeant and transferred a final time, this time to Company F on April 16, 1865. He mustered out on July 1, 1865. The fact that he is promoted twice after his time as a prisoner of war is atypical for the raiders, and the fact that "no evidence" is given against him and he is acquitted of robbery and assault make it unlikely that he was one of the raiders, and it is puzzling as to exactly why he was held over for trial. Another William Kennedy, a private with the 132 New York, died in the prison on September 27, 1864.

Peter Gilmore, 145th Pennsylvania, Company J—No record of a prisoner by this name can be found. The letter "J" was not used in identifying companies because it was too easily confused with the letter "I" so there was no Company J in the 145th Pennsylvania Regiment, and the name Peter Gilmore does not appear in the rosters of the 145th. Nor does the name Peter Gilmore appear in the database of prisoners at Andersonville National Historic Site. Consequently, no further information is available.

Owen Farley, news agent of the Calvary Corps, Army of the Potomac—No record of this man can be found.

John Connolly, 52nd New York, Company C—His name also appears on the roles as John Conoly. The inclusion of this man in the trial is curious. He is not found in Andersonville's records, which may be a clerical error, but regimental records indicate that he was captured May 18, 1864, at Spotsylvania, and died at Andersonville of diarrhea on June 15, 1864. If so, this man could not have been arrested and tried as a raider since he was dead when the arrests and trial took place. However, there is no listing for a John Connolly or Connelly dying on June 15 in the prison's Register of Deaths, and no man by that name from New York in the prison cemetery. It is possible that another prisoner assumed Connelly's identity in order to collect double rations and perhaps hide his real identity because of his criminal actions. If this was the case, there's no way of knowing who the man tried might actually have been. A Frank Connelly, also of the 52nd New York, Company C, was captured at Bristoe Station, but he also died before the raiders' arrests, reportedly of diarrhea, on June 16.

William Holdings, 145th Pennsylvania—Probably William Mullings from the 145th Pennsylvania. There is no one by the name of William Holdings in the 145th Pennsylvania, and this man's name changes to Mullings over the course of the article. A soldier named W. Mullings from Pennsylvania died at Andersonville on September 8, 1864, and is buried in grave number 8123.

The raiders graves as they appeared in 1865 (above) and as they appear today (below). At some point, the marker for A. Munn had to be replaced, and so the writing on his marker in incised rather than lettered in relief.

Prior to the arrests, there were many instances in which the prisoners punished any raider they could capture. Shaving half of a man's head and beard served as a visual warning to the other prisoners that this man was a thief and not to be trusted.

John McElroy wrote that Leroy Key fended off a group of would-be assassins with an unloaded gun. Key's version of events was markedly different.

Although John McElroy described lines of raiders and regulators squaring off in a large-scale brawl, not a single prisoner diarist mentioned such an event.

While John McElroy claimed to have taken part in the arrest of a raider named Pete Donnelly, he was only able to identify his accomplice as "Egypt," and there is no independent record of any prisoner named Pete Donnelly having been held at Andersonville.

Just over a dozen accused raiders out of the roughly 100 arrested were actually tried in a court martial. The rest were forced back into the prison by the guards and had to run back in through a gauntlet of angry prisoners who were waiting for them. At least one of the men forced back into the prison was beaten to death.

Based on the dates of entry in the prison's Register of Deaths, the grave on the right is likely the man killed while "running the gauntlet." The two graves on the left are likely the graves of the two men found buried underneath one of the raider's tents. Their close proximity suggests that their bodies were so decomposed when they were found that it was impossible to tell the two men's bones apart, and so they are buried, as they were found, together.

| 6 | 5 H. Art'y. | R. I. |

Charles F Curtis

Art., Co. A, 5 Reg't R. I. H. Art'y.

Appears on

_✓_ Company **Muster Roll**

for _July & Aug_, 186_4_

Present or absent _present._

Stoppage, $ _100_ for _____

Due Gov't, $ _100_ for. _____

Remarks: _____

Book mark: _____

Despite being allegedly executed at Andersonville on July 11, 1864, Charles Curtis's compiled military service record clearly shows him "present" in July/ August, 1864, and beyond.

This 1864 photograph shows the southwest corner of the stockade, which is notable for being the section of the prison where the African American prisoners, the raiders, and John McElroy and his comrades from the 16th Illinois Cavalry lived.

Because their executions happened late in the day, the raiders' deaths were not listed in the prison's Register of Deaths until the following day. The raiders' names appear between two lines near the bottom of the page. Although large pieces of the page recording the raiders' deaths are missing, enough fragments remain to identify the six individual raiders. Surprisingly, none of the six appear to be from the 5th Rhode Island Heavy Artillery, and the second raider listed is from the 76th New York and his last name ends in "ivan," suggesting that Charles Curtis of the 5th Rhode Island Heavy Artillery was not one of the six men hanged and John Sullivan of the 76th New York was.

William Collin's name as it appears on the panel devoted to the 88th Pennsylvania on the Pennsylvania Monument at Gettysburg. Veterans of the battle were adamant that only the names of men who actually fought in the battle be listed, and they would personally chisel off the name of any man who did not actually fight, which appears to be what happened to the name listed immediately below Collins's.

This illustration, which originally appeared in John McElroy's 1879 book, shows a despondent William Collins being led back to the gallows a second time following his botched execution.

&R.

Navy Department,

BUREAU OF EQUIPMENT AND RECRUITING.

Washington, *June 5th, 1889*

Sir:

In accordance with your request of the 25th ultimo the Bureau furnishes the following descriptive list and history of service of

William Ritson,

He enlisted 15th day of May 1861, at Philadelphia. Pa for 3 years, as a Seaman : place of birth, Philadelphia, Pa; age at shipment, 31 years; occupation, None : color of eyes, dark; color of hair, dark; complexion, dark; height, 5 feet 3½ inches; permanent marks and scars about person when enlisted Scar on l. wrist

, served in the following vessels, viz:

US "James Ewin" and "Powhatan" Final disposition not reported.

and ~~was discharged from the U. S. S.~~

, 18 .

Very respectfully,

Geo. C. Bowen, Capt. U.S.N.
Chief of Bureau.

To the Commissioner of Pensions,
Washington, D. C.

Claim No. 5309, Initials:

In 1889, the government's final mention of seaman William Ritson of the USS *Powhatan* stated that his "final disposition not reported." This letter was misfiled in the pension application of another sailor named William Ritterson.

Although John Urban believed that his beating was the incident that brought about the fall of the raiders, he never actually stated that he was "Dowd."

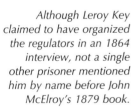

Although Leroy Key claimed to have organized the regulators in an 1864 interview, not a single other prisoner mentioned him by name before John McElroy's 1879 book.

The post in the foreground marks the approximate location of the gallows at Andersonville National Historic Site, with the pavilion surrounding Providence Spring and the reconstructed North Gate in the background.

· 9 ·

"Munn"

Known aliases: A. Munn, A. Muir, Andrew Muir, Andy Muir Meever, Murray, Buer
Assignment: USS *Water Witch*
Rank: Seaman
Place of birth: England
Approximate year of birth: 1842
Enlisted: May 30, 1863, New York City
Age at time of enlistment: 21
Captured: June 2, 1864, at Ossabaw Sound with crew of the USS *Water Witch*
Arrived at Andersonville: June 7, 1864
Assigned Mess at Andersonville: 52nd (?) Detachment, 1st Mess
Approximate age at time of death: 22
Profession: Sailor
Term of enlistment: 1 year
Physical description: 5 feet 5 inches, light blue eyes, auburn hair, ruddy complexion, missing eyelashes

$\mathcal{T}$he most remarkable thing about the man buried with the name "A. Munn" is just how quickly he found himself at the end of a noose.

Although the final raider's grave marker reads "A. Munn/Sea/US Navy," the man buried here was almost certainly known as Andrew Muir throughout his military service. Prisoners who witnessed the execution referred to him as "Muir," "Andrew Muir," or, most specifically, "Andy Muir of the U.S. gunboat *Water Witch*." The misidentification on the grave marker appears to have been a simple misreading of the name "Muir," which was written in cursive in the prison's Register of Deaths. Records also show that Andrew Muir, a seaman on the USS *Water Witch*, was captured on the night of June 3, 1864. This, and that there were no "A. Munns" known to have enlisted in the Union Navy, make it highly probable that the name "A. Munn" actually refers to Andrew Muir.

Most of the witnesses to the execution refer to Munn only in passing. John McElroy mentions his name exactly once, when he lists the names of the six men given the death penalty. Nor does Muir seem to have done anything to draw attention to himself in the final moments of his life.

Perhaps because he was in the stockade for only a relatively brief time, many of the prisoners incorrectly recorded Muir's name in their diaries and early memoirs. G. E. Sabre reported his name as "Andrew Meever"; Eugene Forbes calls him "Murray"; Albert Shatzel's diary appears to call him "Buir."

Also, perhaps because of the brevity of his stay, very few accounts of the raiders provide any details on seaman Muir. The three most detailed known accounts of him are from the unreliable John Ransom, the belatedly published account by Sullivan's former comrade John Worrell Northrop, and brief mentions in the account of the trial in the *Sunday Mercury*.

JOHN RANSOM'S ACCOUNT

The always unreliable John Ransom, who wrote, "Munn, a good looking fellow in marine dress, said he came into the prison four months before perfectly honest, and as innocent of crime as any fellow in it. Starvation, with evil companions, had made him what he was. He spoke of his mother and sisters in New York, that he cared nothing as far as he himself was concerned, but the news that would be carried home to his people made him want to curse God that he had ever been born."

Since Ransom refers to this individual as "Munn" rather than "Muir" is the first indication that Ransom is writing after the event rather than in an 1864 diary as he claimed. Furthermore, we know that Muir was a sailor on the USS *Water Witch*, and that the crew of the *Water Witch* were captured on June 3, 1864, so Muir had been in the prison for about a month when he was executed, rather than the four months Ransom credits him with. Because his rank is given as "seaman," we know that rather than "a poor Irish lad," Muir was a seasoned sailor who'd been at sea for at least three years. He was in his early twenties, somewhat older than the thousands of teenagers who were imprisoned within the stockade. There is no 1860 census record for any Andrew Muir living in New York with his mother and sisters. Ransom's account, therefore, lacks credibility.

JOHN WORRELL NORTHROP'S ACCOUNT

Another detailed account of Andrew Muir is that of John Worrell Northrop, the memoirist who personally knew the raider Sullivan. Northrop did not write his memoir until fairly late, publishing a modified version of his diary in 1904, exactly forty years after the execution. Northrop writes with a flair for the melodramatic: "Sullivan and Muir both said: 'May God bless our souls!'" just before the prop to the gallows is pulled, and he portrays Muir's death as the fulfillment of a prophesy: "It is told of Muir that he was acquitted of a crime in Dublin, Ireland, though he had confessed his guilt to a priest. Since the conviction here he told the story to an Irish friend, adding that after the acquittal the priest told him that death by hanging would be his doom; that the priest's words always haunted him; though he sought to avoid acts tending to their fulfillment, he lost self-control and went wrong. To him he confessed complicity in crimes charged and proved against the raiders."

Northrop's tale, while interesting, is nonetheless questionable, since the name "Andrew Muir" is not found in any court records in pre-1864 Dublin. It is also questionable as to whether or not Muir would have had access to "an Irish friend" "since the conviction" because the convicted men were held outside the stockade from the time they were arrested until they were brought in to be hung. Northrop's story, then, cannot be considered reliable as far as Andrew Muir is concerned.

THE *SUNDAY MERCURY* ACCOUNT

The *Mercury*'s account of the trial of the raiders makes very little mention of Andrew Muir, but it does link him with what is probably the most famous of the raiders' crimes, the attack on a prisoner named Dowd.

> *According to the testimony of Newton Baldwin of the 76th New York: Saw Muir engaged in robbing Dowd. Saw him on top of Dowd, trying to cut out his pocket and fumbling in it. The first time he saw Muir engaged in robbing was when he and the others attacked the orderly-sergeant. Muir had not the same appearance when he attacked Dowd as he had at present. Then he wore whiskers and a moustache; at present they were shaved off.*

WHAT THE RECORDS SHOW

Andrew Muir was already a sailor when he enlisted in the Navy on May 30, 1863, in New York City. He was assigned the rank of "seaman," which indicates that he had at least three years' experience at sea when he enlisted. He gave his place of birth as "England," but some accounts refer to him as Irish, and although "Muir" is a surname more commonly found in Scotland than Ireland, and it is entirely possible that he enlisted under an alias, and that the personal information he gave is questionable. His enlistment record describes him as having blue eyes, auburn hair, and standing five feet five inches, which suits someone from the British Isles, particularly Ireland or Scotland, but his physical description also mentions a curious feature about him: he had no eyelashes.

Muir was assigned to the sidewheel steamer, USS *Water Witch*, which was part of the North Atlantic Blockading Squadron. Disciplinary actions were recorded in the *Water Witch*'s ship's log, and Andrew Muir's name is duly recorded among them. "16 Nov 1863 Andrew Muir, seaman, returned on board having broken his liberty put in double irons by order of Commander." It can't be determined by the listing whether crewman Muir had belatedly returned from liberty on his own, or if he'd been forcibly retrieved, but his commander's punishment, the same that he'd given to two crew members, Thomas Gibbings and Francis Carroll for fighting six days before, indicates that whatever the circumstances, Muir had drawn his commander's anger and had been forced to pay the consequence.

Muir may be the most tragic of the raiders because his one-year enlistment in the Navy was technically up when he was captured. He'd enlisted for a term of one year on May 30, 1863, but the Union Navy was short-handed and would not release the sailors whose terms had expired until replacements could be had. This led to extremely low morale among the men who were anxious to return to civilian life, and the captain had reluctantly let 20 members of the crew leave at the end of May, leaving a short-handed crew and even more resentment among the enlisted men who remained behind.

This unhappy ship was boarded by Confederate forces on the night of June 3, as she lay at anchor in her customary spot in Ossabaw Sound, off the coast of Georgia. *Water Witch*'s officers and a few of her crew put up a gallant fight, killing the attackers' commanding officer Lieutenant Thomas Pelot and the expedition's hired pilot, slave Moses Dallas. The attack, however, was not the Union Navy's finest hour, as many of the *Water Witch*'s crew, having already reached the end of their enlistment, decided not to join the fight. The commander of the *Water Witch*, Lieutenant Commander Austin Pendergrast, wrote in his official report that while the ship's officers fought gallantly, "the men seemed paralyzed with fear, and remained under the hurricane deck without giving the officers the least support, though they were ordered out by Acting Assistant Paymaster Billings and Acting Ensign Hill." They likely regretted their decisions not to fight when they reached Camp Sumter. By the reckoning of one of the ship's Confederate boarding party, it only took them 10 or 13 minutes to secure the ship.

It's not known for sure if Muir was one of those hiding under the hurricane deck or cowering below, but according to the ship's officers, the majority of the enlisted men did not actively participate in fighting, and it seems likely that Muir did not actively engage in defending the ship. Muir was captured along with the rest of the surviving crew of the *Water Witch*, 13 officers and 49 men, and was quickly sent to Camp Sumter along with most of the crew.

One of the most remarkable things about Andrew Muir is how quickly he went from being a "fresh fish" to being hanged as a raider. Another sailor, prisoner Frederic Augustus James of the *Housatonic*, wrote in his diary on June 8, 1864: "About a thousand prisoners came in yesterday . . . among whom were some of our crowd of 'blue jackets' who have been at work in the Richmond hospitals & the Crew of the USS *Water Witch*, captured about a week ago near Savannah by seven barges." If Andrew Muir arrived at Andersonville on June 8, then three weeks later he would have been arrested as a raider, and 34 days would pass between the day he first walked in through the north gate and the day he was carried out the south, having been executed.

Perhaps because his time at Andersonville was so brief, very little was written about Muir by the other prisoners. McElroy mentions "A. Muir, United States Navy" exactly once, when he lists the names of the men convicted. Most diarists and memoirists, if they mention him at all do so only in passing, and his name is written in different diaries as "Muir," "Muer," "Buer," and "Murray," which suggests that he was not well known within the stockade.

One curious aspect of Muir is that when he mustered in, his lack of eye lashes was duly noted. Two different prisoners, Newton Baldwin and later memoirist Ed Glennon, both observed that apparently Muir was beardless, which could have spawned the mistaken idea that he was much younger than his bearded counterparts. Baldwin claimed that Muir had shaved his beard to disguise that he was one of the men who had attacked Dowd, which raises the question of where he would have gotten a razor if he and the others were taken out of the stockade without their belongings. Ed Glennon, who wrote a fascinating stream of thought memoir in 1891, recalled that one of the condemned men was a beardless young boy, who looked out of place standing with the others. Although Muir likely was the youngest man hanged, at 22 years old, he was still older than the thousands of teenagers who were held within the prison gates. Interestingly, there is a medical condition known as *alopecia areata*, an immune system disorder in which the immune system attacks hair follicles, causing the hair to fall out. This can cause hair loss over part or all of the body, or can be localized to the eyelashes, eyebrows, beard, or scalp, or any other part of the body. Given that Muir had no eye lashes when he enlisted, it is possible that he suffered from this condition and thus was unable to grow any facial hair. This would account for comments about Muir's seemingly youthful appearance by Ransom and Glennon.

It was Muir's fatal misfortune to have taken part in the attack on Dowd, the one incident that served as a catalyst for the arrests and executions that followed. Four of the men who were condemned and executed—Delaney, Sullivan, Sarsfield, and Muir—were the ones who were identified as having taken part in the attack on Dowd, and all four were sentenced to death. Muir had been in the stockade so briefly that his list of transgressions had to have been less than those of the men he was tried with, but unfortunately for him, he took part in the one incident that had caught the attention of Henry Wirz. Out of the 100 or so men who were actively raiding and stealing from their fellow prisoners, the ones who attacked Dowd who were particularly singled out for the ultimate punishment.

The *Mercury* transcript indicates that Muir took part in the assault on John Dowd, as did Sullivan, Delaney, and Sarsfield. If this was the case, it was a fatal alliance.

NOTES ON CHAPTER 9

Prisoners who witnessed the execution referred to him as "Muir," "Andrew Muir," or, most specifically, "Andy Muir of the U.S. gunboat *Water Witch*"—The man in question is referred to as "Muir" or "A. Muir" by John L. Hoster, William N. Tyler, John Worrell Northrop, Lessel Long, John McElroy, and in the prison's Register of Deaths. He is referred to as "Andrew Muir" by Charles H. Knox, and "Andy Muir of the U.S. gunboat *Water Witch*" by Robert Knox Sneden.

The misidentification on the grave marker appears to have been a simple misreading of the name "Muir," which was written in cursive in the prison's Register of Deaths—Muir's is the only one of the raiders whose entire death listing is intact in the Confederate copy of the Register of Deaths. A careful examination of the page reveals that there is a dot over the third letter in the name, suggesting it should be Muir rather than Munn.

Since the name "Andrew Muir" is not found in any court records in pre-1864 Dublin—The British genealogy site Find My Past contains Irish court records but searching for the trial of an Andrew Muir in Dublin does not return any results.

According to the testimony of Newton Baldwin of the 76th New York—Baldwin was a member of the same regiment as both Sullivan and John Worrell Northrop, but he was from a different company. Baldwin was a member of Company C, while Sullivan and Northrop were with Company F.

The first time he saw Muir engaged in robbing was when he and the others attacked the orderly-sergeant—In his testimony against Sullivan, witness Newton Baldwin states that he saw Sullivan rob an orderly sergeant, assisted by Muir. Although the testimony is not clear on exactly when this attack is supposed to have taken place, it was at least one day before the attack on Dowd, because Baldwin says that the day after the orderly sergeant was robbed, five more men were lured into Sullivan's tent and assaulted. According to the *Sunday Mercury* article, both Sullivan and Muir were tried on the same day and Newton Baldwin's testimony against them and the other men tried on the same day is lumped together in the article.

Slave Moses Dallas—Because the boarding party did not include a pilot, they were obliged to hire slave Moses Dallas, who was an experienced local pilot. Unfortunately, Dallas was one of the first of the boarding party to be killed, shot by the *Water Witch*'s paymaster, Luther G. Billings. Because Dallas was the only pilot the Confederates had, they ran the *Water Witch* aground three times as they made their way to Battery Beaulieu and were forced to jettison cargo each time in order to refloat the vessel. Moses Dallas is rather remarkable, because although he was technically a slave belonging to Harriet Ann Elbert, he owned property, lived away from his owner's land, married, hired slaves to work in his wife's laundry service and negotiated his own contracts independently of his owner, who apparently received no portion of his earnings. The Confederate Navy paid him between $80 and $100 to work as a pilot for them.

The commander of the *Water Witch*, Lieutenant Commander Austin Pendergrast, wrote in his official report that while the ship's officers fought gallantly— This quote is taken from Pendergrast's additional report, written in Washington, DC, or October 22, 1864. Pendergrast was subsequently court-martialed in connection with the loss of the *Water Witch* and was found guilty and sentenced to suspension for two years on half pay and loss of rank. Regardless, the former Naval Academy cadet remained in the Navy and was serving as commander of the receiving ship *Potomac* when he died of pneumonia on October 23, 1874, at the age of 41.

By the reckoning of one of the ship's Confederate boarding party, it only took them 10 or 13 minutes to secure the ship—Taken from the report of Lieutenant Austin Pendergrast.

Later memoirist Ed Glennon—Edward Glennon of the 42nd Illinois Regiment, Company F, began what would ultimately become a three-volume, handwritten memoir in 1891, while a patient at the US Leavenworth National Home for Disabled Volunteer Soldiers in Leavenworth, Kansas. In it, he recorded his experiences as both a soldier and as a prisoner of war at Richmond, Danville, and finally, Andersonville. Glennon's journal remained in the family and was published in 2003 under the title *Surviving Andersonville: One Soldier's Recollections of the Civil War's Most Notorious Camp*.

Although Muir likely was the youngest man hanged—Patrick Delaney and James Sarsfield would have been approximately 23 when they were executed; Sullivan was 27; Collins was 29; and Ritson was 34.

TIMELINE

1864 June 2 Captured along with the rest of the USS *Water Witch* crew while at anchor at Ossabaw Sound in Georgia

1864 June 7 Arrives at Andersonville Prison

1864 June 29 Takes part in the attack and robbery of John Dowd and is arrested

1864 July 1 Tried for the attack on Dowd and at least one other crime; convicted and sentenced to hang

1864 July 11 Executed by hanging

· *10* ·

Other Alleged Raiders

$\mathcal{A}$lthough most people think of the six men who were hanged when they think of the Andersonville Raiders, there were dozens of "raiders" who preyed on their fellow prisoners. Only a few of these men are mentioned by name, however. This chapter attempts to identify the prisoners who various authors have put forth as "raiders." Although there were likely between 80 and 120 raiders at Andersonville when the crackdown came, the names of most of these men, for better or for worse, are lost to history. Most of the names we know of come from the *Sunday Mercury* article, however, some of the names given in the article cannot be verified, and some of the men who were accused in the article were ultimately found "not guilty," and may or may not have actually been raiders. Others, like Dick Allen and Pete Donnelly come from published memoirs, such as John McElroy's. A scant few are named in prisoners' diaries.

THE RAIDERS ACCORDING TO JOHN McELROY

"Dick" Allen

Because of the popularity of McElroy's book, the best known two surviving raiders have to be Dick Allen and Pete Donnelly. John McElroy ends his account of the execution of the six raiders with the ominous sentence, "Pete Donnelly and Dick Allen knelt down and wiped the froth off Delaney's lips, and swore vengeance against those who had done him to death." Dick is a common nickname for Richard, and there were at least two men named Richard Allen imprisoned at Andersonville, but one of them is much more likely to have been the raider McElroy referred to, because Private Richard Allen of the 83rd Pennsylvania, Company E, was in the same regiment and company as Patrick Delaney, the man hanged as a raider.

Allen's service record is similar to Delaney's. Twenty-four-year-old Richard Allen, a brown-haired, blue-eyed, light-skinned shoemaker was drafted into the army, on September 9, 1863, the day before Patrick Delaney, and he deserted his regiment the same date as Delaney, on October 14, 1863. Like Delaney, Allen was sent to Belle Isle for the beginning of his imprisonment and was transferred to Andersonville on March 19, 1864.

John McElroy tended to describe every raider he named as a "leader" of a band of thieves, and "Dick" Allen was no different. "One day I saw 'Dick Allen's Raiders,' eleven in number, attack a man wearing the uniform of Ellett's Marine Brigade. He was a recent comer, and alone, but he was brave. He had come into possession of a spade, by some means or another, and he used this with delightful vigor and effect. Two or three times he struck one of his assailants so fairly on the head and with such good will that I congratulated myself that he had killed him. Finally, Dick Allen managed to slip around behind him unnoticed, and striking him on the head with a slung-shot, knocked him down, when the whole crowd pounced upon him to kill him, but were driven off by others rallying to his assistance."

The *Sunday Mercury* relates that Allen was tried, found guilty, and punished in conjunction with the raiders' trial. It summarizes the testimony of Daniel Hayes of the United States, Company L, saying that Hayes "swore that one day last week, Allen and his party, including Curtis, came to his tent. He then forced a man named Prentis out of the tent, threw him down on the ground and, threatened his life unless he would tell where the other watch was—in the custody of a friend. Prentiss [*sic*] got the watch from the friend, came out and handed it to Allen and Curtis. . . . The jury returned a verdict finding Richard Allen and Thomas F. O'Connell guilty of robbery and assault; and they were sentenced to be handcuffed and shackled during their imprisonment." This account undermines McElroy's story of Dick Allen swearing to avenge Patrick Delaney's death, because it's difficult to exact vengeance when you are handcuffed and shackled and standing in front of 26,000 angry men.

But McElroy's tale does not end with the hanging as far as Dick Allen is concerned. McElroy writes that the remnants of the raiders were among the first to leave Andersonville because "their relations to the Rebels were such that they were all given a chance to go with the first squads," although it's not known exactly when Allen left Andersonville. Both Allen and McElroy were sent from Andersonville to Camp Lawton at Millen, Georgia, another open stockade prison. McElroy himself arrived at Millen on October 11, 1864, a few days before two of the reported hangmen from the raiders' execution, Corporal Ned Carrigan and a man referred to only as "Sergeant Goody," arrived there. According to McElroy, the raiders were still a functioning group and out for vengeance:

> *The Raiders knew that Goody had come in before we of his own battalion did. They resolved to kill him then and there, and in broad daylight. He had secured in some way a shelter tent, and was inside of it fixing it up. The Raider crowd, headed by Pete Donnelly, and Dick Allen, went up to his tent and one of them called to him . . . Goody, supposing it was one of us, came crawling out on his hands and knees. As he did so their heavy clubs crashed down upon his head. He was neither killed nor stunned, as they had reason to expect. He succeeded in rising to his feet, and breaking through the crowd of assassins. He dashed down the side of the hill, hotly pursued by them. . . . We snatched up our clubs and started after the Raiders, but before we could reach them, Ned Carrigan, who also comprehended what the trouble was, had run to the side of Goody, armed with a terrible looking club. The sight of Ned, and the demonstration that he was thoroughly aroused, was enough for the Raider crew, and they abandoned the field hastily.*

McElroy goes on to say that, unlike Henry Wirz, the commandant at Millen was sympathetic to the complaints of the men persecuted by the raiders.

> *He sent in a squad of guards, arrested Dick Allen, Pete Donnelly, and several other ringleaders, took them out and put them in the stocks in such a manner that they were compelled to lie upon their stomachs. A shallow tin vessel containing water was placed under their faces to furnish them drink.*
>
> *They staid [sic] there a day and night, and when released, joined the Rebel Army, entering the artillery company that manned the guns in the fort covering the prison. I used to imagine with what zeal they would send us over; a round of shell or grape if they could get anything like an excuse.*
>
> *This gave us good riddance—of our dangerous enemies, and we had little further trouble with any of them.*

Because Richard Allen is a fairly common name, it's not possible to definitively track him outside of his military career, however, in the 1870 US census, there is a man named Richard R. Allen living with his family in Frankford, in Philadelphia County, Pennsylvania. This Richard Allen is 30 years old in 1870, the same age the prisoner of war would have been, and he's got a wife, Martha, and a three-year-old son named Morton, whose September 15, 1867, birth would be in the realm of possibility for a father who was away at war until 1865. Moreover, the Richard R. Allen family only appears in Frankford on the 1870 US census, then eventually end up in Chester, Pennsylvania, about 30 miles from Philadelphia where Dick Allen, the raider, entered into the Army. This could all be coincidental, but the 1870 census raises one more surprising coincidence: Richard R. Allen and his family are listed immediately below a family named Delaney, with a 50-year-old named Daniel Delaney, who is presumably the father, and several children ranging from 5 to 19 years old. There is no proof that Patrick Delaney, the raider, was connected to this family, but given the apparent relationship between Patrick Delaney and Dick Allen, it is a curious circumstance, indeed.

Although Allen served in the same company as Patrick Delaney and McElroy depicts him as one of the two men who swear vengeance over Delaney's dead body, McElroy more often associates Allen with another prisoner, "Pete Donnelly." There are many "Peter Donnellys" in the Union army, but none who served with the 83rd Pennsylvania, nor does the trial transcript mention a man by that name as being tried as a raider.

Pete Donnelly

Pete Donnelly is noteworthy in John McElroy's book as the man that Leroy Key sent young McElroy to "arrest," accompanied by a large, taciturn man whom McElroy identifies only as "Egypt." When McElroy goes to get Donnelly, the man refuses to accompany him. Initially, Donnelly refuses to go, saying "Well, you don't think you can take me unless I choose to go! You haint got anybody in that crowd big enough to make it worth while for him to waste his time trying it out."

The conversation deteriorates until:

> *"Finally Pete thrust his fist in my face and roared out:—"By _____, I ain't going with ye, and ye can't take me, you _____"*
>
> *This was "Egypt's" cue. His long left arm uncoupled like the loosening weight of a pile-driver. It caught Mr. Donnelly under the chin, fairly lifted him off his feet and dropped him on his back among his followers. It seemed to me that the predominating expression in his face as he went over was one of profound wonder as to where that blow could have come from, and why he did not have time to dodge or ward it off.*
>
> *As Pete dropped, the rest of us stepped forward with our clubs, to engage his followers, while "Egypt" and one or two others tied his hands and likewise secured him. But his henchmen made no effort to rescue him and we carried him over to headquarters without molestation.*

McElroy describes Donnelly as "a notorious character, and leader of a bad crowd," and states that he knew him at Pemberton Prison, a building that sat adjacent to Libby Prison. But Donnelly does not seem to have been convicted during the trial because, according to McElroy, he appears at the foot of the gallows swearing vengeance for Patrick Delaney. McElroy concedes that Donnelly "was more 'knocker' than Raider." Except for his arrest, Pete Donnelly is always mentioned in conjunction with Dick Allen. According to McElroy, Donnelly is punished by the prison commandant at Camp Lawton after leaving Andersonville and ultimately ends up joining the Confederate Army.

No one named Donnelly is mentioned in the *Sunday Mercury* article on the trial of the raiders, and while there are several Donnellys held at Andersonville, no record can be found for a Pete or Peter Donnelly. It is possible that this was a nickname, but without knowing what this man's actual first name was, there's no way to learn more about him.

It is also possible, however, that McElroy misremembered Donnelly's name, since nearly a decade and a half had passed between the events at Andersonville and McElroy's reporting of them. McElroy associates "Pete Donnelly" with raider Dick Allen, but the *Sunday Mercury* mentions a Thomas O'Connell of the 9th Maryland being tried at the same as Allen. The names Donnelly and O'Connell are not dissimilar, and it's possible that after a decade and a half, McElroy could not quite recall the name of the raider associated with Dick Allen, and so he came as close as he could, and assigned the man the first name of "Pete." It's impossible to know for sure if "Pete Donnelly" and "Thomas O'Connell" refer to the same man, but Thomas O'Connell and Dick Allen are both found guilty on the same day and are sentenced to be handcuffed and shackled, apparently for the remainder of their time as prisoners.

Thomas O'Connell

Thomas O'Connell, of the 9th Maryland, Company D, is cited in the *Sunday Mercury* as being tried for robbery and assault along with Charles Curtis and Richard "Dick" Allen, but details about his crimes are scant. He's charged with "the same offense as those previously tried" ("assaulting with intent to murder (if necessary) and highway robbery"). We're told that "Other witnesses testified to other charges against Curtis Allen, and O'Connell" and that "The jury returned a verdict finding Richard Allen and Thomas F. O'Connell guilty of robbery and assault; and they were sentenced to be handcuffed and shackled during their imprisonment."

Whatever crimes O'Connell committed are not specified, although one witness refers to "Allen and his party" robbing him of a watch. Given the way that Allen and O'Connell's names are linked together when the judgment is reported and that they share the same punishment, it seems likely that O'Connell may have been included in Allen's party of thieves.

Thomas O'Connell of the 9th Maryland fought with the regiment's D Company. Regimental records state that he was "Taken prisoner, October 18,

1863, Charlestown, Va (now West Virginia); prisoner of war records show him sent to Baltimore on November 29, 1864, for M.O. (Muster Out); no further record A. G. O., War Department."

Dailey

Another alleged raider who, according to John McElroy, managed to escape punishment by currying favor with his captors was a man identified only as an Irishman named "Dailey." McElroy writes that the raiders, after being stopped at Andersonville, rose up again in force at the prison in Camp Lawton, in Millen, Georgia, where many of the prisoners were sent after leaving Andersonville. "Our old antagonists—the Raiders—were present in strong force in Millen. Like ourselves, they had imagined departure from Andersonville was for exchange, and their relations to the Rebels were such that they were all given a chance to go with the first squads. A number had been allowed to go with the sailors and marines on the Special Naval Exchange from Savannah, in place of sailors and marines who had died. On the way to Charleston, a fight had taken place between them and the real sailors, during which one of their number—a curly-headed Irishman Dailey, who was in such high favor with the Rebels that he was given at the place of driving the ration wagon that came in the North Side at Andersonville—was killed, and thrown under the wheels of the moving train, which passed over him."

The order for the sailors to leave Andersonville came on September 20, 1864. The sailors immediately implemented a plan to rescue as many soldiers as possible by giving them the identities of dead sailors and taking them with them when they left the camp. Although McElroy implies that the prison authorities "allowed" the men to go in the place of sailors and marines who had died in captivity, this was not the case. The sailors themselves hatched the plan to take as many soldiers with them as they could by giving them the identities of their deceased comrades, a plan which they kept secret from the Confederates. Knowing this, and given McElroy's penchant for inventing stories, it is almost certain that he fabricated this event as well. Without a first name, a regiment, or a precise place of death, it's impossible to identify the man referred to, and the raider named Dailey may or may not have ever existed.

Heffron

John McElroy also tells the story of a raider who turned on his own, but with dire consequences. "One of the Raiders—named Heffron—had, shortly after his arrest, turned State's evidence, and given testimony that assisted materially in the conviction of his companions. One morning, a week or so after the hanging, his body was found lying among the other dead at the South Gate. The impression made by the fingers of the hand that had strangled him were still plainly visible about the throat. There was no doubt as to why he had been killed, or that the Raiders were his murderers, but the actual perpetrators were never discovered."

There was a prisoner named "Heffron" at Andersonville, a man named B. Heffron of the 90th Illinois Cavalry, but a more likely candidate for the man McElroy refers to would be James Hafran, a private in the 70th Illinois Cavalry, Company I. Hafran died at Andersonville on July 23, 1864, and is buried in grave 3825 under the name J. Hoffman. The similarity of names and the date of death "a werk or so after the hanging" make Hafran a possible match for the man McElroy refers to, although "J. Hafran" is listed as having died of dysentery rather than strangulation, and there is no one named Heffron (or anything similar to Heffron) mentioned as testifying at the Raiders' trial according to the *Sunday Mercury*, although mention is made of additional witnesses who are neither named nor quoted.

As is often the case with McElroy, there are reasons to be skeptical of this story, which originates in McElroy's book and is not related in any prisoner's diary or earlier memoir. There are no incidents of death by strangulation in the Register of Deaths, either during July or at any other point during the prison's tenure.

McElroy names one other villain in his piece, and, although this man isn't, strictly speaking, a raider, McElroy writes about him with the same contempt that he holds for the men who preyed on their fellow prisoners.

Pete Bradley

"Pete Bradley" is the name of the man John McElroy says defended the raiders in their court trial. Not exactly a raider, McElroy refers to him as "a foul mouthed, long-tongued Tombs shyster." "The Tombs" is a nickname for the municipal jail in New York City. Located in Manhattan, during the time of the Civil War it was known both for its unhealthy conditions (it had been built on a filled-in pond and within 10 years of its 1838 opening was sinking into the ground) and for the large-scale corruption that took place within its walls. Since McElroy describes him as a "shyster," this implies that Bradley took part in this corruption, and that his legal dealings may have been less than honest.

McElroy implies that Bradley was with him at one of the Richmond prisoner-of-war camps, probably Belle Isle. He claimed that Bradley was the judge of a fistfight at Andersonville that McElroy declared "rather tame," but he reported that Pete Bradley would beat back spectators who got too close with a heavy club and described Bradley as "A long-bodied, short-legged hoodlum, nicknamed 'Heenan.'" "Heenian" is likely a corruption of the word "Fenian," and the Fenian brotherhood was one of the predominantly Roman Catholic groups of Irishmen rebelling against English rule in Ireland, frequently through violent means.

McElroy writes that he encountered Bradley again after leaving Andersonville, when they were both sent to Savannah. There, he describes Bradley as standing on a little platform within the stockade and giving a speech urging the Union soldiers to threaten to join the Confederacy unless they were promptly exchanged, concluding with the exhortative, "And now, fellow prisoners, I propose to you this: that we unite in informing our Government that unless we are exchanged in thirty days, we will be forced by self-preservation to join the Confederate army." This results in such an uproar that the Rebel guards rush in with guns drawn to save Bradley from being torn apart.

But McElroy gets one more dig in at Bradley.

> *Imagine my astonishment, some time after getting out of prison, to find the Southern papers publishing as a defense against the charges in regard to Andersonville, the following document, which they claimed to have been adopted by "a mass meeting of the prisoners":*
>
> *"At a mass meeting held September 28th, 1864, by the Federal prisoners confined at Savannah, Ga., it was unanimously decided that the following resolutions be sent to the President of the United States, in the hope that he might take such steps as in his wisdom he may think necessary for our speedy exchange or parole."*

Thereafter follows a list of six resolutions demanding an accounting and redress by the Federal government for the lot of the prisoners, and the document is signed "P. Bradley, Chairman of Committee in behalf of Prisoners."

McElroy disavows any knowledge of such a committee and ends the chapter by declaring it "a brazen falsehood."

Interestingly, this newspaper article is the most compelling evidence that "P. Bradley" existed. His name does not appear in any known Andersonville document, and although he would have had to have practiced law in New York City in order to serve as a lawyer at the "Tombs," no lawyer by this name appears in the New York City directory. There was a Peter Bradly who served in the 62nd New York Regiment, but that man died of disease in Philadelphia on August 26, 1862, and was a shoemaker rather than a lawyer, so he was not the man McElroy referred to. No other contemporary prison source mentions a Pete Bradley acting as the raiders' defense lawyer. The *Sunday Mercury* states that they were defended by Henry Higginson. Warren Lee Goss claimed that the raiders were defended by "An able lawyer, an officer of the rebel guard, conducted the defense, afterwards stating to me that he had no doubt of the guilt of those who suffered punishment." Charles Hopkins implied that the raiders had more than one lawyer representing them, "Attorneys were a-plenty in that Bullpen capable of taking almost any case to Court. . . . Good, capable attorneys were assigned to the culprits."

It is not known who wrote the document signed P. Bradley. Without a first name or regiment, tracing the author is impossible. The piece was printed in part or in its entirety in several newspapers in Indiana and Ohio. It's not inconceivable that McElroy came across this article shortly after his release from prison and wanted to discredit it because it reflected poorly on the men who chose "death before dishonor," and what better way to discredit it than to place the words in the mouth of a man who McElroy used as an example of deceit?

There is no proof that anyone named Peter Bradley from a New York regiment was ever a prisoner at Camp Sumter. The name does not appear in any known record, and so Pete Bradley appears in the National Park Service's Database of Prisoners held at Andersonville Prison as a "possible prisoner," because his presence at Andersonville can't be substantiated. Although it's possible that Pete Bradley was a prisoner who slipped through the clerical cracks and records of him were lost, given that there is no record of a lawyer named Pete Bradley in New York City around the time of the Civil War and McElroy's penchant for fabrication, it's also possible that the "foul-mouthed, loud-tongued Tombs shyster" existed only in John McElroy's fertile imagination.

THE *SUNDAY MERCURY*'S RAIDERS

John McElroy's version of the history of Andersonville notwithstanding, the single largest source of names of accused raiders comes from the court transcript given in the *Sunday Mercury*, which lists 14 names of men accused of raiding. This figure is consistent with several prisoners' estimate of the number of men held over for trial. Of the 14 accused, one man had his case suspended, three men were acquitted, four men were convicted and sentenced to wear a ball and chain, and six men were sentenced to hang. Those convicted fall into three categories: those who took part or were associated with the men who robbed and assaulted John Doud; Mosby, who is identified as the "leader" or "chief" of the raiders by most sources; and "Curtis," who seems to have been singled out by the members of the 16th Illinois Cavalry—three of the four quoted witnesses against him were either members of the 16th or shared a tent with a member of the 16th, and the fourth witness's regiment is not made clear in the article.

Given all of the furor over the arrests of the raiders, it's surprising to read that any of them were found not guilty, but according to the article, at least three (Owen Farley, William John Kennedy, and Patrick Murphy) and possibly four (Peter Gilmore) of the fourteen men accused were acquitted of charges of robbery and assault. It's not clear how Owen Farley came to be arrested, but the other two men acquitted both came from the same regiment as a man who was convicted of a lesser charge. Patrick Murphy and William Kennedy were members of the 52nd New York, the same regiment John Connolly was, although where Kennedy and Connolly were both members of Company C, and Murphy was from Company B. Peter Gilmore, the accused whose case was suspended with no known resolution, was a member of the 145th Pennsylvania, the same regiment (albeit a different company) that William Mullings served with. These acquittals raise the horrifying possibility that other innocent men may have been scooped up during the arrests as well, and then forced to run the gauntlet where they were beaten (and in one case, reportedly killed) by a mob of angry prisoners armed with clubs when they were sent back into the stockade. Little information is available on the four men charged but not convicted, but what little can be discovered about them follows.

Peter Gilmore

The *Sunday Mercury* mentions a man named Peter Gilmore of the 145th Pennsylvania, Company J, as being one of the men tried along with the raiders. This man is mentioned in the testimony of Ramiro Spicer in conjunction with the attack on Dowd. Spicer states that Gilmore was present along with Sullivan and Delaney but stops short of saying that he saw Gilmore take part in the assault. According to the *Mercury*, Gilmore's case is "suspended" and apparently was never revisited.

The regimental information given in the newspaper article for Gilmore is an apparent error; regiments skip over designating their companies with the letter "J" to avoid confusion with the letter "I." There are no records in the 145th Pennsylvania's muster rolls for a man named Peter Gilmore, although there was a Thomas J. Gilmore in the 145th who was a prisoner from May 5, 1864, to December 9, 1864, and who mustered out with his company on June 12, 1865.

Owen Farley

The *Sunday Mercury* mentions an "Owen Farley, news agent of the Calvary Corps, Army of the Potomac" as one of those being tried. However, no record can be found for a man named Owen Farley who worked as a news agent with the cavalry corps for the Army of the Potomac. A man by that name enlisted in the 51st New York, Company H, on August 3, 1864, and went missing on September 30 of that same year at Poplar Grove, Virginia. But these dates fall after the trial of the raiders, making it unlikely that he was the man indicated in the article.

According to testimony given by Newton Baldwin, Farley was "frequently" present at robberies committed by Sarsfield, Sullivan, Delaney, and Muir, but Baldwin "never saw Farley do anything." Consequently, he was acquitted.

William John Kennedy

William John Kennedy, of the 52nd New York Regiments, is mentioned in the *Sunday Mercury* account of the raiders' trial, although no details of his suspected crime are given, and the account concludes, "There was no evidence against Kennedy and Farley," and so he is found not guilty.

The regimental history for the 52nd New York states that 22-year-old William Kennedy enlisted in Brooklyn as a substitute for a term of three years. He mustered in as a private in Company C and was captured in action on December 2, 1863, at Mine Run, Virginia. He apparently spent time at Andersonville before being paroled, although there's no date given for his parole in the regimental history. Kennedy then transferred to Company G on August 15, 1864, which suggests that he may have been paroled within a month of the hangings, but it was not unusual for a man to be transferred to another company in absentia. Kennedy was transferred to Company C on September 17, 1864, and was promoted to corporal before being transferred back to Company B on March 10, 1865. Finally, he was promoted to sergeant on April 16, 1865, and mustered out with his company on July 1, 1865, near Alexandria, Virginia. He is the only known man who was allegedly accused of being a raider to have received a promotion after his time as a prisoner of war.

At the end of the transcript of the second day of the trial, court reporter Edward Wellington Boate wrote, "There was no evidence against Kennedy and Farley." Given all this information it seems likely that William Kennedy may have been falsely accused of having been a raider.

Patrick Murphy

According to the *Sunday Mercury* article, Patrick Murphy of the 52nd New York Regiment, Company B, stood trial alongside Sarsfield, charged with taking part in the attack on Dowd. According to Dowd's testimony, after trying to sell a watch to Dowd, Sarsfield left and returned with Murphy, who was from the same regiment as William Kennedy. After two other witnesses stated that Murphy did not take part in the actual attack on Dowd, Murphy was acquitted.

There is no record of a Patrick Murphy serving with the 52nd New York, but there is a record for a soldier named Peter Murphy in that Regiment, and records show that he was a prisoner at Andersonville. Peter Murphy enlisted in Brooklyn for a period of three years as a private on September 14, 1863. He was captured in action at Bristoe Station, Virginia, exactly a month later, on October 14, 1863. He arrived at Andersonville on March 12, 1864, and shortly after the raiders' trial, he enlisted in the Confederate Army, serving with the 10th Tennessee Infantry. On August 8, he transferred to Company D and was recaptured on December 28, 1864, at Egypt Station, Mississippi. Murphy is one of the few that had the great misfortune to have been held in both Union and Confederate prisoner-of-war camps. He was confined at the prison at Alton, Illinois, on January 23, 1865. He was officially transferred to Company G, 5th United States Volunteers (Confederates), on April 4, 1865. No further information is available.

CONVICTED OF LESSER CHARGES

The men who were convicted of robbery and assault but not condemned to hang were all found guilty of robbery and sentenced to either wear a ball and chain for four months (if the only crime they were convicted of was robbery) or to be handcuffed and shackled for the remainder of their time as a prisoner (if they were convicted of both robbery and assault). There is no reason to doubt that these sentences were carried out, just as the hangings were.

John Connolly

John Connolly of the 52nd New York Regiment, Company C, is mentioned in the *Sunday Mercury* article, but no specific details of the crime he was accused of are given, simply that Henry C. Higginson, the defense attorney at the raiders' trial, "called several witnesses for the defense, the effect of whose evidence, while it left the case against the other prisoners untouched, was to clear Connolly and Mullings from the most heinous crimes of assault with intent to murder." Higginson was apparently successful in clearing Connolly of the assault charge, but was not successful in getting him acquitted of robbery, because the jury found "Connolly and Mullings, guilty of robbery; sentenced to wear a ball and chain 25 lbs weight, for four months."

The problem with this account is that the records indicate that John Connolly of the 52nd New York died at Andersonville on June 15, 1864, two weeks before the arrest of the raiders. It's not known if it's the date of death or the identification of the man who was tried that's an error. It may be that another prisoner assumed Connolly's identity after his death in order to draw his rations, and that this second prisoner may have given Connolly's name when he was arrested.

William Holdings/Mullings

The name William Holdings of the 145th Pennsylvania Regiment, Company G, is mentioned among those tried on the second day of proceedings in the *Sunday Mercury* article, and then never mentioned again. The listing is likely an error because the name William Mullings, which is not mentioned in the list of those being tried, is subsequently mentioned in the body of the article, while the name William Holdings is not. There was no man by the name of Holdings in the 145th Pennsylvania, but records indicate that a William Mullings of the 145th Pennsylvania, Company G, was a prisoner at Andersonville.

According to the *Sunday Mercury*, William Mullings of the 145th Pennsylvania, Company G, "acted as a runner for the gang. He went out, up, and brought to the tent the man intended to be robbed. Mullings picked up two of the five men robbed in Sullivan's tent. Whenever a lot of prisoners came into the prison Mullings would go among them, asking if they wanted to buy blankets or rations. By this means he decoyed them into Sullivan's tent, where they could be robbed. . . . Mr. Higginson called several witnesses for the defense, the effect of whose evidence, while it left the case against the other prisoners untouched, was to clear Connolly and Mullings from the most heinous crimes of assault with intent to murder . . . Connolly and Mullings, guilty of robbery; sentenced to wear a ball and chain 25 lbs weight, for four months."

Unfortunately, this turned out to be a life sentence for Mullings. He died two months later on September 8, 1864, and is buried in grave number 8125.

There are a few other mentions of prisoners robbing and assaulting their comrades within the stockade, but whether these men were associated with the bands of thieves remains to be seen. Given that most accounts of the numbers of raiders active within the prison range upward from 80, it is inevitable that many raiders were not held over for trial. At least some were

punished by the prisoners without the benefit of a trial even before the raiders' arrests; several prisoners wrote in their diaries of would-be thieves being
seized and publicly punished. Some of the accused predators mentioned are
discussed next.

Scotly

In his diary entry for June 30, the day after the assault on Dowd, and the same
day as the trial of James Sarsfield and Patrick Delaney, a prisoner from the
145th Pennsylvania, Samuel Foust wrote, "Scotly taken out as raider." There
are no other details given. There is no record of a prisoner named Scotly at
Andersonville, but there was a man named David Scott in the 145th Pennsylvania who died at Andersonville on September 21, 1864, who may or may
not have been the person Foust was referring to. There is no other record of
a man named Scotly or Scott being arrested as a suspected raider, and since
this man's name does not appear in the court transcript, he likely was not tried
and was turned back into the stockade soon after.

Staunton

Some prisoners believed that some of the raiders could escape prosecution
either by bribery or by having curried favor with their Rebel captors. Charles
Hopkins, for example, recalled that seven men were arrested and taken out
of the stockade, but the unnamed "worst of the lot" turned state's evidence
and testified against the others, thus saving his own neck. This supposition,
made at least 35 years after the fact, is not supported by the other prisoners
who wrote that considerably more than seven suspected raiders were arrested.

Early memoirist Warren Lee Goss wrote that some of the raiders were
used bribery to avoid severe punishment by the regulators. "In the case of
Staunton, a big brute, and tool of the rebels, who killed a man, as mentioned
in preceding pages, it was rumored that his money, procured by dicker with
prisoners, obtained him a mild sentence and punishment." Unfortunately,
Staunton is never mentioned by name in the preceding pages of Goss's book,
so it's impossible to know exactly what Goss is referring to.

Later in his memoir, Charles Hopkins refers to a man with a similar
name, "Stanton," saying that Stanton aligned himself with Big Pete's police
force and used that position to abuse his fellow prisoners, although he seems
to have been more of a sadist than a thief. According to Hopkins, this man
met his end at Camp Parole in Maryland, shot and killed out of revenge by a
nameless Pennsylvania soldier who had been victimized by him.

Stanton meets a different end according to prisoner and artist Robert Knox Sneden, writing an "enhanced" version of his diary after his release, although he, too, says that Stanton was brought to justice in the end. His diary entry for December 18, 1864, says that "Several of the Regulators, or police, who were in powers at Andersonville and 'Camp Lawton' have been arrested for cruelty toward us while there, and Stanton, who was the most cruel, is in irons."

Records only show one prisoner named Staunton, and several Stantons, but without a first name of regiment, it's impossible to identify exactly who this man was.

Mat Crane

The November 22, 1864, issue of the *New York Times* reprinted excerpts from the diary of Sergeant Major Alfred Letteer, of the 77th Pennsylvania, at one-time a prisoner at Andersonville, with an introduction stating that Letteer "died in hospital in Savannah." The entry for Thursday, July 7 reads: "Some men were sent in this morning that were taken out suspected of being 'raiders.' No charges were preferred and no evidence called on, so they were sent back to camp. 'Mat. Crane,' one of them, has been heard by one of the detectives to say that he will 'drive a knife to my heart' before he leaves the camp. I am on my guard for him and his party of desperadoes, and with my friends will give them a hearty welcome the moment they wish to attack."

There is no record of a Mat or Matthew Crane at Andersonville, but a prisoner named Nathaniel Crane, 73 Pennsylvania, Company H, was captured at Missionary Ridge, Tennessee, on November 25, 1863. He was a private and was held at Andersonville and survived.

Interestingly, there is an account of Nathaniel Crane being arrested for drunkenness in the November 23, 1889, *Pittsburgh Dispatch* (page 7), titled "An Ancient Warrior: Tramping to Washington to Collect a Pension, He Falls by the Wayside." The article reads:

> An old couple were last night arrested by Officer Hutchison and sent to the Seventeenth ward police station charged with drunkenness. The pair were Nathaniel Crane, aged 73 years, and his wife, Sarah Crane.
>
> Both lived in St. Joe, Mich., [sic] and had walked all the way to Pittsburgh, doing a little peddling on the way. Crane wished to reach Washington, D.C., to collect a pension claim of $2,500. He has the necessary papers with him. He served through the war with Company H, Seventy-third Regiment, Pennsylvania Volunteers; was a prisoner at Andersonville prison and was wounded in the thigh.

Last night Crane stated that he was very poor and had to resort to peddling to work his way to Washington, but when he reached this city he got a little drink and it unnerved himself and his wife also.

Nathaniel Crane's pension applications indicate that he was a soldier with the 10th Pennsylvania Infantry, Company G, and the 66th Pennsylvania Infantry, Company E, before transferring to the 73rd Pennsylvania Infantry, Company H. He enlisted on August 6, 1861, and had achieved the rank of corporal when he was taken prisoner on November 25, 1863. Crane was a prisoner of war until November 19, 1864. He mustered out at the completion of his term on May 25, 1865.

Although it's questionable whether the newspaper had the correct age—for Crane to have been 73 in 1889, he would have had to have been born in 1816, making him 48 during the summer Andersonville Prison was in operation, and thus older than most of the other prisoners. There is no way of knowing if Nathaniel Crane was the person Letteer referred to in his diary as "Mat Crane." Without having the actual diary, it's impossible to know if the "M" was a misreading of the letter "N" or not. The newspaper account, however, with its mention of drunkenness and that Matthew Crane was walking from Michigan to Washington in hopes of collecting a huge pension rather than traveling by train, suggests that Matthew Crane was probably not a pillar of society, which would be in line with the type of person who would stoop to robbing his fellow prisoners.

Crowly

In *Battlefield and Prison Pen, Or Through the War and Thrice a Prisoner in Rebel Dungeons,* John W. Urban recalls his attack on the day the raiders were arrested:

The fellow whom I had taken by the throat was a New York a ruffian by the name of Crowly. Crowly and fifty of his comrades were soon under arrest.

It was about this time that I saw my old enemy, Crowley, taken to the place of punishment and receive ten strokes well laid on for stealing a fellow-prisoner's tin cup. I always did think he got off too easy when he stole our watch, and I am afraid I was uncharitable enough to wish the number of lashes twenty instead of ten.

Records reveal two soldiers named Crowley who fought for the state of New York and ended up at Andersonville: Michael Crowley, a private with the 182nd New York Infantry who was captured at the Battle of Cold Harbor on June 3, 1864, and later paroled, and Charles Crowley of the 2nd New York Heavy Artillery, a private with the 2nd New York Heavy Artillery, who died October 22, 1864, and is buried at the Andersonville National Cemetery in grave number 11297. The regimental history for the 2nd New York lists Charles Crowley as "Age, 31 years. Enlisted, December 3, 1863, to serve for three years; no further record."

NOTES ON CHAPTER 10

He then forced a man named Prentis out of the tent—The man Hayes refers to is likely William S. Prentice of the 16th Illinois Cavalry, Company I. It's difficult to tell from the way the testimony is related, but Hayes may have been Prentice's tent mate.

"Sergeant Goody"—"Sergeant Goody" is likely Sergeant Walter Goode, who enlisted with his bother Walter, a private in the same company.

Accompanied by a large, taciturn man whom McElroy identifies only as "Egypt"—"Egypt" is a nickname for someone from Southern Illinois, which is sometimes known as "Little Egypt." One of the major cities in this area is Cairo, Illinois.

McElroy describes Donnelly as "a notorious character, and leader of a bad crowd," and states that he knew him at Pemberton Prison—McElroy states that Pemberton Prison was the first prison he was held at. Pemberton, on the campus of Libby Prison in Richmond, Virginia, was one half of a building that was formerly used as a warehouse. The other half of the building was a separate prison, known as the "Crews" building.

This figure is consistent with several prisoners' estimate of the number of men held over for trial—Warren Lee Goss estimated that 15 men were tried as raiders. Samuel Melvin wrote that 14 were taken out for Wirz to determine what to do with them.

Samuel Foust—Sergeant Samuel D. Foust of the 145th Pennsylvania, Company I, was captured at North Anna River, Virginia, and died at Andersonville on November 14, 1864. He is buried in grave number 12025.

Scotly—Private David Scott of the 145th Pennsylvania, Company G, was captured at the Battle of the Wilderness on May 5, 1864. and died at Andersonville on September 21, 1864. He is buried in grave number 9411.

The sailors themselves hatched the plan to take as many soldiers with them as they could by giving them the identities of their deceased comrades, a plan which they kept secret from the Confederates—This plot by the sailors to rescue soldiers using the identities of dead sailors and marines is confirmed by Wilbur Hale, a beneficiary of the plan in a chapter he contributed to Cornelius Van Santvoord's book, *The One Hundred and Twentieth New York State Volunteers*. It is also confirmed in the pension application of sailor and Andersonville POW Robert Scanlin, and in the book *The Story of a Strange Career Being the Autobiography of a Convict: An Authentic Document* by Anonymous (the author was George Anderson).

There are no incidents of death by strangulation in the Register of Deaths, either during July or at any other point during the prison's tenure—The cause of

the raiders' deaths is listed as "asphyxiation." A single other instance of death by asphyxiation occurs in the Register of Deaths, in the case of William Erek, who died
on June 20, 1864, when the wall of the well he was sleeping next to collapsed, burying
him alive. There are no other incidents of asphyxia in the register, nor are there any
instances where the cause of death is given as strangulation or any other discernable
form of homicide. There is also some evidence that a prisoner named Robert Shellito,
of the 150th New York may have committed suicide by hanging himself from his tent
pole in August 1864.

· *11* ·

"Dowd"

$\mathcal{A}$s the prison population grew, and the prisoners' circumstances became increasingly desperate, it was inevitable that things would reach the breaking point, and that point came during the afternoon of June 29. On that day, the raiders staged a robbery in broad daylight, and when the intended victim, a man identified as "Dowd" resisted, he was so badly beaten that even the Rebel camp officials knew that something had to be done to stop the prisoner-on-prisoner crime that was occurring within the stockade.

Eugene Forbes gives the most detailed diary account of the events surrounding the attack:

> *Wednesday, Jun 29—About two P.M. two men came along, trying to sell a watch; Dowd asked to look at it, and did so, after which they went away; in a short time they returned with reinforcements, and attacked him as he sat in his tent, with clubs, brass knuckles, &c.; he defended himself bravely, and they again departed; he came out of his tent, and put on his pants, when they again attacked him, and finally got him down, took his watch, cut out his money, (which he had sewed in the waistband of his pants,) to the amount of $170; he was badly cut up, but finally got away and reached the gate, and reported to Capt. Wirz, who came up with him and demanded that the robbers should be given up, under the penalty of no rations for one week; in a short time a guard came in, and took eight men from a tent near the dead line on our side; very soon the camp was in an uproar, for the men came into the arrangement, and the raiders were hunted from one end of camp to the other; by dark the tumult was nearly over, but the raiders were not all caught yet; about 50 were taken outside; the issuing of rations stopped. . . . Large quantities of clothing, blankets, &c were found in some raiders' tents.*

According to Forbes's diary, one of his friends, Samuel Oakley "Oak" Bellerjeau, went out to testify against James Sarsfield, one of Dowd's attackers the

133

next day, perhaps providing Forbes with insights to the attack that other prisoners would not have been aware of.

In 1882, a man named John Wesley Urban, of the 1st Pennsylvania Reserves (later the 30th Pennsylvania Infantry), wrote a memoir titled *Battle Field and Prison Pen.* Urban had read Robert Kellogg's prison memoir, and particularly his account of the assault that had sparked the downfall of the raiders, and wrote that he had been the victim in question, which he detailed in his own book:

> *For some time the robbers appeared to have things all their own way, but a storm was brewing. Had they been wise they would have averted the consequences by stopping their miserable system of robbery and oppression. But very little, however, appeared to be accomplished towards suppressing the raiders, until at length an event occurred that in the end put a stop to their deviltry.*
>
> *Robert H. Kellogg, Sergeant-major of the Sixteenth Regiment Connecticut Volunteers, who was in the prison at the time, and is the author of the interesting work called "Life and Death in Rebel Prisons," writes of that affair in the following words:*
>
> *"These new-comers afforded the raiders, or camp-robbers, fresh opportunities to continue their work. They seized upon one of these, and it soon proved to be a robbery in earnest. After severely beating and cutting his head, they took his watch and $175 in money. He entered a complaint to Captain Wirz, and the whole camp being aroused, collected around with clubs and began to arrest the gang as fast as possible," etc.*
>
> *I was the soldier the Sergeant refers to as being robbed and beaten by the raiders. Mr. Kellogg is correct in his statement, with the exception of the taking of the money. I had none at the time of the assault, so could not have been robbed of any. In justice to the Sergeant, I will say that I have carefully read his book, and the work is a faithful, reliable account of the terrible sufferings of the prisoners and he deserves the thanks of every survivor of rebel prisons for the truthful manner in which he has shown their friends the terrible course of treatment the rebel authorities adopted.*

Over 35 years after his imprisonment and eight years after the appearance of John Urban's book, another prisoner, Charles F. Hopkins of the 1st New Jersey, sat down with his diary and memories to pen his own memoir of his wartime experiences. Hopkins had read several of the Andersonville memoirs that had been published by other prisoners by this time, and when he came to write about the Dowd incident, he wrote a detailed, embellished version of the original story, reflecting the belief that "Dowd" had actually been John Urban, and claiming that "Urban" had been a German prisoner who had made his way to the gate after the assault and managed to attract the attention of

Henry Wirz, who happened to be in the vicinity. Urban reportedly told Wirz, a Swiss native, in German what had befallen him, and this account immediately spurred Wirz into action. The unspoken implication is that Wirz, a foreigner, would take action to protect a fellow German where he would take no action to protect the native Americans within the stockade. There is, however, no evidence to suggest that John W. Urban spoke German (according to census records, he was born in Pennsylvania as were his parents and grandparents. He never claims to have spoken German in his book. Nor does Hopkins seem to realize that the name of the prisoner beaten was recorded by prison diarists as "Dowd" rather than Urban, suggesting that he was drawing on Urban's book rather than on recollections and diary when he wrote this account.

Although he's long been credited with being "Dowd," Urban never identifies himself by that name in his book, nor does he ever claim that he was using an alias while at Andersonville. He simply states that he was the victim Robert Kellogg wrote about, and Robert Kellogg also never used the name "Dowd" in his account, although it seems clear that he is writing about the "Dowd" incident. If one continues reading Urban's account of his assault, however, it becomes apparent that Urban is not talking about the same incident as Kellogg. Urban writes that he was watching a group of Rebel soldiers digging something, when he was suddenly surrounded by three men, one of whom, a man he identifies as "Crowly," attempted to pickpocket Urban's watch. Urban reports that he grabbed Crowly by the throat, and someone—apparently one of Crowly's accomplices—begins to beat Urban, who cries for help. But when the Rebel guards approach, Crowly immediately claims that Urban had attacked him, showing the handprints on his throat as proof. Both men are eventually returned to the stockade, the situation apparently unresolved, and Urban says that that incident was the impetus that the regulators needed to begin their crackdown on the raiders.

This account is markedly different from Kellogg's story, most notably in that Urban never claims to have spoken to Henry Wirz. Urban follows the McElroy version of events where the prisoners themselves provide their own salvation from the raiders without Rebel assistance. Urban's story differs from the one Kellogg tells in that Urban claims only a watch and no money was stolen, and that he never claims to have had any direct contact with Wirz, while according to Kellogg's unpublished diary, "The raiders pitched on a newcomer today in broad daylight & robbed him of $175 and a watch, after beating his face and head all to pieces. I believe he complained to the Captain, for very soon a crowd got together with clubs, &c., and as fast as they [could] caught a raider. He was passed outside the gate & given up to the tender mercies of the Rebels." Nor does Kellogg ever allude to the regulators, saying instead that "the whole camp" is spurred to go after the raiders armed with clubs. Hopkins's account, where Urban attracts Henry Wirz's attention by speaking German, has no support in either Urban's book or Kellogg's.

While the details of Urban's story don't match with the other prisoners' accounts of "Dowd," there is another prisoner whose story does match. John G. Doud, a man "of good and temperate habits," was a 41-year-old farmer in Avoca, New York, when he received a notice telling him that he'd been drafted. Two weeks later, Doud's widowed mother, Sabra, appeared before Justice of the Peace S. D. Lewis, and gave a statement attesting to her financial dependence on her son. "With the use of form 39 my son John is notified that he was on the 14th day of July legally drafted in the service of the United States for the period of three years, in accordance with the provisions of an act of Congress for enrolling and calling out the national forces and for other purposes. I am dependent on my son John's labor for my support, I am a widow 61 years of age. I have no income of my own that equals one fourth of my necessary expenses, I have no other son in this state to help me. The above being my circumstances—dependent as I am, I choose that my son John stay at home with me."

Sadly, Sabra's request to keep her son home with her was denied, and John was enrolled with the 97th New York. Before leaving, he "left orders for his mother to continue to purchase supplies for her maintenance while he was in the service" at Sylvester Peek's local store, and promised to send back portions of his pay to help meet her expenses. As a member of the 97th New York, he would have fought at Bristoe Station and Mine Run before being captured on May 6, 1864, at the Battle of the Wilderness. Mortimer Wood, another member of Doud's company, would later testify on behalf of Sabra Doud's effort to secure a pension: "I was a private in the 97th Reg NY Vols and was acquainted with John G Dowd who was a comrade of same company. We were taken prisoner at the Battle of the Wilderness on or about 6 May 1864 and was sent to Andersonville Prison together where we remained for about Four Months. While in the prison he was beaten by a party of Prisoners who beat his head and body fearfully and he never recovered from the effects of same. He was very much disabled and robbed of a Considerable [amount of] money and his watch. I was present at the time and know the facts."

Another Andersonville survivor who knew Doud, Hiram T. Wood, testified that,

> I was taken prisoner at Drury's Bluff of Fort Darling on James River Virginia on or about 16th May 1864 and was taken to Richmond, Virginia, where I remained about eight days and, then sent to Andersonville Prison where I remained about four months. While there I became acquainted with John G. Dowd who was a private of Co D 97 NY Vols who was a prisoner who informed

me that he was captured in the battle of the Wilderness. On or about the 1st July 1864, there was a riot amongst a party [of] New York roughs prisoners and they attacked this John G. Dowd and he was badly beaten and robbed of his money and Watch he was much disabled he was taken outside by Captain Wirtz [sic] who thought he was nearly killed and I never see him afterwards til I met him at Avoca, Stueben, NY in July 1865 just after his discharge.

These two accounts place Doud in the right circumstances and approximately the right time to be the man who was beaten by the raiders so viciously that the sight of him prompted Henry Wirz to begin an immediate crackdown on the raiders. Given these accounts and the discrepancies between Urban's version of the story and statements made by other prisoners, "Dowd" is not likely to be John Urban but is probably John G. Doud. John G. Doud is also identified by name, company, and regiment in the *Sunday Mercury* article, which gives his account of his attack and is remarkably like the recounting given in Eugene Forbes's diary.

John G. Dowd, 97th NY, Company D, was the first witness. The appearance of this man excited the horror and pity of everyone present. His head and face, arms, legs, and body generally bore marks of the most brutal violence. He testified as follows—On the 28th of June, about one o'clock, I was sitting in my tent, when Sarsfield came along, crying out "Who wants to buy a watch?" (Sarsfield's object was to find out who had money.) I asked him what his watch was worth, and he replied, twenty dollars. Sarsfield left, and soon after returned with prisoner Murphy. Sarsfield renewed the offer to sell the watch, and while doing so, the other prisoner grabbed at my pantaloons, which I had in my hand, cleaning. In the scuffle, I was struck with "brass knuckles" in the face, by Sarsfield, as I believe. I then took my knife out of my pocket to defend myself. Several others then attacked me and one of them snatched the knife out of my hand, and, in doing so, cut me across the hand. Sarsfield had a dagger in his hand, and threatened if I resisted he would cut my heart out and throw it in my face. I was frequently struck with the "brass knuckles." I saw one of the men (not on trial) take hold of the chain of my watch and draw it out. I was then knocked down and turned over. They took hold of my watch-pocket and turned it out. It contained a pocket book containing $136, which the raiders carried off.

Eugene Forbes wrote in his diary the day after the attack that "Dowd moved his things outside today, where he has liberty to the extent of one mile." That's the last mention of him until his parole at Jacksonville, Florida, on April 28, 1865. Perhaps because of his injuries, he was kept at Andersonville until the prison camp closed. He mustered out of the 97th New York on July 17, 1865.

John Doud made his way back to Avoca, New York, a broken man; emaciated, sickly, and suffering from trouble with his liver and his bowels. No longer capable of the hard, physical labor demanded of a farmer, John Doud set up a small cooper's shop to support himself and his widowed mother. He succeeded for a time, but the man who had never had to consult with a doctor before the war needed frequent medical care after it. Even so, he worked to support his mother at the cooper's shop until he was physically no longer able to do so. No fewer than four different doctors testified as to his declining medical condition for his mother's pension application. One of them, Christopher Patterson, wrote, "I commenced treating him July 31, 1869 saw him every day up to September 5. I treated him for disease of the glandular structure & liver & glands of the bowels. I was obliged to use a large sized catheter to throw water up the bowels to move them for weeks the disease was in my opinion a chronic disease of the glands of the bowels and liver. He was a man of good and temperate habits." Another, Peter R. House, testified that he'd known Doud for 24 years and that Doud went into the army sound, but came out of it, he "found him suffering from chronic disease of the liver, believes it to have been Atrophy with Lesions of the alimentary canal, and that of pain in the head, as an associated condition of that of the liver & bowels . . . in part of 1868 to 1869, he was confined to his bed and great suffering until his death."

It was a long, slow, agonizing death. Doctor A. U. Brown, a physician called into consult during the last month of Doud's life noted that near the end, "he was in a state of general marasmus, scarcely an organ in the system performing its normal function." It's impossible to know how much of his physical condition was due to the abuse he suffered at the hands of the raiders and how much was a result of deprivations all prisoners suffered at Andersonville, but undoubtedly, it was his time at Andersonville Prison that contributed to his early death. Sabra Doud outlived her son by 13 years, and eventually had to sell her house to support herself, and when that money ran out, she applied for, and received, a pension in the name of her lost son. John Urban, just 20 years old when he was a prisoner at Andersonville, was credited with being the man who was responsible for the raiders' downfall, lived until 1918, dying at the age of 74, while John Doud, the man whose beating brought about the end of the raider's reign, lay all but forgotten in his grave in Avoca, New York.

NOTES ON CHAPTER 11

Samuel Oakley "Oak" Bellerjeau—He was a member of the 11th New Jersey Infantry, Company D.

Suggesting that he was drawing on Urban's book rather than on recollections when he wrote this account. The attack that prompted the arrests is not recorded in Hopkins's diary—Hopkins's memoirs, written sometime after 1900, are flawed by the vagaries of memory and influenced by the prison memoirs—both good and bad—that came before him. As far as the raiders are concerned, he states that seven were arrested, but that one turned state's evidence and wasn't convicted. He misidentifies Sarsfield as "Champlin" and states that "Muer" was captured in Albemarle Sound rather than Ossabaw Sound. He states that "Keyes" oversaw the regulators. He is slightly confused when writing about the number of raiders taken out of the stockade and says that the man who assaulted "Urban" was taken out of the stockade, along with seven others, for trial, then a few lines later says that seven men were taken outside. He also says that the "bull pen" was full of lawyers, and that these men were "eloquent" in the defense of the accused, even though they knew that they were guilty, but there's no indication that Hopkins heard any portion of this eloquence himself.

Mr. Kellogg is correct in his statement, with the exception of the taking of the money—Most accounts of the attack on Dowd, including Robert Kellogg's, Eugene Forbes's, John McElroy's, and the *Sunday Mercury*'s, mention that a large sum of money was taken.

Charles F. Hopkins of the 1st New Jersey, sat down with his diary and memories to pen his own memoir of his wartime experiences—Hopkins's memoir was combined with his prison diary and published as *The Andersonville Diary and Memoirs of Charles Hopkins*, edited by William B. Stymple and John J. Fitzpatrick in 1988.

Urban reportedly told Wirz, a Swiss native, in German what had befallen him—As far as can be determined, Doud, who, like his parents was born in New York state, did not speak German, nor does John Urban mention this detail in his account.

"Crowly"—No other known account mentions a man by this name as being a raider. See chapter 10, "Other Alleged Raiders."

A man "of good and temperate habits"—Several different people used this term to describe Doud in his mother's pension application.

A statement attesting to her financial dependence—A statement confirming this request by S. Lewis is part of John G. Doud's compiled service record.

On the 28th of June—This is probably an error by Doud. Most other accounts put the date of attack as June 29, 1864.

Eugene Forbes wrote in his diary—See Forbes diary, entry for June 30, 1864.

John Urban, just 20 years old when he was a prisoner—One prisoner, a man named John Duff, referred to the victim of the beating as an "old man." This description certainly seems more appropriate for the 42-year-old Dowd than for the 20-year-old Urban.

• *12* •

A Clearer Picture

It was just his luck to run into the Rebels.

Luck hadn't been on Willie Collins's side since he'd first joined the army more than two years before. He'd enlisted in October 1861, then gone AWOL shortly after mustering in, but the army had found him and returned him to his regiment, the 88th Pennsylvania, where he was soon transferred to Company D, which had a reputation of being made up of troublemakers and "hard cases." He'd had the misfortune to be shot in the thigh and captured at the end of August 1862 at the Battle of Second Manassas but had been paroled on Grovetown Battlefield three days later. Because of his injury, he was sent to Baltimore, to the confiscated former home of Maryland Confederate captain (later general) George H. Steuart, which was being used as a Union military hospital. Collins found the hospital more to his liking than life in the infantry and exaggerated the severity of his injury to avoid being sent back to his company; but his injury wasn't bad enough to keep him from slipping out to frequent the local taverns. Even then, sometimes he'd get so drunk and belligerent that the prison guards would find him and confine him to the guard house. To be sure, he was a noticeable man, six feet tall and close to two hundred pounds with red hair and beard. He managed to slip away when a military escort came to the hospital to accompany the recovered soldiers back to their units in January 1863, and was nowhere to be found until after the escorts left. He had the misfortune to be spotted unawares by one of the assistant surgeons while walking in town, as well as any able-bodied man could, and without his customary limp. The assistant surgeon, fed up and irate, wrote to the provost marshal, asking that the belligerent "source of annoyance" be returned to his company by special escort at the soonest possible date, and so the reluctant Collins rejoined his regiment, which had taken part in the

140

battles of Antietam and Fredericksburg without him. He rejoined the 88th on March 24, 1863, having missed close to six months of service.

Collins's finest moment in the Union army came on July 1, 1863, when his regiment, the 88th Pennsylvania, took part in the first day of the Battle of Gettysburg. The men of the 88th took on Alfred Iverson's North Carolina Brigade, charging across an open field while under enemy fire, and the men of Company D were the first ones over the wall to take on the enemy. Collins rose to the occasion, perhaps aided by his big size, he fought competently and attracted the notice of his superiors, earning a promotion to corporal on July 1, 1863. The second day of the battle found the men of the 88th fighting on Cemetery Ridge, and they ended the battle holding their position at Ziegler's Farm on July 3–6. Nearly half of the 249 men of the 88th were battle casualties, with 18 men killed, 50 wounded, and 53 missing—a casualty rate of 48.5 percent.

Collins went on to fight with the 88th Pennsylvania at Chancellorsville, surviving his third major battle intact. His luck ran out on October 12, 1863. The regiment was on night maneuvers, rapidly moving back and forth against the Rapidan River near Stevensburg, Virginia, in anticipation of an encounter with Confederate forces. On the moonless night of October 12, 28-year-old Collins became separated from his regiment and was never seen by them again. He encountered Rebel troops and was captured. After fighting at three of the major battles of the war, Collins went missing as his company was moving into position in anticipation of another battle. The 88th recorded him as a deserter.

William Collins was not the only man to be captured in that area. Just a day or two before he disappeared, a man called Sullivan, a substitute who had been with the 76th New York for just a month, deserted near Culpeper, Virginia. Sullivan was a small man, just five feet, three and a half inches tall with blue eyes, dark hair, and a light complexion. He gave his age upon enlistment as 26 years old. An Irish immigrant, "John Sullivan" was likely an alias given because he'd intended to desert when he enlisted, and had only signed on to collect the money draftee William Oliver, the son of a local judge, had paid him to take his place in the army. "John Sullivan" was as common a name among the Irish as "John Smith" was with the English, and by the time he joined his company, Sullivan was already obscuring even that identity by telling his comrades that his first name was "Cary." His career as a bounty jumper and deserter was scuttled when, after deserting, he too, was captured. Two days after Collins went missing, a soldier named Patrick Delaney was one of a dozen recently arrived draftees from the 83rd Pennsylvania who fell out while marching "double quick." They tossed away their guns and set off to the north, planning to go home to Pennsylvania. Delaney was an immigrant, and not a soldier by choice, but rather a victim of a recent innovation in American warfare—a forced draft. Rather than stay in a war that they hadn't voluntarily joined, Delaney and the others planned to simply walk away. Unfortunately, Delaney and the others were also picked up by some of the Confederates who were in the area.

It can't be known for certain if Collins, Sullivan, and Delaney met while en route to one of the Richmond, Virginia, prisons, but given that they were captured within a few days and 40 miles of each other, it's very possible. All three ended up at Belle Isle, a Confederate prison camp about 70 miles southeast of Culpeper, which, as the name suggests, was located on an island in the Richmond section of the James River.

At Belle Isle, some of the prisoners began to turn on their comrades. A diarist named J. Osborne Coburn wrote in his diary that "raiders" robbed him of the better part of four loaves of bread while he carried it back to the men of his mess. This pattern of prisoner on prisoner crime may have begun even before the soldiers reached their regiment. Patrick Delaney's commanding officer described the drafted men in his company as "the grandest scoundrels that ever went unhung . . . rioters, gamblers, thieves, pickpockets and blacklegs. . . . On board the boats that took them to Alexandria [Virginia], they fought, gambled, and stole from each other. Some of them stole several hundred dollars at a time." Collins adopted the nickname "Mosby" after a Confederate colonel, whose style of striking the enemy with small, fast, unexpected raids rather than traditional battles was one that Collins, a former city kid from Philadelphia, taught the others how to emulate. Men who carried out these unexpected attacks were commonly known inside the prisons as "raiders."

The men continued their thieving ways following their arrival, settling in the southwest corner of the prison. By staying close together, they could not only assist each other in the commission of crimes but protect each other in the event of a pursuit. The southwest corner, one of the few places within the stockade that couldn't be seen from the hilltop Star Fort where the prison officials kept their headquarters, soon developed a reputation as a "tough neighborhood" that other prisoners tended to avoid. Newcomers to the camp, however, were easy marks for men with criminal intentions. The raiders would frequently lure the "fresh fish" inside their tents with the promise of assistance, then once they had them out of sight, they'd rob them, taking anything of value. Other times, they might simply wait until their victims slept or were absent and simply make off with their watches, blankets, or other possessions. Other victims were simply scammed by the thieves, who might ask to see an object by offering to purchase it and simply refuse to return it once they had possession, or offering to make change for a large denomination dollar bill and then keeping it without making change.

Because the scammers were physically backed up by the other raiders, there was little that the victims could do to get their money or possessions back. At this point the raiders were considered more of a nuisance than a serious threat, but that would change in May 1864.

The "Plymouth Pilgrims" were 2,364 Union soldiers who had been captured at Plymouth, North Carolina, on April 20, 1864. As it happened, many of the soldiers captured had just been paid and had received up to three months back pay, as well as enlistment and reenlistment bounties. As part of their terms of surrender the Plymouth captives were allowed to keep their cash and property, which was unusual. As a result, the stylishly dressed "Pilgrims" entered Andersonville with an influx of cash that would have been in the hundreds of thousands of dollars range in modern currency. This changed prison life at Andersonville. A "market street" ran perpendicular to the north gate and suddenly the prison economy flourished as prisoners sold and traded what they could within the stockade. With the increase in wealth, however, came an increase in crime. Prisoners' diaries began to mention raids by bands of thieves that became increasingly more brazen. The thieves would work in tandem, going out and offering an item up for sale as a way of identifying men who had money. If a person asked to see the item they were offering, that marked him as a potential victim. The raiders might go back for reinforcements and bide their time until they found their victim alone and vulnerable, then swoop in, snatch whatever money or possessions their victim might have, and race back to the southwestern corner of the stockade where their encampment was, with their fellow raiders blocking any pursuers or helping to protect their fellow thief once he reached the relative safety of the raiders' corner of the camp.

But raiding, while sometimes profitable, was by no means a safe or easy occupation, and the other prisoners began to band together to protect each other. If a raider tried to steal from a member of the Plymouth Pilgrims, for example, that man could muster assistance from the other members of his company by simply shouting "Plymouth!" to bring assistance running. Raiders were sometimes captured by the men they'd sought to steal from. Raiders who were caught might be "roughed up" or have half of their head and beard shaven off as a visible warning to the other prisoners that this man was a known thief. They might be whipped, bucked, and gagged, or forced to march around the camp by their captors to the jeers and taunts of the other prisoners. Despite this, as conditions in the camp worsened and the stakes grew higher, the frequency and brazenness of the raiders' crimes grew. Spotting a potential victim during the day, five or six raiders might sneak into his tent at night and their sleeping victim might awaken to find a knife or razor at his throat, his assailants demanding that he hand over his property. If a man resisted, the raiders would not hesitate to use physical violence to subdue him, and rumors began to swirl around the camp that the raiders would go so far as to commit murder in the commissions of their crimes.

On the first of June, a sailor from the USS *Powhatan*, William Ritson, was transferred to the stockade along with other sailors who were captured on September 8, 1863, at the Second Battle of Fort Sumter. Perhaps because of his inclination to rob his fellow prisoners, Ritson used an alias, the name of an actual soldier with the 5th Rhode Island Heavy Artillery, Charles F. Curtis. The real Charles Curtis was currently located in North Carolina, where he was frequently out on sick leave at the hospital in Morehead, North Carolina. The sailors captured along with Ritson knew him, of course—some of them had sailed on the *Powhatan* with him, and they'd been held together more or less during the first three months of their captivity until Ritson and 14 other captives from Second Sumter had been sent to Salisbury Prison as hostages for the lives of a Confederate privateer and his crew—but sailors were a distinct minority at Andersonville, with only about 200 of the thousands of prisoners being from the Navy. When Ritson began stealing from the other prisoners, most of them knew him only by his assumed alias of "Curtis."

James Sarsfield, a member of the 76th New York who would be listed on prison records as "John Sarsfield," arrived at Camp Sumter shortly after the Plymouth Pilgrims, having been captured two weeks later, on May 5 at the Battle of the Wilderness. Like Delaney and Sullivan, he was an Irish immigrant, but the 22 or 23-year-old, brown-haired, gray-eyed man with the light complexion who stood just five feet, three and half inches tall was neither a bounty jumper nor a deserter; like Patrick Delaney he had been drafted. Although the raiders would later be characterized as "New Yaarkers," the 22-year-old Sarsfield is apparently the only one of the six men who would be hanged to live in New York City, coming from the borough of Brooklyn. He joined his regiment at roughly the same time Delaney joined his, and may even have traveled aboard the same ship—another member of the 76th New York who arrived at about the same time as Sarsfield wrote that there was so much theft and violence onboard that brought him to Alexandria, Virginia, that he considered himself lucky to have escaped with his life. Sarsfield had been with his regiment for eight months when he was captured in battle and was listed as "present" for all of them. His company listed him as first "missing in action," then on detached service as a prisoner of war. There's nothing in his service record to indicate that he was any sort of a discipline problem, but his criminal activities as a prisoner of war began not long after his arrival at Andersonville Prison. Between his arrival in the third week of May and his arrest as a raider on June 29, just five weeks had passed.

But Sarsfield was not the most recent arrival of the raiders when their end came. That distinction goes to Andrew Muir, a seaman from the USS *Water Witch*. The tragedy of Andrew Muir wasn't how quickly he fell, but the fact that, by his reckoning, he shouldn't have been there at all. His year of enlistment was already up when a Confederate boarding party seized the *Water Witch* on the night of June 2, 1864, and he'd simply been waiting, like most of the crew, unwillingly, for replacement sailors to arrive so that he could be transported home and mustered out of service. In fact, many members of the *Water Witch* crew were so disgruntled at this forced extension of their time with the Navy, that they simply refused to fight, leaving that to the officers and those whose term of service was still in play. Some members of the crew reportedly even hid beneath the hurricane deck of the ship, rather than join in the fight. It was a choice they surely regretted once they saw what awaited them within the prison stockade. Diarists would mention that the crew of the *Water Witch*, with Muir almost certainly among them, arrived at Andersonville on June 7.

By the end of June, there were probably between 80 and 200 raiders operating within the prison. Some, such as Delaney, Sullivan, and Sarsfield, worked together in the commission of their crimes, but it is also likely that some men, driven to desperation by their situation, operated independently of the raiders' organization of small bands of criminals, but were lumped in with them when the term became used to describe any prison thief. This still represents a very small percentage of the prisoners. On the day of the hanging, the prison's morning report would state that there were a little over 26,000 men held within the stockade. Using the highest estimated number of raiders—John McElroy's 500—this means that the raiders were outnumbered by at least 52 to 1. Because of this, while their crimes were certainly escalating in frequency and violence, the raiders were unlikely to have been a dominant force within the stockade.

The raiders' crime spree ended abruptly on June 29, 1864, with a particularly brazen crime, committed in broad daylight. At about one or two in the afternoon, an older prisoner, 42-year-old John G. Doud of the 97th New York, who'd been one of the "Plymouth Pilgrims," was approached by James Sarsfield, who offered to sell him a watch. Doud asked to look at it and declined to buy, but this was enough to mark him as a victim. The raiders knew that he possessed enough cash to purchase a watch, and so Sarsfield set off, probably back to the raiders' section of the camp in the southwest corner, and gathered reinforcements to back him up, among them Sullivan, Delaney, and Muir. They found Doud in his tent, literally with his pants off, caught in the act of cleaning them. At first they pretended that they still wanted to sell Dowd a watch, probably hoping to grab his money when he produced it to make the purchase, but when he again declined, they demanded that he hand over his money anyway. He refused to hand over his money—as one of the Plymouth Pilgrims, he had just been paid before being captured, and currently had $136 sewn into the waistband of his pants, money that he had intended to send to his widowed mother back in Avoca, New York. When Doud refused to hand over the money, the raiders attacked him, viciously beating him with clubs and brass knuckles. In the tumult, the tent was knocked down. Doud managed to get his pants back on and grab his knife as the raiders left the tent, only to be attacked again when he emerged. One of the raiders snatched Doud's knife, cutting him across the hand as he pulled it away. Sarsfield pulled out a dagger of his own and snarled that he would cut Doud's heart out and throw it in his face if he didn't produce the money. The gang of raiders began to viciously beat Doud again. He fought as best he could, but Doud was outnumbered by men armed with weapons while he had none. This time his assailants managed to get him down. They flipped him over and took his watch, then cut his money out of his pants. They left him, in the words of prisoner Robert Kellogg, "after beating his face and head all to pieces."

Somehow, Doud made it away from his tent and to one of the prison gates, where he managed to attract the attention of prison commandant Captain Henry Wirz. Wirz reportedly took one look at the brutally bruised and beaten Doud and demanded that the men responsible be handed over to him at once, ordering the prisoners' food rations be withheld until those responsible were in custody to strengthen his demand. But it wasn't necessary. When Wirz sent in guards to retrieve the men responsible, other prisoners had had enough of the raiders, and eagerly pointed them out. Doud was removed from the stockade, both to receive medical attention and for his own safety. It would later be reported that he would be given liberty to move around the outside of the stockade for up to one mile. Perhaps because of his injuries, Doud would be among the last of the Union prisoners to leave Andersonville. He would finally be paroled on April 28, 1865.

So many men were identified as raiders—accounts range from 50 to over 100—that Wirz could not hold them all, and somehow made the determination as to who the worst of the offenders were. These 15 or so suspects were ordered held within the confines of the south gate. The rest of the accused were forced back into the prison, where the other prisoners were waiting for them. The aggrieved prisoners armed themselves with sticks and clubs, whatever could be found at hand, and formed a double line just inside the south gate. As each man was returned to the stockade, he had to run "the gauntlet" of men seeking to get payback by beating them as they desperately ran past. Reports were that at least one of these returning raiders was beaten to death on the spot.

Wirz consulted his superior, General John Winder about the situation, and the following day Winder issued General Orders Number 57, which authorized the trial and punishment of the "evil disposed persons" accused of "assaulting, murdering and robbing their fellow prisoners." The arrests continued. One prisoner reported in his diary that three of the men involved in the attack on Doud had been captured the night before, and that "the fourth and worst one" had since been caught. At nine o'clock on the morning of June 30, Henry Wirz sent for the sergeants of the mess to be called together and escorted to his headquarters. A jury was selected, made up of sergeants of the mess who were relative newcomers to Camp Sumter based on the idea that they knew the least about the accused raiders and thus could give them the fairest trial possible. The longest held member of the jury had been there since May; the most recently arrived had entered the stockade just eleven days before. They were men from a variety of different states and regiments.

The first trial began that very day, roughly 24 hours after Doud had first been approached by Sarsfield. Although pains had been taken to secure the fairest jury possible, the men selected to serve as judge and attorneys for the defense and prosecution were something less than qualified. The judge was apparently a Missouri farmer with no legal experience. The defense lawyer, Henry Higginson, was a con man with a penchant for self-glorification; he would be part of a delegation of six prisoners released a week later to carry a petition asking for the resumption of prisoner exchanged to Washington, DC, and was awarded a brevet promotion to major by the governor of Illinois. In 1865, he would testify at the trial of the Lincoln assassination conspirators saying that the prison guards had shown him a letter signed by John Wilkes Booth. His sole qualification in terms of being a lawyer seems to have been the fact that his father had been the sheriff of Pekin, Illinois; after the war, Higginson would work as an insurance agent. In the trial of William Collins, Higginson would decline to address the jury at all on behalf of the man he was supposed to be defending. The prosecuting attorney, Sergeant O. W. Campbell was a private school teacher who would survive Andersonville, only to die on his way home. The court reporter, who went by the alias Edward Bates, was a reporter with the *Sunday Mercury*, a weekly newspaper based in New York City. His real name was Edward Wellington Boate, and he would later go on to testify as a witness for the defense in the war crimes trial of Henry Wirz.

Although the initial plan had been to begin with the trial of William Collins, the case was postponed so that more evidence could be collected and the trial proceedings began with the trial of James Sarsfield on charges of "assaulting with intent to murder (if necessary) and highway robbery." Sarsfield was tried along with another man, Patrick Murphy of the 52nd New York, although one of the witnesses would state that Murphy had not been present when the attack on Doud took place, and so he was acquitted.

The first witness to testify against Sarsfield was Doud himself. "The appearance of this man excited the horror and pity of everyone present," recorded the court reporter. "His head and face, arms, legs, and body generally bore marks of the most brutal violence." Three other men's testimonies were recorded as well; two claimed to have witnessed Sarsfield's assault on Doud, one claimed to have been robbed by Sarsfield himself. By that evening, James Sarsfield had been found guilty and sentenced to hang for his crime.

The second day of trial saw the rest of Doud's alleged assailants put on trial. Delaney, Sullivan, and Muir stood trial along with two more men from the 52nd New York, William John Kennedy and John Connelly (which may be either an alias or a clerical error, as regimental records indicate that John Connolly of the 52 New York died on June 15, two weeks before). Owen Farley, a news agent with the Cavalry Corps; and two men from the 145th Pennsylvania, Peter Gilmore and William Holdings (whose name apparently changes to Mullings later in the court transcript) were also tried that day.

No evidence was produced against Kennedy and Farley, and acting defense attorney Higginson focused his questions on clearing Connelly and Holdings/Mullings from the capital charge of assault with intent to commit murder. Connelly and Holdings/Mullings were found guilty and sentenced to wear a ball and chain for four months. Gilmore's case would be suspended with no conclusion reached. Witnesses stated that Delaney, Sullivan, and Muir were all physically involved in the attack on Doud, as well as other robberies. All three were found guilty and sentenced to hang.

On July 2, the third and final day of the trial saw Richard "Dick" Allen of the 83rd Pennsylvania, a comrade of Patrick Delaney placed on trial along with Thomas O'Connell of the 9th Maryland and William Ritson, who the trial transcript referred to as "William Wrixon, alias Curtis, United States steamship *Powhattan*." Four witnesses were called, two of whom testified that Allen and Curtis had worked in tandem to rob them of a watch, with Curtis allegedly echoing Sarsfield's threat to Doud that he would "cut out his (Prentiss's) heart" as well as cut his throat if Prentiss did not produce the watch. A third witness stated that he had been robbed of a watch and $70 by an unidentified accomplice inside Curtis's tent.

Perhaps the most curious testimony is that of James Marion Friend, who like the witness who said that Curtis had threatened to cut out his heart and slit his throat, was from the 16th Illinois Cavalry, the regiment that 15 years later would be given credit for bringing down the raiders in Friend's comrade John McElroy's best-selling book. According to Friend's testimony, Curtis and Patrick Delaney snuck into Friend's tent at night and woke him up by holding a razor to his throat and accusing him of having robbed them of a blanket. According to Friend, he denied having stolen from them, and in response, they slashed his face with the razor, and when he put his hand up defensively, they caught him between the finger and thumb with the razor, causing a deep gash. According to Friend, he then managed to crawl out of his tent and tried to toss his wallet into the space between the dead line and the stockade wall, but he didn't throw it far enough and one of his assailants picked it up, saying "God damn you, that is all we wanted."

At no point in the recorded testimony is Ritson associated with the attack on Doud. There may have been bad blood between him and the members of the 16th Illinois Cavalry. Both Leroy Key and John McElroy of the 16th called "Curtis" the "chief" of the raiders, even though most other sources assign this designation to Mosby, the alias of William Collins. Both Key and McElroy state that Key was accosted by Curtis and an armed gang, although the particulars of their stories disagree. Also startling is Friend's statement that his wallet contained $449 because he had been "trading a little." At a time when a private such as Friend would have been paid $13 a month for his service, this raises questions as to how Friend could have come by such an amount in the first place. It's worth noting that two of the witnesses against Curtis—James Marion Friend and William Prentice—were members of Key and McElroy's 16th Illinois Cavalry while a third witness, Daniel Hayes, of one of the US regiments, was apparently Prentice's friend and possibly his tent mate. In the end, the testimony against him was enough to convict Ritson, and like Delaney, Sullivan, and Sarsfield before him, he was sentenced to hang. Dick Allen and Thomas O'Connell were found guilty of robbery and assault, although the specifics of O'Connell's crimes are not recorded, and both were sentenced to be handcuffed and shackled for the remainder of their imprisonment.

Only William Collins remained to be tried. His reputation was not so much as a thief himself, but rather as an organizer of thieves. Most of the prisoners who named a raider in their diaries wrote about "Mosby," the chief organizer of the raiders. In addition to being charged with robbery and assault, he was also accused of "being the leader of a gang of thieves." One of the three witnesses whose testimony against him is recorded, admitted, "I know Mosby did not take part in the robberies himself, but I know him to be a planner of robberies for others." The testimony against him accused him more of running scams than violent robberies, and witnesses said that Collins was the leader of a band of thieves and stole from little boys. His defense lawyer apparently did not put up much of a contest against the allegations against Collins: "Mr. Higginson said that after he had heard of Mosby's character, he declined to address the jury in his defense." Not surprisingly given his reputation, "The jury found Mosby guilty of robbing and assaulting his fellow-prisoners, and with being a leader of an organized band of thieves, robber, and garrotters, and he was sentenced to be hanged."

The newspaper account of the trial concludes with, "There were several others tried, and found guilty, and sentenced to wear ball and chain for terms varying from ten days to the remainder of their imprisonment."

The six condemned men were placed in stocks outside the prison walls. The Confederate officials now had to decide—should they follow through on General Order number 57 and proceed with the punishments prescribed by the prisoners, or were they obliged to protect all of the men in their custody? For just over a week, the matter was considered and debated. Finally, on Sunday, July 10, General John Winder issued General Order Number 61: the executions would proceed. And so the following day, wood to construct a gallows was placed inside the camp and Father Peter Whelan, the Catholic priest who tended to the prisoners, was notified. Five of the six men condemned, except William Collins, were Catholic. Whelan agreed to accompany the condemned men to the gallows, to offer what comfort he could. The six men, perhaps buoyed by the delay between the sentencing and its execution, doubted that they would be hanged. They didn't believe that the prisoners' court-martial had the authority to execute them, and surely the Rebels would not follow the edict of its prisoners. They began to think that the trial was an elaborate hoax, meant to scare them from their criminal ways.

The evening of July 11 was a sweltering one, with a rain in the morning that left all those in the stockade miserable. At a little before 5 o'clock, prison guards released the condemned men from the stocks, and joined by Father Whelan on foot and Henry Wirz riding on the back of his gray horse, they were marched toward the south gate of the stockade. A few musicians joined them, playing the "Dead March" on their drums as they went. Whatever the six men had been expecting, it wasn't the sight of well over 20,000 men sitting on the two slopes that led down to the prison's narrow stream, each one turned to face a rude wooden gallows that had been constructed just to the south side of the stream, not far from where the raiders had their camp. As they halted in front of the gallows, Henry Wirz made a short speech, saying that he was returning the six men to the prisoners in the same shape in which he'd received them, and bade the prisoners to do what they would with them. He asked God for mercy for them all, then turned and rode out of the stockade, followed by the guards.

The awful reality of what was about to happen now fell upon the six men. Limber Jim and his assistants stepped forward to bind the hands of the condemned, but William Ritson suddenly bolted, running toward the only place not full of prisoners—the filthy, fetid stream. Without hesitation, he charged into it, wading through the other side and slogging forward. He made it to the other side and was still dodging his way through the crowd when he was finally grabbed by the other prisoners. He was brought back, his hands bound, and he was forced to mount the gallows with the others. Meal sacks, in the place of hoods, were placed over their heads and the nooses affixed around their necks. The hangmen got down off the gallows, a signal was given, and the prop that supported the board on which the six men stood was yanked away. The six bodies fell, but to everyone's horror, one of them suddenly plummeted back to earth—William Collins, "Mosby," the big six-footer from Philadelphia. The executioners removed the hood and hurriedly checked on him and found to their dismay that he was still alive. He was revived and looked around in dismay; his executioners stood around him and his five compatriots now hung, dead or dying, above him. Earnestly, Collins began to plead for mercy, and argued that it was "unlawful" to hang him a second time. Although his cries were described as "piteous," mercy was not to be found. Another rope was fetched, another noose tied, and he was once again forced back up the steps of the gallows and was "launched into eternity," this time fatally.

The bodies were left hanging for some 15 or 20 minutes; long enough to make sure the men were dead. Then they were cut down and some of the prisoners filed past to look at the bodies; a brutal visual reminder on the wages of sin. Then the prisoners went back to their struggle to survive and the six bodies were carried out, finally leaving the stockade forever.

The bodies were carried to the prison's "dead house," a rude shed where the bodies were identified and listed in the prison's Register of Deaths. Here was a problem. Eight of the sailors who had gone out to work at the prison hospital had been captured along with William Ritson and had lived in close quarters with him for months. Any one of them may have been the one to identify his body for the clerk who had the onerous task of listing the prison's dead. Unfortunately, the clerk knew that one of the men hanged was "Curtis" of the 5th Rhode Island; but Sullivan had taken great pains to conceal his identity, going so far as to offer protection to the men from his company if they promised not to reveal his identity as Sullivan the deserter, because desertion was a capital offense in the Civil War Army. Both "W. Rickson, USN"—a clerical variation of Ritson's name—and "Chas. Curtis, 5 Rhode Island" were listed among the dead, while Sullivan's name was omitted. When the six raiders were buried, the prisoners in the burial party made a point of burying them apart from the other prisoners. The six were not included among the "honored dead," being buried instead a few dozen yards to the north of where the dead were currently being laid to rest. The burial party did not foresee that more dead would eventually fill in the empty space between the graves they were currently digging and the place where the raiders lay, and that there would be thousands more dead buried beyond where the raiders lay.

The year after the prison closed, an expeditionary task force from the US government that included Red Cross founder Clara Barton and prison clerk Dorence Atwater arrived to create a national cemetery and to mark the graves permanently. Using the Register of Deaths, they marked as many of the graves as possible with the names of the dead. Thanks in large part to Atwater's own copy of the list of deaths, they did a commendable job; only 460 of the 12,920 prisoners' marble grave markers bear the legend "Unknown." The raiders' graves were marked with the names listed in the death register, with three of them incorrect: "Chas Curtis/5 RI" "W. Rickson/USN" and "A. Munn/ USN"—a misreading of "Andrew Muir." The name "Sullivan" is missing altogether. These errors were recorded on the marble markers that identified the men buried beneath them. Most of the gravestones at Andersonville National Cemetery include a grave number along with the name and regiment of the deceased, but the six graves set apart from the rest and partially hidden behind a tree have no such numbers. The surviving prisoners did not wish the raiders to be counted among the honored dead who lie there.

The prison stockade site and Andersonville National Cemetery, along with the National POW Museum, now comprise Andersonville National Historic Site, which is administered by the National Park Service. The Park Service's policy is that the cemetery is a historic site and should not be altered, save for the addition of more deceased veterans, and so the existing grave markers are not changed, even if they are believed to be incorrect. Each Memorial Day, all graves of the honored dead in the National Cemetery are marked with flags, except the six; the graves of the men hanged as raiders go unadorned. Their sins are not forgiven and never will be.

Appendix A

The Transcript of the Raiders Trial

$\mathscr{T}$he record is APZ 479-1865, pertaining to Dorence Atwater, Co. R, 2nd New York Cavalry.

SUNDAY MERCURY NEWSPAPER

The following article is taken from the August 20, 1865, issue of the *Sunday Mercury*. A clipping of this article is referred to in the Compiled Military Service records of Patrick Delaney, William Colling, and John Sullivan, and is located at the National Archives in Washington, DC (File APZ (EB) 1865, Entry 409, Records of the Adjutant General, Group 94). The clipping originally appeared in the appendix of the book *Ghosts and Shadows of Andersonville: Essays on the Secret Social Histories of America's Deadliest Prison* by Robert S. Davis. A copy of the *Sunday Mercury* for the date in question is also held on microfilm at the New York Public Library, and the article can be found on page three of that newspaper. Although it is inaccurate on several counts, it offers one of the very few alleged accounts of what happened during the trial of the accused "raiders."

ANDERSONVILLE PRISON.
Was Captain Wirz Guilty of the Enormities Charged to Him?

A THRILLING EPISODE OF PRISON LIFE.
How an Organized Gang of Ruffians Preyed upon Their Fellow-Prisoners.

SIX OF THEM SENTENCED TO BE HANGED
Detailed Statement of the Whole Proceeding, by the Official Reporter of the
  Court

&c &c &c

The treatment said to have been received by Union prisoners at the hands
of the Confederate authorities at Andersonville, seems to be among the
bitterest subjects now connected with the late war. Various accounts have
been published describing Captain Wirz, the Commandant of the prison,
as a monster, in comparison with whom Nero would not be a circumstance;
others—and these the most intelligen[t] and trust-worth, and who had
superior opportunities of knowing the facts, both from actual confinement
for months in the Andersonville stockade, and subsequently by intimate
intercourse with Captain Wirz for months have boldly come forward and
defended him from the charge of cruelty to his prisoners; and while admit-
ting the fearful suffering—which, indeed, it would be hard to overdraw—
endured by the unhappy men in that wretched "d—d bul[l]pen," to use
Wirz's own words, maintain that such sufferings were solely the result of
poverty and want of resources in the Confederacy.

Before coming to our present purpose in giving the particulars of a
thrilling episode of prisoner-life, which had hitherto been but briefly al-
luded to by the press, we may be permitted to refer to some of the statements made against Captain Wirz, especially to one which bears upon
the very subject of this trial. A person in the *Washington Chronicle*, who
appears to have been a prisoner at Andersonville, but whose statements are
as nonexistent with the facts as that a horse-chestnut and a chestnut horse
mean the same thing, makes several charges against Captain Wirz. Next to
malignity, stupidity is the most intolerable thing to deal patiently with. This
person, who signs himself "S. H, Co. C, Eighth Pennsylvania Cavalry," says
that the "raider at Andersonville [*sic*] were deserters from the United States
Army that they were known to be so by Captain Wirz," and that "they received favors from the Rebel authorities that were not accorded to the loyal
Union prisoners"—such as permission to go outside the stockade to work,
obtain better rations than the other prisoners, and even permitted to bring
plenty of wood on returning every evening.

The writer of this article, happening to know all facts in connection with
the modus operandi of the machinery in Andersonville brands every one of
the foregoing statements as shameful, ignorant falsehoods.

Again, "Wirz was aware of the existence of this gang and their depredations, and although their poor victims time and again complained of them to
him, the hardened villains took no notice of their complaints, encouraging

their oppressors in their inhuman barbarities." The truth is that Wirz, whenever he heard of an act of oppression by one man—any man—toward another, would be down upon him like a thunderbolt. Wirz had his failings, but his worst fault was impulsiveness. And to charge him with contriving at raiders, is a piece of donkeyism that his most inveterate enemies in Washington, when his trial comes on, will not be guilty of.

A long paragraph in the same article headed, "An Outbreak," described the attacks of the raiders which brought on the trials and execution which it is our object to describe. There was no "outbreak." It was the mere culmination of a system carried on in the camp by a set of scoundrels and thieves. If the founders of the prosecution against Wirz have no better grounds to go upon than such statements as we have referred to, the sooner they abandon their case the better.

Captain Wirz or the authorities at Andersonville never gave the slightest encouragement to desertion. We happen to know, having seen some fifty letters per day from prisoners at Andersonville, addressed to Captain Wirz, offering to take the oath of allegiance to the Southern Confederacy. The letters were handed by Captain Wirz to use [illegible], and were destroyed, and never [illegible].

"Well," said Wirz, "only think of a United States soldier in prison deserting to the Confederacy. The fellows only want to get away. Damn your deserters. I don't like them, North or South."

One charge against Wirz is that the stockade was only 200 yards wide by the same number long. Another, when smallpox broke out, Wirz had the men inoculated in the filthiest matter he could find.

The stockade by measurement, was twenty nine acres in extent. When the smallpox broke out at Andersonville, the most salubrious spot outside the stockade was selected, to which the patients were removed, and the most experienced physicians appointed to attend them. The result was less than forty deaths from smallpox at Andersonville.

As to inoculation, it can be affirmed that not a single person was inoculated at Andersonville, unless perhaps by his own desire; but the person who makes the statement we refer to must have had Belle Isle, or some other Confederate prison in his imagination.

On this subject, we will merely say, that as Captain Wirz's trial will, in all likelihood, take place in a few days and that witnesses are summoned from all quarters against him, it would show a higher sense of fair-play and self respect, on the part of the high-tened [*sic*] and honorably-[enacted? conducted?] press to abstain from publishing such stupid lies about the helpless prisoner who cannot defend himself until he appears before the bar of public jury.

If Captain Wirz is condemned after a fair trial, and after his witnesses get a fair opportunity of telling all they know about him, let him be dealt with as his conduct deserves. But if the newspapers not so clamorous to condemn Wirz had been only one-tenth as zealous in trying to urge the Executive to exchange the Andersonville prisoners, the Federal Government would not have to answer before their God for at least 11,000 lives ruthlessly thrown away.

The Raiders—Their Trial
Toward the close of the month of June, 1864, when there were some 35,000 Union prisoners at Andersonville, some four of five hundred gougers, robbers, mugger, garroters, and (if in the execution of their infamous proceedings murder became necessary), murderers, banded themselves into a regular organization. Men were beaten and robbed and knocked down in broad daylight. At night, when a man retired to his poor quarters, he was awoke by finding a ruffian's knee on his stomach, brandishing a knife over him and other ruffian holding him down by the throat, and threatening that if the poor wretch made any resistance his "bloody heart would be cut out." A reign of terror spread itself over the prison. Men lay down in the miserable tents at night in terror; and they woke in the morning unrefreshed, the terrors of the banditti still haunting them. It was a terrible time. But what appeared to be every man's business was nobody's business; and no man dared grapple with this inhumane organization. Just as a compact band of guerillas may at any moment descend from a mountain upon an unsuspecting and unarmed village. At length a man named Dowd was attacked before his own tent by a dozen of the band, and all but murdered; he was robbed of money, watch, etc. He was brought next morning before Captain Wirz, and having stated his case, his appearance, broken face, eyes swollen, head strapped up, and his shins all kicked and bruised, all seconding his appeal to the captain.

Capt. Wirz—"By God, until every scoundrel of that gang is brought out of the stockade, I swear I shall not permit a single ration to be sent into the stockade. Until you hear from me send not a ration into the stockade. The d____d cowards! Thirty five thousand soldiers and yet not have the pluck to defend themselves against the damn scoundrels, the bloody Yankee thieves, that are preying on their poor fellow prisoners. Bush, give me my pistols!"

Bush gave Wirz his pistols, and he proceeded to the stockade; and the gang, under the pressure of hunger, began to be brought out. Some three thousand men formed themselves, after a long dead silence of hunger and thought, into a vigilance-committee, and some one hundred and three villains were taken out, amid the triumphant shouts of the poor fellows in the stockade, and placed in ball and chain.

On the representation of the facts at headquarters, the following order was issued:

ORDER AUTHORIZING THE FORMATION OF A COURT TO
  TRY THE RUFFIANS
CAMP SUMTER, ANDERSONVILLE, Ga, June 30, 1864
GENERAL ORDER NO. 57,
  I. A gang of evil-disposed persons among the prisoners of war at this post, having banded themselves together for the purpose of assaulting, murdering, and robbing their fellow-prisoners, and having already committed these offenses it becomes necessary to adopt measures to protect the lives and property of the prisoners against the acts of these men; and in order that this may be accomplished, the well-disposed prisoners may, and are hereby authorized to establish a court among themselves for the trial and punishment of all such vile offenders.
  II. On such trials, charges will be distinctly made, with specifications, setting forth time and place, a copy of which will be furnished to the accused.
  III. The whole proceedings will be properly kept in writing, the testimony fairly written out as nearly in the words of the witnesses as possible.
  IV. The proceedings, findings, and sentence in each case will be sent to the commanding officer for record, and if found in order, and proper, the sentence will be ordered for execution.

By order of
John H. Winder, Brig. Gen.
W. S, Winder, A.A.G

To Capt. HENRY WIRZ, commanding, etc.

  The morning on which the order was issued, about three hundred sergeants, the head of every ninety men in prison, were summoned to Captain Wirz's headquarters, when the order was read for them. Every man of the three hundred approved of the formation of the court for the trial of the raiders, and gougers, and garroters. Twenty-four were selected from the number, from which twelve were balloted for a jury, as follows:

Members of the Jury.
  Sergeant George W. Merwin, Fifth Michigan Cavalry, Company B, Foreman; Benjamin Bartlett, Sixty-seventh Pennsylvania, Company K; Thos. C. Hurlburt, First Connecticut Cavalry, Company B; J. Weston Dana, Fifty-sixth Massachusetts, Company K; J. S. Banks., Third Ohio Cavalry, Company I; Thomas J. Shepard, Ninety-seventh Ohio, Company E; John

S. Benjamin, Sixty-fourth New York, Company E; Egbert Webb, Fifth Michigan Cavalry, Company H; Wm. C. Messick, The Michigan Cavalry, Company H; Stephen T. Brown, Seventieth New York, Company C; Henry Miller, First Michigan Sharpshooters, Company I; Samuel West, Seventh New York Heavy Artillery, Company H.

Edward Wellington Boate, Forty-second New York, was unanimously appointed official reporter of the Court.

Sergeant O. W. Carpenter, Seventh Michigan Cavalry was appointed to prosecute; and Private (since Major) H. O. Higginson, Nineteenth Illinois, Company K, was assigned as counsel to defend the prisoners.

The best and most convenient arrangement that could be made at the time was to try the prisoners before the above jury, who after the verdict constitute themselves into a court of twelve and then after due deliberation decided upon the punishment to which each convicted person was sentenced.

First Day's Proceedings

William Collins, alias Mosby, 88th Pennsylvania, Company D, was the first of the prisoners tried, but as it was understood that more evidence could be had than what was brought against him the first day, his case was postponed. (Mosby was subsequently tried, found guilty and hanged.)

Patrick Murphy, 52nd NY, Company B, and John Sarsfield, 140th NY, Company C, were charged with assaulting with intent to murder (if necessary) and highway robbery. They pleaded not guilty.

John G. Dowd, 97th NY, Company D, was the first witness. The appearance of this man excited the horror and pity of everyone present. His head and face, arms, legs, and body generally bore marks of the most brutal violence. He testified as follows—On the 28th of June, about one o'clock, I was sitting in my tent, when Sarsfield came along, crying out "Who wants to buy a watch?" (Sarsfield's object was to find out who had money.) I asked him what his watch was worth, and he replied, twenty dollars. Sarsfield left, and soon after returned with prisoner Murphy. Sarsfield renewed the offer to sell the watch, and while doing so, the other prisoner grabbed at my pantaloons, which I had in my hand, cleaning. In the scuffle, I was struck with "brass knuckles" in the face, by Sarsfield, as I believe. I then took my knife out of my pocket to defend myself. Several others then attacked me and one of them snatched the knife out of my hand, and, in doing so, cut me across the hand. Sarsfield had a dagger in his hand, and threatened if I resisted he would cut my heart out and throw it in my face. I was frequently struck with the "brass knuckles." I saw one of the men (not on trial) take hold of the chain of my watch and draw it out. I was then knocked down and turned over. They took hold of my watch-pocket and turned it out. It contained a pocket book containing $136, which the raiders carried off.

Sergeant Joseph Rivers, 22nd NY. Co. M, swore that on the 26th inst., while looking for some of his boys, he was met by a man who brought him to his tent to sell him a blanket. Outside the tent they met Sarsfield, opposite his tent, who said he had a better blanket to sell; called witness a s-n of a b—h, and dragged him back into the tent and assaulted witness with a screw. Sarsfield took witness by the pocket, and took of it $50.04, together with some small articles, a spoon, a comb, etc. He also took his haversack and blouse, in which there was tobacco. They then tried to knock him down, tried to pull him down by his hair. He made a struggle and ran away.

R. C. Spicer, 76th New York, Company E, swore that he was present at the attack on Dowd. Murphy was not there; but he recognized Sarsfield as one of the men who attacked Dowd with a knife, with which he struck him on the head. Sarsfields character is that of a thief and a robber; he goes about choking and robbing men and threatening to cut their throats if they say a word or make any resistance.

N. Baldwin, 76th New York, Company C, while proving that Murphy did not take part in the riot, swore that Sarsfield was one of the men who attacked Dowd; witness stated that he knew Sarsfield to be a robber; the day before he decoyed five men into his tent, and, with the other, swore he would kill those five men into his tent, and with others, swore he would kill those five men if they made any noise, and then robbed them.

Joseph Terril, 101st Ohio, Company E, swore that he knew Sarsfield, who was generally seen in company with two men, one of them named Delaney; witness saw as many as twenty or thirty men a day come out of Sarsfield's tent, their pants nearly torn off; the first that would be heard, after these men entered the tent, would be the man gasping for breath; Sarsfield and his gang raided on witness one night.

The result of the examination into this case was the acquittal of Murphy, and the conviction of Sarsfield, who was sentenced to be hanged.

Second Day's Proceedings

William John Kennedy, 52nd New York, Company C; Patrick Delany, 83rd Pennsylvania, Company E; John Sullivan, 76th New York, Company F; Peter Gilmore, 145th Pennsylvania, Company J.; Owen Farley, news agent of the Calvary Corps, Army of the Potomac; William Holdings, 145th Pennsylvania, Company G; John Connolly, 52nd New York, Company C (Frank Connelly, 52 NY); Andrew Muir, United States steamer Waterwitch, [*sic*] were next put on trial.

The chargers were similar to those in the previous case.

The prisoners pleaded not guilty.

N. Baldwin, of the 76th New York, Company C, swore that Sullivan's business was that of robbing the prisoners and that he was one of those who attacked Dowd. He struck Dowd, who had his pants off, and with his tent torn down, Dowd was imploring Sullivan to let him put on his pants. Witnesses saw Sullivan rob an orderly—who had come in that evening, and was induced to go to Sullivan's tent. Witness tented within a dozen yards of Sullivan. Next day five more men were taken at different times to Sullivan's tent, when they were robbed by Sullivan, Delany, and Sarsfield. These men (so robbed) had only just come into the camp. Witness saw one man stretched in the tent. Sullivan and another of the prisoners were holding him down, and they threatened to cut his throat unless he lay still. This was of daily occurrence. Delaney was generally present at these robberies. Sarsfield generally did the cutting out business, while the others held down the victims.

Sergeant Carpenter—Why did not the men in the neighborhood clear out that gang?

A: Well, there were so many of them, and they were all so armed with clubs, that people were afraid of them. Sullivan carried a club with an iron nut at the end of it. Saw Delany rob a watch from a man on the street a few days ago. He came up to the man, who had a stick of wood on his back, and said, "This is a good hat you have on." The man clung to the hat. Delany then grabbed the watch and carried it off. The man dropped his wood, and some other person came up and carried it off. The prisoner, Mullings, acted as a runner for the gang. He went out, picked up, and brought to the tent the man intended to be robbed. Mullings picked up two of the five men robbed in Sullivan's tent. Whenever a lot of prisoners came into the prison Mullings would go among them, asking if they wanted to buy blankets or rations. By this means he decoyed them into Sullivan's tent, where they could be robbed. (The newcomers were those among whom the robbers plied their infamous trade, as they were ignorant of the robberies carried on by the band of scoundrels.) The general conversation of these men was about robbing, and how much they took from such and such a man. Heard one of the fellows say, "I got $20 out of that fellow; I got nothing out of that other son of a b—h." Saw Muir engaged in robbing Dowd. Saw him on top of Dowd, trying to cut out his pocket and fumbling in it. The first time he saw Muir engaged in robbing was when he and the others attacked the orderly-sergeant. Muir had not the same appearance when he attacked Dowd as he had at present. Then he wore whiskers and a mustache; at present they were shaved off. Never saw Farley do anything, although he was frequently present among the gang when the robberies went on. Witnesses stated that Delaney, Sullivan, and Muir were all physically involved in the assault on Doud and other crimes. All four were found guilty and sentenced to hang.

R. E. Spicer recalled: saw Sullivan, Delaney and Gilmore rob a man the day before; he resisted, when Sarsfield came up and brandished a knife at him; Sullivan was also engaged in the attack on Dowd.; saw Delaney in Sullivan's tent take hold of men, gag them; and take their money away. By "gagging" he meant putting something in their mouth, so that they could not cry out. While robbing on those occasions, heard them threaten men that if they made any noise they would cut their throat; one day last week, while they were robbing a man in Sullivan's tent, witness heard one of the gang say two or three times "Here is a razor, cut his throat." Sullivan, Delaney, and Gilmore were present at the time; Sullivan carried a club with a knob of iron at the end; a few nights previously, Delaney went to rob a man who had a watch; some of the persons in the next tent made noise, and his purpose was defeated. The next night, between 11 and 12 o'clock, Delaney came to that tent, told one of the men in it to "come here"; the man hesitated. "Are you not coming?" said Delaney; the man was lying down in his tent at the time, he rose, when Delaney struck him on the head with a club having an iron knob in the end; he then struck another of the men in the same tent; Delaney then came to a boy fifteen years of age who was lying outside the same tent and beat him with the wooden end of the stick; saying that if he heard any more noise, he would knock his brains out and "let every man mind his own business"; knew Delaney to shove men into the tent, and rob them; knew him to draw men into the tent by telling them he had something to sell them.

Joseph Farrel, 101st Ohio, Co. B, swore that some night ago a gang came to mug him; but he could not identify any of them among the prisoners. A few days ago he saw a man go into Sullivan's tent with a watch in his pocket, and saw him leave without the watch. While the man was in the tent, he heard a scuffle, and soon after he saw the man's feet sticking out from under the tent, and heard him gasping for breath.

This closed the prosecution.

Mr. Higginson called several witnesses for the defense, the effect of whose evidence, while it left the case against the other prisoners untouched, was to clear Connolly and Mullings from the most heinous crimes of assault with intent to murder. There was no evidence against Kennedy and Farley.

The jury, after an hour's deliberation, returned the following verdict: Kennedy and Farley, not guilty; Connolly and Mullings, guilty of robbery; sentenced each to wear a ball and chain 25 lbs weight, for four months; Gilmore's case suspended; Sullivan, Delaney, and Muir guilty of all the charges, sentenced to be hanged by the neck until dead.

Third Day's Proceedings

Richard Allen, 83rd Pennsylvania Company E; William Wrixon, alias Curtis, United States steamship Powhattan; Thomas F. O'Connell, 9th Maryland, Company D, were put on their trial charged with the same offence, as those previously tried.

Daniel Hayes, United States, Company L, swore that one day last week, Allen and his party, including Curtis, came to his tent and took a watch belonging to the witness, which was hanging up in his tent. He then forced out of the tent a man named Prentiss, threw him down on the ground and threatened his life unless he told where witness's other watch was. Allen and Curtis did this. They then forced Prentiss to accompany them, Prentiss promising that he would tell where the other watch was deposited if they would spare his life. Prentiss pointed out where the other watch was—in the custody of a friend. Prentiss got the watch from this friend, came out, and handed it to Allen and Curtis.

On cross-examination, it appeared that this witness was not inside his tent when this robbery was committed. He was some twenty yards from it. But he saw the watch taken.

Mr. Higginson—Is it not singular that you and your party did not make some resistance to save your watch? A. There were upward of twenty men in the gang in that same tent, and they were all dangerous men, armed with weapons.

William Prentiss, 16th Illinois Cavalry, Company I, the man referred to in the evidence of the last witness, confirmed the statement of Hays [*sic*]; adding at [*sic*] when Allen & Curtis demanded the second watch, he tried to escape from the tent, but was taken hold of, jerked down, four of five of the gang having hold of him and threatening that if he did not give information where the other watch was they would cut his throat. Curtis, alias Wrixon, said he would cut out his (Prentiss's) heart. They had their knives out ready to do so, and he expected to be murdered every moment. They had him by the throat and their hands on his mouth. While accompanying them to where the second watch was deposited, they said if witness "went down there and got them into a mess, they would not give two cents for his life!"

James M. Friend, of the 16th Illinois Cavalry, Company I, stated that, last Saturday night, while he was lying in his tent, Curtis and a man named Delany came and woke him up. They asked him who was lying in the back of his tent? Witness replied "No person." Curtis then charged the witness with having been down to their quarters and robbed them of a blanket. Having denied this, Curtis struck him in the face with a razor and cut him. The wound was a ghastly one, across the side of the cheek. Witness put up his hand, and received a gash between the thumb and first finger. They then made several passes of the razor at him, but he succeeded in creeping away from them on his all fours, and tried to throw his pocketbook into the "dead line," but did not succeed in throwing it far enough, and so he picked it up again, when one of them grasped it from him, saying, as he did so, "God d—n you, that is all we wanted." There were four hundred and forty nine dollars in the pocketbook. He had been trading a little.

J. P. Erwin, 103rd Pennsylvania Regiment, Company B, swore that Wrixon, alias Curtis, had some weeks previously choked him down, when he was robbed of a watch and seventy dollars. While buying some beans he had a ten-dollar bill in his hand, which was snatched from him; Curtis, is at that moment came up, and he took him to his (Curtis's) tent; and while there, Curtis choked him down and somebody else came up and robbed him.

Other witnesses testified to other charges against Curtis, Allen, and O'Connell.

This closed the prosecution.

Witnesses were called for the defense, but the testimony was vague, and only went to prove that they never saw the prisoners guilty of any crime.

The jury returned a verdict finding Richard Allen and Thomas F. O'Connell guilty of robbery and assault; and they were sentenced to be handcuffed and shackled during their imprisonment. Wrixon, alias Curtis, they found guilty of all of the charges preferred against him, and he was sentenced to be hanged.

Wrixon denied that he was guilty, adding:—"I am not a citizen of the United States. I am a deserted from the United States Army, and took the oath of allegiance, and demanded to be tried by a court of Confederate officers."

Upon this statement, the Court ordered the official reporter to make a note of the prisoner's objection to his trial and conviction.

This was made out, and the prisoner brought to the headquarters under the escort of Confederate officers.

On coming before Wirz:

Wirz—"Well, my man, what is the matter?"

Curtis—"I am a deserter. I wish to be tried by Confederate Officers."

Captain Wirz—"Take this man before General Winder, and make the official reporters not concerning Curtis's objection."

Brought before General Winder:

Winder—"Well, what do you want? Have you been tried?"

A: Yes, sir but I am a deserter from the United States service, and I deny that they have any power to try me down there."

General Winder: "Let me see. What have they done to you down below?"

Curtis: "They have sentenced me to death."

General Winder:—"Well, what do you want me to do?"

Curtis:—"I want to be tried by Confederate officers."

General Winder:—"Very well; I cannot get Confederate officers to try you, but I shall try you myself, and from all that I have heard of your case, I shall order you to be shot. The Yankees have sentenced you to be hanged. Which do you choose?"

Curtis hung his head, and he was brought down to the stocks.

William Curtis [*sic*], alias Mosby of the 88th Penn. Company D was again put on trial on charge of robbing, assaulting, and with being the leader of a gang of thieves.

Charles W. Ross, of the 5th Ohio Cavalry, identified the prisoner, who went by the name of Mosby, called after the celebrated Confederate raider of that name. Saw him engaged in several raids in the prison. Saw him take biscuits from a man who was peddling them in the street. Had seen him decoy men into his tent who had only come into the camp the same day. This man complained of having his watch and ten dollars taken from him. Saw Moseby instigate other men to rob the prisoners—little boys. Saw him point out where to go and and rob persons. Saw one of those men strike a little boy who had a box of peanuts for sale, and then rob the boy of his box of peanuts, and tell the boy, who began to cry, to dry up, or he would whip him.

Cross examined—Why did you not go and raise a crowd to try to put down those men?

A: I did not do so, as I was too much interested in keeping quiet. He had too strong a gang for me. I often heard Mosby called the head of a gang. I swear he was the head of a gang of thieves.

George Ogleby, of the 4th Kentucky Cavalry, Company A—I know the prisoner at the bar as "Mosby." Saw Mosby come up to a German who was buying some onions, asking the person from whom he sought them could change the bill. He said no; but said this man (pointing to Mosby) could, the onion seller passing the bill at the same time to Mosby, who carried it off and lay down in his tent. The German demanded his change. The onion seller said he knew nothing about it. Mosby came back from his tent, and the German asked him for his bill. "Get along," Mosby said, "I know nothing of your bill." A crowd gathered around them. Mosby told the German to clear out, or he would give him a thrashing. The German went away and did not get the bill. It appeared to me that the onion seller and Mosby were acting in concert. Both their tents joined one another.

Joseph Ackers, of the 14th Connecticut, Company I, testified that he knew the prisoner. Knew a man to be robbed one night in his tent. It was midnight. Heard the man cry in his tent. Just before the cry he saw Mosby creep along the tent and then get inside. I know Mosby did not take part in the robberies himself, but I know him to be a planner of robberies for others. I know it because I heard him lay the plans to rob persons. When any person came along who had things for sale, Mosby's gang would go along, he leading the way, and take the articles from the owners by force and violence sometimes. Saw the gang attack parties selling articles, when a fight ensued, Mosby taking part in the fight. Heard Mosby tell his men to be ready to go round at night, and take boots or shoes or any other articles they could find.

James Keating, of the 42nd New York, Company [?], was called for the defense. Said: I heard Mosby say he would not go hungry while he could steal anything. He was called a raider, a name which he deserved.

Mr. Higginson said that after he had heard of Mosby's character, he declined to address the jury in his defense.

The jury found Mosby guilty of robbing and assaulting his fellow-prisoners, and with being a leader of an organized band of thieves, robber, and garrotters, and he was sentenced to be hanged.

There were several others tried, and found guilty, and sentenced to wear ball and chain for terms varying from ten days to the remainder of their imprisonment, but the six convicted and sentenced to death were regarded as the ringleaders of the organization.

There were about ninety others remaining untried, all well known thieves, but it was considered that the execution of half a dozen would be sufficient to strike terror in the hearts of the other evil-doers; and the smaller fry were, after a warning, turned into the camp.

In the meantime, the report of the proceedings was prepared, amply setting forth the pros and cons—the evidence for the prosecution and that for the defence [*sic*]. When prepared, it was sent forward to General Winder.

In the meantime, the convicts were placed in stocks, awaiting the decision at Headquarters.

It would be impossible to describe the feeling which pervaded the camp at this moment. Wagers were offered by every man who had a dollar, whether or not the convicts would be ordered for execution. It was evident that the culprits themselves did not believe they were to die; although a worthy priest named Father [Peter] Whelan, from Florida, who had been attending the prisoners for several months before was unceasing in his labors in trying to impress upon them the real nature of their position.

APPROVAL OF THE SENTENCE BY THE COURT

At length, after a suspense of three or four days, as everybody began to think the sentences would not be put in execution, an orderly from General Winder entered Captain Wirz's office with the following document:

HEADQUARTERS POST ANDERSONVILLE, GA.,
July 10, 1864

GENERAL ORDERS, No., 61

The Court authorized by General Order, No 57, June 30, 1864 having tried and sentenced the following men named the following men to the punishment attached and set opposite their respective names, the Court is authorized to execute the sentence in the above cases:

Patrick Sarsfield, to be hanged; John Sullivan, to be hanged; Patrick Delany, to be hanged; Andrew Muir, to be hanged; William Wixon [*sic*], alias Curtis, to be hanged; William Collins, alias Moseby, to be hanged. By order of Brig Gen. JOHN H WINDER. Robt. W. Brown, Lt. Col and Adjt.

THE EXECUTION

Capt. Wirz had the convicts brought to his headquarters, and informed them of their doom; telling them that before sunset the next day, they would be in eternity. He told them therefore to prepare themselves for their fate; and that he would send for whatever clergyman they might desire should be with them at their last moments.

Next morning, a scaffold was commenced to be erected in the prison on a spot where every prisoner in the camp could have a sight of the execution, which was ordered to take place at 4 o'clock in the afternoon of Monday, July 11.

A detachment of Confederate soldiers, with Captain Wirz at their head, rode toward the stocks where the six unhappy men were held. The stocks were unlocked and the six convicts were led back into the prison, preceded by Father Whelan (the only clergymen who could be had to attend them), who offered up fervent prayers as the cortege moved in. Having arrived at the foot of the scaffold, Curtis made a bolt through a cordon of Union prisoners several ranks deep, with staves in their hand, being a portion of the vigilance-committee detailed for the duty to keep order during the execution. Curtis was soon brought back and pinioned. The convicts, having ascended the scaffold, Father Whelan begged of the crowd to forego the execution—to have mercy on them. But not a single voice of the thousands were raised on their behalf. The prisoners begged for mercy; but the cry was, "The mercy you showed to your fellow prisoners." After half an hour's delay, mealbags were drawn over their heads and faces, and they were launched into eternity, amid the stillness of death which reigned over the awe-stricken camp, with its thirty-eight thousand spectators of the terrible set of retributive justice which had fallen over the miserable criminals.

The rope on which Mosby hung, broke when he was swung off, and he fell heavily to the ground. Some voices said, "Don't hang him," but they were unheeded, and he was soon once again on the scaffold, and he shared the fate of his companions. After the execution, a man could take a dollar on the tip of his finger, and no one would dare touch it. No more beating, gouging, garroting, or mugging was experienced, and every man slept at night without apprehension.

NOTES ON APPENDIX A

A person in the *Washington Chronicle*—It is not known what piece in the *Washington Chronicle* Boate is referring to.

George W. Merwin—A sergeant with the 5th Michigan, Company B, Merwin was also known as George Kelly, the surname of his stepfather. He survived the war but died shortly after from chronic diarrhea on April 9, 1865, in Vicksburg, Mississippi.

Benjamin Bartlett, 67th Pennsylvania, Company K—This man's name appears on the regimental rosters, but no further information is available.

Thos. C. Hurlburt, First Connecticut Cavalry, Company B—Actually Thomas E. Hurlburt. He was a quarter-sergeant with the First Connecticut Cavalry, he was captured at Old Church, Virginia, on June 10, 1864, just 19 days before the arrests of the raiders. He was exchanged on November 19, 1864, and died April 8, 1879.

J. Western Dana, 56th Massachusetts, Company K—James Weston Dana is listed as a sergeant with the 55th Massachusetts, and having been taken prisoner at Petersburg on June 17, 1864, just 12 days before the arrests of the raiders. He was paroled at Vicksburg, Mississippi, on April 27, 1865. He mustered out on May 12, 1865.

J. S. Banks, Third Ohio Cavalry, Company I—Private John S. Banks was a private with the 3rd Ohio Cavalry. He enlisted on September 2, 1861, and survived Andersonville, mustering out on May 24, 1865. He died on June 7, 1920.

Thomas J. Shepard, 97th Ohio—No information on this man can be found.

John Benjamin, 64th New York Company E—Benjamin enlisted in the army as a corporal on September 10, 1861, in Ithaca, New York. He was promoted to sergeant a year later, on December 16, 1862. He was wounded in action on May 12, 1864, at Spotsylvania and was captured on June 18, 1864, just eleven days before the raiders' trial. He survived Andersonville and mustered out at Elmira on July 6, 1865.

Egbert Webb, Fifth Michigan Cavalry, Company H—Egbert Webb was a sergeant with the 5th Michigan Cavalry when he was taken prisoner at Trevilian Station, Virginia, on June 11, 1864, just 18 days before the arrests of the raiders. He survived the war and made it home, applying for an invalid's pension in 1882. He died in Monroe, Michigan, on June 22, 1906.

Wm C. Messick, 7th Michigan Cavalry, Company H—He survived Andersonville and was still living as of 1889.

Stephen T. Brown, 70th New York, Company C—Brown, a 34-year-old farmer from Shelly, New York, enlisted on September 18, 1861, and reenlisted on January 4, 1864. He was captured at Petersburg, Virginia, on June 16, 1864, just 13 days before the arrest of the raiders. He also appears on company rolls as Stephen T. Brown and W. Brown. He survived Andersonville and applied for an invalid's pension on July 24, 1874.

Henry Miller, First Michigan Sharpshooters, Company I—Henry H. Miller was a private with the First Michigan Sharpshooters, Company I. A note on his Civil War Service index card says to also see USSS (US Sharpshooters) and 117 USCT (117th Regiment, US Colored Troops). Company K of the First Michigan Sharpshooters is noteworthy because it was the largest all-Indian regiment in the Union army. It is not known what Henry Miller's race was.

Samuel West, Seventh New York Heavy Artillery, Company H—The 21-year-old enlisted on August 12, 1862, was promoted to corporal six days later, and to first sergeant on June 1, 1864. He was captured in action on June 16, 1864, at Petersburg, Virginia, just 13 days before the arrest of the raiders. West was paroled on February 27, 1865, at Northeast Ferry, North Carolina, and mustered out on May 21, 1865.

Edward Wellington Boate, 42nd New York, Company K—An Irish immigrant, Boate enlisted under the name Edward Bates on July 11, 1863. He was captured in action on October 14, 1863, at the Battle of Bristoe Station, his first military engagement. Like raiders Sullivan, Collins, and Delaney, he was sent to Belle Isle before being transferred to Andersonville. Shortly after the raiders' trial, he was part of a delegation of prisoners released from Andersonville to carry a petition to Abraham Lincoln asking for supplies for the prisoners to be sent to Andersonville and also for a resumption of prisoner exchanges. The group never met Lincoln. Boate fell ill before reaching Washington and was discharged for disability on November 15, 1864. Following the war, he testified on behalf of Henry Wirz at his trial, defending Wirz, who, Boate said, was blamed for circumstances beyond his control. Boate was extremely critical of Union officials and blamed them for letting Union prisoners languish. This made him a very unpopular public figure. Boate died on September 19, 1871, at the age of 49.

Sergeant O. W. Carpenter, Seventh Michigan Cavalry—Sergeant Otis W. Carpenter was captured at the Battle of Trevilian Station, Virginia, on June 11, 1864, meaning that he was in Andersonville Prison for less than 18 days when he reportedly served as a court official at the raiders' trial. Although the *Sunday Mercury* says that he was the prosecuting attorney at the trial, the regimental history of the Seventh Michigan states that Carpenter served as Advocate General. Carpenter survived Andersonville, but died in a military hospital in Annapolis on December 6, 1864, before he could get home.

Private (since Major) H. O. Higginson, 19th Illinois, Company K—Private Henry Higginson was paroled shortly after the raiders' trial as part of the same delegation as Edward Wellington Boate, charged with taking a petition to Washington asking for the resumption of prisoner exchanges and aide to those who were being held as prisoner of war. He later testified at the trial of the Lincoln assassination conspirators, claiming that a guard had showed him a letter signed by John Wilkes Booth, an assertion that seems unlikely at best. He was later given a brevet promotion by the governor of Illinois but left the military not long after his return from Fort Sumter and spent the end of his life in a series of soldiers' homes.

R. C. Spicer 76th New York, Company E—Although some records say this man's first name was Ramira, according to one of his descendants, he was actually Ramiro Ernest Spicer.

N. Baldwin, 76th New York, Company C—Newton Baldwin, of Sullivan's regiment.

Joseph Terril, 101st Ohio, Company E—Company records say that the correct spelling of this man's name was "Terrill."

William Prentiss, 16th Illinois Cavalry, Company I—His name was Private William S. Prentice of the 16th Illinois Cavalry.

J. P. Erwin, 103rd Pennsylvania Regiment, Company B—Private John P. Erwin, of the 103rd Pennsylvania.

Appendix B

Published Diaries and Memoirs
of Andersonville 1865–1870

*S*urprisingly few prisoner-of-war memoirs were published in the five years immediately following the end of the war, and the war-weary nation did not take particular notice of them. They were not best sellers. It wasn't until after John McElroy's best-selling 1879 book that a glut of POW memoirs were published. Not all the early memoirs mentioned the raiders. The writers may not have been present at the prison when the arrests and executions took place, or they may not have considered the subject matter suitable for the sensibilities of the gentle readers back home. Some early published memoirs, such as A. O. Abbott's and Willard Glazier's, made no mention of the raiders of the execution at all.

EUGENE FORBES: *DIARY OF A SOLDIER, AND PRISONER OF WAR IN THE REBEL PRISONS*, 1865

Thursday, May 26—Some of the dirtiest men were sucked and scrubbed today, and some of the "raiders" bucked and gaged, and their heads shaved.

Friday, May 27—A "raider" was caught last night, and kept prisoner until daylight, when he was bucked and gagged, his head shaved, and afterwards marched around the camp; he took it very coolly. A fight occurred between a party of "raiders" and some of the "raidees," in which the latter got the worst of it; one man is said to be pretty badly hurt. . . .

Thursday, June 9—The "raiders" held high festival last night; one man was wakened by them, and found the edge of a knife across his throat, and was told that death was his portion if he uttered a cry; they relieved him of a blanket and some money; the mark of the knife was still on his throat this morning.

Saturday, June 11—A speculator, selling sugar at 25 cts. Per spoonful, was set upon, beaten by the raiders and his sugar taken after a hard struggle . . . .

Saturday, June 18—One man slept in the much box last night; he was surrounded by five or six men during the night, and his pocket was cut out; another, walking around with a blanket on his shoulders, was seized by four men, and his blanket taken away. At eleven o'clock today a man was knocked down and robbed of his watch and $80. . . . Went to see Mat. Hill; he lives near the "raiders."

Tuesday, June 22—Brown, of our detachment, has been shamefully treated by some of the men. He has chronic diarrhea, and having met with an accident, washed his pants and drawers and hung them up to dry. Some scoundrel stole them, leaving him with nothing but a shirt. One of our men gave him a pair of drawers, and he now lives near the runlet, his feet awfully swollen and gradually sinking under disease. Our own men are worse to each other than the rebels are to us. . . . Heard a chase after a raider after we had turned in; don't think they caught him.

Sunday, June 26—A party of raiders "cleaned out" Tarbell, McNees and Nelson of 57-1; they took boots, blankets &c. . . . A "raider" as caught and his head shaved this morning; he sold his pint cup for $1.50, and then went at night and stole it back.

Monday, June 27—A "raider" was chased early this morning, but I do not know if he was captured. . . . A fine prospect of a general row this afternoon; the raiders were out in full force; an orderly sergeant was enticed into their tent, and robbed of $50; the raiders near the gate were contemplating an attack on this part of camp last night; the sailors and raiders in this corner combined their forces, sent out skirmishing parties, and made arrangements to repel the attack, but the fight did not come off.

Wednesday, Jun 29—About 2 P.M. two men came along, trying to sell a watch; Dowd asked to look at it, and did so, after which they went away; in a short time they returned with reinforcements, and attacked him as he sat in his tent, with clubs, brass knuckles, &c.; he defended himself bravely, and they again departed; he came out of his tent, and put on his pants, when they again attacked him, and finally got him down, took his watch, cut out his money, (which he had sewed in the waistband of his pants,) to the amount of $170; he was badly cut up, but finally got away and reached the gate, and reported to Capt. Wirz, who came up to him and demanded that the robbers should be given up, under the penalty of no rations for one week; in a short time a guard came in, and took eight men from a tent near *the dead line on our side; very soon the camp was in an uproar, for the men came into an arrangement, and the raiders were hunted from one end of the camp to the other; by dark the tumult was nearly over, but the raiders were not all caught yet; about 50 were taken outside; the issuing of rations stopped . . . Large quantities of clothing, blankets, &c were found in some raiders' tents. Capt. Wurtz deserves great credit for his prompt action in the matter, and will probably be successful in checking the positions of these thieving scoundrels.*

Thursday, June 30—The crusade against the raiders continues, and several were taken today; three of those who robbed Dowd are reported to be among the number; the fourth and worse one has been caught since the above writing; they are now pretty well cleared out; the sergeants of the messes (90) were called up at 9 A.M. and taken to Capt. Wirz's headquarters, where 24 of them were selected, their names taken, and 12 drawn by lot as a jury for the trial of the principal raiders; this P.M. the trial is progressing; this course is pursued to prevent retaliation on the part of our Government, to whom the whole proceedings are to be sent; it is an act of justice on the part of Confederate authorities which the men have not expected, they supposing that no notice would be taken of their complaints; but the reverse has been the case, and we can now feel secure the attacks of daylight assassins or midnight murderers; the issuing of rations was promptly commenced as soon as the men known as ringleaders were captured. . . . Oak. went out as a witness; towards night news came in that Sarsfield, one of the principals, who said he would "Cut out Dowd's heart and throw it in his face," had been convicted and sentenced to be hung; the trial of the others will come off tomorrow. . . . I forgot to mention in connection with the raiders that large amounts of money were discovered in their tents today, as well as watches, jewelry, and articles of all descriptions. . . . Dowd moved his things outside today, where he has liberty to the extent of one mile.

Friday, July 1—The raid on the raiders continues, though in a less violent degree than on previous occasions.

Monday, July 4—A raider caught stealing a blanket, was tried by one of the committees, his head shaved, and shown around camp.

It's interesting to note that Forbes describes an attempted robbery by a raider on July 4th—before the execution but after the wide-spread arrests of the raiders on June 29th and 30th. Clearly, not all of the thieves in camp had been arrested, nor did the arrest of the raiders completely halt the crimewave within the prison.

Monday, July 11—About five o'clock, a rebel guard was seen marching toward the stockade, preceded by a drum corps, playing the "Dead March," and conducting six prisoners. They entered the gate at the southeast part of the stockade, when Capt.

Wurtz [sic] *(commanding the camp) delivered the prisoners over to a body of the Regulators, headed by "Limber Jim." A gallows had been previously erected in the street leading from the southwest gate. The prisoners names were given as follows: "Moseby," "Murray," "Terry," "Sarsfield," "Delainey" and "Curtis." They were all of Irish birth or extractions, except "Moseby," who was English. "Limber Jim," with his assistants, proceeded to bind the prisoners' hands, the Captain having withdrawn the guard to the outside, leaving the condemned to be disposed of by our men. When Curtis was about to be bound, he exclaimed, "This cannot be," and made a dash through the crowd and toward the creek; he succeeded in reaching the other side, but was arrested and brought back. Shortly after five o'clock, the whole six were swung off, but "Moseby's" rope broke, bringing him to the ground, but he was soon swung up again. After having hung bout fifteen minutes, they were cut down, when the crowd quietly dispersed. So endeth the raid on Dowd, three of his principal assailants being among those executed. And it is hoped that it will also end the system of organized robbery and ruffianism which has so long ruled this camp. "Limber Jim" and his assistants were taken out of the stockade after the execution, and it is supposed they will be employed outside.*

CHARLES SMEDLEY: *LIFE IN SOUTHERN PRISONS:* *FROM THE DIARY OF CORPORAL CHARLES SMEDLEY, OF COMPANY G, 90 REGIMENT OF PENN'S VOLUNTEERS*, 1865

5th day, 5th mo. 26th. This was a very hot day. There are some men here just like skeletons, they are so gone with chronic diarrhea. The boys caught some of the raiders and punished them by shaving their heads.

4th day, 6th mo. 29th Was very warm, had a thunder storm in the evening. Am weaker than ever and can hardly get along. Did not get any rations because some of the men took the "raiders" in hand, and, after knocking down, and I guess killed some, arrested sixty and gave them over to the old captain. It is said he shot one. Last night they killed a man, and an Indian killed one of them.

2nd day, 7th mo. 11th. . . . Six of the "raiders" were hung inside the stockade, by our own men, at five o'clock this evening. The rope of Moseby broke when the drop fell, and let him to the ground; they made him mount the scaffold and try it the second time. One broke loose before he mounted the scaffold and ran through the crowd, but was arrested. I was down helping to draw rations and saw the execution.

LIFE IN SOUTHERN PRISONS. FULTON TOWNSHIP,
PENNSYLVANIA: THE LADIES AND GENTLEMEN'S
FULTON AID SOCIETY WITH PEARSOL GEIST PRINTERS,
THE DAILY EXPRESS, 1865

ROBERT KELLOGG: *LIFE AND DEATH IN REBEL PRISONS,* 1865

To add to our sorrow and indignation, we found a large gang of desperadoes among our own men in camp, whom we called "Mosby's Raiders," and who lived by robbing and beating, sometimes almost murdering their comrades in misfortune. They attempted to carry out their plans in a thieving raid upon us, probably meeting with a strong temptation in the looks of our overcoats and blankets, but we were out in a twinkling, prepared for our defense, and they, seeing an overpowering force, beat a hasty retreat. We would fain believe that such men are an exception among Federal soldiers, but it may be we can not tell how harsh treatment, and long continued neglect and abuse, would degrade manhood in any case. We, as a regiment, presented a united front, and were therefore too strong for them. . . .

It was not infrequent that one of the camp thieves or "raiders" would be arrested in his prowling operations at night, carried to the brook, to endure the process of "gagging" and "bucking" having' one side of his head shaved, and this not being considered sufficient punishment, he would finally be thrown into the swamp, there to consider the propriety of discontinuing his "raids" for a season. Truly, "the way of transgressors is hard. . . ."

So much rain seemed to hold the pugilistic element in check, but the "raiders" eventually meant to make up for lost time. On the return of a pleasant morning, they had five distinct fights before roll-call, which was in the early part of the day; but one must remember we had no laws but those of our own making, and these could not be enforced with authority they thought binding . . . .

Now we would see a "raider" led by our tent in chains, with his head shaved, to some place of punishment . . . .

These new comers afforded the "raiders" or camp-robbers, fresh opportunities to continue their work. They seized upon one of these, and it was soon seen that it was

A ROBBERY

in earnest. After severely beating and cutting his head, they took from him his watch and $175 in money. He entered a complaint to Captain Wizz, and the whole camp being completely aroused, a crowd collected, armed with clubs, who began to arrest the gang as fast as possible. As soon as one was caught, he was handed outside to the care of the rebels, who were to watch over them until they could be tried by our men. A few, against whom positive proof could not at once

*be brought, were sent into prison again, where they had to run the gauntlet be-
tween a long line of enraged men, who, armed with heavy clubs, dealt blows at
the miscreants as they ran past.*

*One man was killed while undergoing the punishment. About fifty of the
band were caught, and the prospect was good that the infernal proceedings which
had so long been continued would come to an end.*

*All through the next day they were hunted with great success. The Rebel
Quartermaster, rebel sergeants and guard, went into the prison, and, piloted by a
notorious character known as "Limber Jim" and his comrades, they soon ferreted out
the infamous scoundrels. They were taken outside, where they were to be tried by a
jury of twelve men selected from the newly arrived, who of course would know the
least about them, and would therefore be more impartial in rendering the verdict.
Beneath their tents were found knives, pistols, watches, money, &c, and it is said
that buried beneath one tent was the body of a man who was supposed to have been
murdered by them.*

*It was a day of great excitement, and one which we thought would place an
effectual barrier against such operations in the future. . . . .*

The 12th was a day of unusual excitement

A GALLOWS

*had been erected on the south side of the prison, and it was said that half a dozen of
the camp-robbers, who had been tried and found guilty, were to be hung. At half-
past four in the afternoon, Capt. Wirz came in with the six, under a rebel guard,
and turned their over to the Police, or Vigilance Committee. They had been convicted of murder and robbery, and were sentenced to be hung until they were dead.*

*Upon giving them up for punishment he made the following remarks: "These
men have been tried and convicted by their own fellows, and I now return them
to you in as good condition as I received them. You can now do with them as your
reason, justice, and mercy dictates. And may God protect both you and them."*

*The Catholic priest begged hard that their lives might be spared, but finding
himself unsuccessful in this, he turned his attention to their spiritual condition, and
spent a season in prayer for them. They themselves seemed strangely unconcerned,
apparently thinking it was simply an affair got up, thoroughly to frighten them,
and they appeared to cling to the idea, even until they had ascended the platform
erected for their execution. As they were about mounting the scaffold, one of them
broke from the men who were holding him, and ran through the crowd, across the
swamp, to the opposite hill-side, as if by one desperate effort he would escape his
fearful doom, that began to take on the semblance of reality. He was captured, however, and led back; and as he was securely placed with the other five, such forlorn
to wretchedness, such miserable hopelessness, was visible in his countenance, as is
impossible to describe. Opportunity was given them to speak, if they had any thing*

they wished to say. They said a few words, bidding their comrades take warning by their fate. One, mindful of his relatives in this last hour, wished a friend to call upon them in New York City, if he should live to get home. These words ended, meal-sacks were drawn over their heads, the fatal ropes were adjusted, and as the drop fell, the rope around the neck of the leader of the gang broke, thus setting him free. He was at once taken up, had it re-adjusted, and was pushed off; the whole six were thus suddenly launched into the eternal world. It was a sad spectacle to see their bodies swinging in the air, but we felt it to be just, and another illustration of the truth, that "The way of transgressors is hard."

Their depredations had been carried on so long, and with such a bold hand; they had become so reckless of human life and property, it was necessary that an example should be made of them in such a way as to make a lasting impression upon all those who should be similarly inclined. Prisoners were coming in every day. Of course the crowd comprised all classes and dispositions, and it was desirable to have some system of law and order that would control the mass.

The knowledge of such a fact would, at least, inspire the newly-arrived with something of wholesome fear, and the general tendency would be to keep in check a like outburst. Although the "raging element" had been comparatively small, it had been productive of most unhappy consequences, and we longed to have it shorn of its power, and severe measures were alone requisite for its accomplishment.

JOSEPH FERGUSON,
LIFE-STRUGGLES IN REBEL PRISONS, 1865

There were desperate characters in the prison, who committed acts of violence, outrage, and murder. Men, who never were honest or good in their manhood, became devils in this pandemonium by no moral or restraining influences, their natured became hardened to vice and crime. For protection, the prisoners organized a police force, who caught six of the most desperate characters. They were tried by court-martial and hung.

ANONYMOUS, *A VOICE FROM REBEL PRISONS*, 1865

But the rebels were not the only ones by whom our situation was aggravated. There were a set of raiders amongst ourselves, who speculated on the feeble and weak, robbing them in every possible way, and living on the distresses of their own causing. Complaint was made to Capt. Wortz, who had charge of the stockade; and he ordered all rations stopped until the guilty ones should be discovered. This, or course, made all use their energies to detect the thieves; and after going without rations for three days, seven of the ringleaders were caught and delivered to the captain, who placed them outside under guard to remain until the day of trial, when they were conducted inside, tried, and condemned before a jury selected from among ourselves, and afterward hung—the captain furnishing the wood with which to build the gallows. After that, we were not troubled with raiders.

HENRY DAVIDSON, *FOURTEEN MONTHS IN SOUTHERN PRISONS; BEING A NARRATIVE OF THE TREATMENT*, 1865

Nothing but discouragement met us at every turn; we were not even safe from the deprivations of the prisoners themselves. We were cautioned particularly against the "raiders," a class of depredators with which every army abounds and of which no military prison is ever free, who under cover of darkness, were wont to search the camp and steal such few useful articles as they would take unobserved from their fellow. We were assured we must keep the strictest guard over our effects at all times, or the raiders would get them, and we be left destitute. . . .

In the early part of the summer, the camp was infested by gangs of thieves and marauders, who committed their depredations upon the peaceably disposed, both in the open light of day and in the darkness of the night. Men were robbed of money, watches, rings, and blankets, openly and by stealth; some, who were known to have money, disappeared mysteriously and were never heard of afterwards; assaults were frequently made in the streets, the victim knocked down and terribly beaten with clubs, and his pockets rifled of their contents; it became necessary for the prisoners, in lying down to sleep, to attach their valuables to themselves, in such a manner that they could not be taken, without arousing the slumber and to such a pitch of confidence and desperation did the ruffians reach, that no one felt secure in retaining anything of value upon his person, either by day or night. These villains were called Mosby's Raiders, Mosely's Gang, or more frequently, "Raiders" they seemed to have a regular organization, with leader and subordinate officers, and single resistance to their assaults was useless, for the gang was always ready to support any of its members when occasion requires. Occasionally a raider was caught by a strong force of prisoners and "bucked" or gagged but this punishment was little regarded, and the criminal after being released signalized his repentance by knocking down and robbing the first man that came his way. They had means of knowing and marking the man who had money; and secretly arranging their plans, waylaid him when he was off his guard, or picked his pockets in the crowd upon the market, or while at the creek for water; but the more usual method by which they operated was by open assault; in these cases, the place where the intended victim concealed his money was first discovered, when he was surrounded by the gang, one of whom seized him by the throat, to prevent his crying out, while the remainder relieved him of his treasures. For a long time no notice of these enormities was taken by the prison authorities; in fact, had they been disposed to take the matter in hand for correction, they would undoubtedly have failed in accomplishing any good result, on account of the difficulty of identifying the miscreants.

Some time during the later part of June, their villainies reached a climax; one afternoon, a man was assailed by the gang, knocked down, beaten with clubs until he was covered with blood; his bones were broken; deep cuts made upon his body with the bludgeons, and his watch and sixty dollars in money taken from him. This brutal act aroused the whole camp, for if such atrocities were longer permitted to pass unpunished, every man was liable to similar treatment, at any time; a number of the prisoners, among them the victim himself, represented the facts to Gen. Winder, and appealed to him for protection; but he refused to do any more in the matter than sanction any action the prisoners themselves might adopt. At the request of the latter, a force of Confederate soldiers was sent into the prison and eighty-six men arrested, taken out and placed under a strong guard. The prisoners within the stockade demanded a trial by jury for these men, and their demand was acceded to by Gen. Winder. For this purpose, Capt. Wirz summoned all the Sergeants of detachments and divisions, laid the matter before them, and proposed that they request each of their respective divisions to select one man to represent it. This was accordingly done, when these representatives chose twelve of the most unprejudiced from among the men in the stockade to act as a jury, selecting for the purpose, those who had but recently arrived, and had, for that reason, seen but few of the raiders' operations; a presiding officer was appointed; counsel assigned both for the prosecution and the defence [sic], and a clerk, or Secretary designated to record the proceedings in full.

When all the preliminaries were perfected, the accused were separately tried; the assault upon the man as described above, being the particular crime in question. The trial was held in the little enclosure around the North gate, and continued about a week; men were summoned from the stockade as witnesses, and closely and rigidly examined by the counsel for the defence [sic], who had been an Attorney before entering the army; and every precaution was adopted in sifting the evidence, so as to ensure a fair hearing for the accused. When all the witnesses had been examined, the judge summed up the evidence, and presented it to the jury, who, after daily considering it, found six men guilty, upon the specifications presented at the trial. The six convicted men were, thereupon, sentenced to be hung, and the 11th day of July was named for their execution. When the trial was completed, the prisoners were placed in the "laying down stocks" and under strong guard to prevent their escape, where they were retained until the day of the execution. Meanwhile, the prisoners in the stockade, had procured lumber of the prison commander, and about midway the South section of the enclosure, and a little South of the wagon road, had erected a scaffold of sufficient height, that all within could witness the execution, and ropes were formed by splicing cords belonging to shelter tents, and such other things as could be adapted to the purpose. When all was in readiness, the criminals were brought in and delivered into the hands of the prisoners, by Capt. Wirz, with these words: "Here, men, I bring you back the prisoners in as good condition as I received them; you can take them and do as you please with them, and may God help you." They were then taken in charge by the prisoners and conducted to the scaffold, where they were placed upon the drop, their hands and feet fastened in the usual manner, a cap drawn over their faces and the noose slipped over their heads. At the signal, the trap door was sprung, and five of the guilty men swung off into eternity. The rope of the sixth broke, and falling to earth, he made an effort to escape, but he was soon retaken and securely suspended by the side of his fellow criminals. The bodies remained hanging for half an hour, when they were taken down and placed in the "dead house," from where they were soon conveyed to the grave-yard, and buried. A full account of the proceedings from the beginning of the trial to the burial was written by the Clerk of the Court, and transmitted by flag of truce to the Government at Washington.

It is painful to record this event, to contemplate these men, who disgraced the colors they wore, by their atrocious deeds; but justice to the prisoners themselves requires that a full statement can be published. Some of the prisoners within the stockade, disapproved of the proceedings, considering that they had no right to interfere, to the extent of depriving their fellow-men of life; the criminals themselves threw their principal defence [sic] upon this point, although each asserted to his innocence to the last moment. There is no doubt that this terrible retribution was both just and necessary. Their lawless depredations had spread a complete terrorism throughout the stockade; no one felt secure at any time, either in his treasures of his life, either by day, or by night; they had prosecuted their villainous calling so long, and with such impunity, that they seemed to have abandoned all precautions for concealment in their operations. It was a matter of necessity that condign punishment should be inflicted upon the guilty parties, in order that the peaceably disposed might enjoy the limited rights allowed them, unmolested. There was surely no reason why this additional horror should be added to the already overwhelming wretchedness we were forced to endure; and the inalienable right of self-preservation, secured to us alike by natural and human law, demanded the infliction of the punishment these guilty men suffered.

There is no doubt that these men were guilty of the crime of which they were convicted. The evidence before the jury was both voluminous and explicit; they were impartial men who had not suffered in any manner from their depredations. They had ample time to consider and weigh the testimony; and more than all, some of the ill-gotten [sic] gains were found in the possession of the accused, and identified by those from whom it had been taken. A less complete chain of circumstances had often led to the conviction of murderers in the Courts of Justice.

Of the character of these men, little need be said; that they were ruffians before entering the army, was evident from the ease and method with which they entered upon their career of crime, at Andersonville, and the entire absence of all restraint against a full and free indulgence in their vicious propensities, left an open field for their operations. The ease with which they effected their crimes and the good living consequent upon their possession of ready means, with which to patronize the sutler and the markets, were allurements which they neither tried nor wished, to resist. The consequences of their wickedness fell upon their own heads, and the justice of their sentences is vindicated by the necessities of the case.

The course pursued by the Confederate authorities in the matter, is also deserving of credit. It was well known to them as it was felt by the prisoners, that light or temporary punishment would not answer the purpose; and they did not wish to bear the responsibility of inflicting a severe one. They therefore turned the accused men over to trial and punishment by their fellows, only placing within their reach such facilities as were necessary for carrying out the sentence, whatever it might be. The names of the men who were executed, are in my possession, but consideration for their friends, if any such remain, induces me to withhold them; a fuller statement that this, can be found among the papers in the War Department at Washington.

After the execution of the raiders, quiet and security prevailed among the prisoners. Little acts of petty larceny occurred, as is usual in all camps, however well regulated, but nothing of particular value was stolen, and no more brutal assaults were made for the purpose of robbing the victim. A police or vigilance committee, was organized, or rather organized itself, among the prisoners, for the preservation of order in the camp. The purpose for which it was designed was good, but there were acts of meanness perpetuated by these policemen, that deserve the severest censure; for many a poor fellow, unable to help himself, was unmercifully beaten by them, without any reason for their so doing. Yet on the whole, they performed their disagreeable duty with as much lenience, perhaps, as could be expected, although sometimes failing to discriminate between the innocent and the guilty. In virtue of their office, they received an extra ration, daily.

WARREN LEE GOSS, *THE SOLDIER'S STORY OF HIS CAPTIVITY AT ANDERSONVILLE, BELLE ISLE AND OTHER REBEL PRISONS*, 1865

It was rumored around camp, from time to time, that raiders and flankers were organized for the perpetration of outrages, and of protecting themselves against the punishment of such acts. Although there was no definite organization among us, it was agreed upon that these villains should be promptly dealt with; that when any of the Plymouth prisoners could identify a "raider," or was attacked or robbed by one of them, he was to call out loudly "Plymouth!" when every one of the boys within hearing were to turn out to his assistance. In accordance with this agreement, we heard one morning the rallying cry, and captured a fellow who was caught in the act of stealing a blanket. The boys gathered around him, not knowing what to do with the Tartar now that they had caught one. He sat gnashing his teeth, threatening his captors with the vengeance of a band, which he said was formed for mutual thieving, if they should injure or inflict punishment upon him. Feeling some reluctance to proceeding against him, they were about to release him without punishment, otherwise than a few kicks, when a corporal of Company G, second Massachusetts heavy artillery, familiarly known in prison as "Big Peter," came into the crowd, and taking the raider fearlessly in hand, inflicted summary punishment upon him by shaving half of his head and face, giving no heed to the desperado's savage gnashing of teeth and threats of vengeance, except to thump his head at each beginning and repetition of them. After dealing out justice in this off-hand manner, and an administrative reminder (in the rear) from a pair of the heaviest of cowhides, the thief was released, with admonitions to sin no more.

This, I believe, was the first instance of formal punishment for such misdemeanors; and thereafter Big Pete, by virtue of these services, became the terror of evildoers. Pete exhibited so much courage at this time, and subsequently so much good sense and natural judgement, that he gradually became the administrative power for the punishment of offenses committed. He performed for us the services of shaving, and in a dignified, impartial manner gave the culprit a trial—hearing the statements of both sides before pronouncing judgement and inflicting punishment, both of which, however, were often condensed into the last act. Few exceptions were taken to his rulings, for who could object to the persuasive arguments of one who wore such heavy boots?

The incident narrated was the beginning of a power in camp to punish offenders, which finally provided us with an effective police organization. Pete was an uneducated Canadian—a man of gigantic stature and great physical strength, of an indomitable will, great good nature, and with innate ideas of justice, in the carrying out of which, he was as inflexible as iron. A blow from his fist was like that from a sledge-hammer, and from first to last he maintained so great a supremacy in camp that no description of the prison at that time would be complete without a sketch of him. His trials were often intensely grotesque and amusing to spectators, but not generally so to the culprit. I took pains to follow some of his trials, and I must say, in justice, I never knew him to make a wrong decision, although baffled in his purpose by ingenious lies, he had a talent for detecting them and sifting out the truth. Thus, at last, by common consent, if any one had complaints to make, he carried them to the "shebang" of Big Peter. He either went himself, or sent some of his adherents, who returned with the accused; witnesses were then summoned and punishments dispensed. Justice was being dealt out in this manner, when one morning it was announced—to our sorrow we found it carried into practice—that our rations were to be stopped on account of men missing from the stockade—supposed by the rebel authorities to have escaped by means of tunnels. Investigation led to no new discoveries, and after twenty-four hours extra starvation, they were again issued as before, it being impossible to discover the missing men, or any modes, by which they could have escaped.

    About this time, the raiders, under the leadership of Mosby, became exceedingly bold, attacked the new comers in open daylight, robbing them of blankets, watches, money, and other property of value. Rumors of frightful import were circulated through the camp of men murdered for their blankets, watches, money, and other property of value. After this, more men were missing at morning roll-call, of whom there could be no reasonable account given. Under Big Peter a company was organized, armed with clubs, who proceeded to the shelter formerly occupied by the missing men. Inquiries being made among those who were living near, no information could be obtained, otherwise than the fact that outcries were heard during the night, and that there was a scuffle near; but scenes of disorder being common during the night, they had taken but little notice of them, since, as peaceable men, they wished to avoid all wrangling. Nothing at first could be found, in the shelter formerly occupied by these men, to excite suspicion. Most of the crowd had dispersed, when one of the men, on his hands and knees at the entrance, looking down into the grave-like hole which formed the principal part of the abandoned dwelling place, saw a piece of blue cloth, partially covered with dirt. Seeing in this the element of a patch, for the repairing of his shattered wardrobe, he pulled at it, and found it fastened to the ground. This excited his curiosity, also his desire for possession; and he began to dig and pull, until further progress was arrested, and he started back with horror and the unexpected appearance of a human hand. A crowd had gathered around, and speedily a dead man was unearthed, whose throat had been cut in a shocking manner, and his head bruised by a terrible blow. In the same space, beneath him, was found another victim, with his throat cut. The news of these horrible murders spread through the prison as if by telegraph, and a large crowd soon assembled around the scene of these atrocities. The police proceeded to the shelter of several notorious thieves and bad characters of the prison, and arrested them. Through information, or clew gained of one of these, they were induced to dig in the shelter of some of those arrested, which resulted in the discovery of money, watches &c., in many cases identified as the property of the murdered men.

    Rapidly after the perpetration of these cold-blooded atrocities, strong police forces were formed under Big Peter as chief of police. Afterwards a judgeship was established in prison, and there were two regular practicing attorneys, who took fees of Indian meal, beans, and small currency in payment for services rendered; and sometimes, it was said, bribed the judge and chief of police. In the case of Staunton, a big brute, and tool of the rebels, who killed a man, as mentioned in the preceding pages, it was rumored that his money, procured by dicker with prisoners, obtained him a mild sentence and punishment. Not to digress further, the supposed murderers, some fifteen in number, were arrested, and after gaining sufficient evidence, consent was obtained of the prison authorities for their trial. Besides this was obtained the privilege of conducting the trial under guard, in a building outside the prison. The accused were also held in custody through the kindness of Wirz, the commandant. A jury of men was empaneled, composed of prisoners just captured, who had never been in the prison, and who, therefore, could not have formed prejudices on either side. The trial lasted through a number of weeks. Competent men were appointed to defend the prisoners by the authorities. An able lawyer, an officer of the rebel guard, conducted the defence, afterwards stating to me that he had no doubt of the guilt of those who suffered punishment. The prosecution was conducted by men selected from among the prisoners. Six of them were pronounced by a jury guilty of murder.

On the 12th of the month, Captain Wirz, accompanied by a guard, brought the prisoners into the stockade, where, on the south side, near the gate, and the scene of the murder, a gallows had been erected. Here he turned the offenders over to the prison police, with a short speech, in which he stated that they had been impartially tried and found guilty of atrocious murders, and that he left their punishment in the hands of the prisoners of the stockade. He then turned, and followed by his guard, left the prison.

GILBERT E. SABRE,
NINETEEN MONTHS A PRISONER OF WAR, 1865

Chapter 21

Raiding at Sumter—Detection of a Number of "Raiders"—Their Trial—Sentenced to be hanged—Their Execution—The Effect of extreme Measures.

The system of "raiding," which was carried on with so much annoyance at Belle Isle, was practiced, with even greater industry, at Camp Sumter. The class of vagabonds who thus indulged their thieving propensities, spent their nights in prowling through the camps, carrying off every thing they could lay their hands upon.

The sick and helpless were particularly annoyed by their depredations, but every one suffered more or less. It was impossible to possess anything, unless it was closely watched. While one man was absent, it became necessary for a comrade to remain as a sort of guard to the property. At length, the evil became so great that it was determined to set a terrible example.

Quietly, one afternoon, a small number of prisoners held a secret meeting to consider the nuisance and adopt measures to stop it. After exchanging views upon the subject, it was determined to organize a small and reliable detective force, to keep watch and draw out any suspected parties, in hopes of discovering the ring leaders.

The same night, the detectives commenced their duty. A close surveillance was kept upon different parts of the camp, but morning came without making any discoveries. The following day passed in mixing with several suspected parties, but without avail. The second night met with the same results. It was not supposed that the raiders got wind of the efforts to find them out, and they had taken the wise precaution of desisting, at least temporarily, from their labors. During the same day, however, a blanket was missing from a poor fellow who was dying of the effects of chronic diarrhoea. The "detectives" immediately started in quest of the "raider." After an hour's diligent search, he was discovered and drawn from his hiding place, not only with the article stolen, but numerous other evidences of his guilt, and which were at once claimed by their owners.

A preliminary examination drew from the man an acknowledgment of his crime, and at the same time the names of a number of others implicated in the same acts were elicited. The entire party was arrested, and a trial called.

On the next morning the sergeants of the different messes were assembled, and, out of this number, twelve were chosen to act as a jury. Several officers were brought down from Macon to witness the trial. Those of the sufferers by the depredations of the "raiders," who were able to attend, were summoned to appear as witnesses, and the accused were permitted to choose their own counsel and witnesses. During the excitement of the arrests, a number of men were held for trial, but who, upon proving their innocence, were at once discharged.

The trials of the "raiders" was conducted with the strictest impartiality. After hearing all the evidence, the respective cases were argued with considerable ability. The verdict given, was for the leading "raiders" to be hanged by the neck until dead, and the remainder to suffer such other punishments as the extent of their crime deserved.

The following were the names of the men condemned to death:

William Collins, alias , 88th Pennsylvania volunteers.
Patrick Delany, 83d Pennsylvania volunteers.
Andrew Meever, United States navy.
Terrence Sullivan, 72d New York volunteers.
John Sarsfield, 140th New York volunteers
Charles Curtis, 5th Rhode Island artillery.

On Monday, July 11, 1864, a rude gallows was erected by our own men on rising ground in the Southwestern portion of the stockade. The gallows was a rude piece of workmanship, build out of material which the rebel officials, but too willingly in this case, provided. It was composed of two heavy, forked logs, which were fixed perpendicularly in the earth, with a strong cross-beam resting in the forks at the top. A platform, about six feet from the ground, was built and supported upon props, which, at the final moment, were to be cut away, and the unfortunate men launched between heaven and earth. Six men from the camp were designated to adjust the ropes about the necks of the condemned, and a seventh detailed to execute the dropping of the platform.

At five o'clock in the afternoon the southwestern gate was thrown open, and the prisoners were marched in under guard of rebel soldiers, commanded by Captain Wurtz [sic], accompanied by the colonel commanding the post. A solemn procession moved in front of the gallows, and halted.

By this time several thousand prisoners had assembled to witness the execution. Many sympathized with the unfortunate situation of their comrades. But the crime of stealing from a fellow prisoner was always regarded as the most unprincipled of acts, but also a matter in which every one who suffered was reduced from a state of deplorable misery to absolute deprivation of probably the last hold he had upon life. The crime was much aggravated by the depredations committed upon the helpless sick. In view of these facts, however benevolent of yielding the wishes of the fellow-prisoners of the condemned, all wished the sentence to be carried to the melancholy end, as a warning, in the future, to others disposed to the same practices.

When the culprits were formed in line the rebel captain stepped forward, and, as near as I could note them, after the affair was over, made the following remarks to those in charge of the execution:

"PRISONERS—I now hand over to you, in the same manner I received them, the men whom you have condemned to death on the gallows."

Then, turning to the culprits, he said:

"You have been arrested and condemned by your own comrades; I now turn you over to them, and leave them to carry out the sentence, or do as they may see fit."

After this, the colonel, captain, and guards immediately left the inclosure.

The condemned now received the consolations of religion, administered by a Catholic priest, who was permitted by the rebel authorities to visit the stockade on different occasions. The priest accompanied the culprits to the foot of the gallows, and engaged in prayer. In the midst of these holy offices, Curtis took occasion to make an attempt at escape. He succeeded in breaking through the crowd, but was immediately pursued and returned.

The prayer being finished, the six criminals, each accompanied by the persons appointed to execute the sentences, stepped up on the platform. The criminals each said a few words, which were scarcely audible, proclaiming their innocence, and begging for mercy.

When they concluded what they had to say, the ropes having been previously adjusted, a sack was drawn over their heads, and the six men who accompanied them descended.

At a given signal, the platform was cut away, and five of the unfortunate men were struggling in mid-air. The rope, however, of the sixth broke, and the culprit fell to earth. He begged piteously to be released, but his comrades were inexorable. Another rope was secured, and, when the five bodies were removed, he was hanged alone.

The bodies of the six men were removed from the stockade, and buried in a separate part of the graveyard, distinct from those who died in camp.

During the execution, I observed outside of the inclosure [sic] the whole of the rebel troops on duty at Camp Sumter were drawn up facing the gallows. This was, as I understood afterwards, a precautionary measure, supposing some treachery on the part of the prisoners.

At first thought, the above action on the part of the prisoners, appears an act of useless severity on the part of comrades of the men so dishonorably and summarily deprived of life. But our experience after in the evil which it was designed to correct, does not justify this opinion. The example of extreme punishment thus placed before the minds of others, of "raiding" proclivities, had a good result. It all at once put a stop to this class of annoyance. During the remainder of the time I remained at Camp Sumter I did not hear of a single article being stolen, and the feelings among all classes of prisoners were stronger and more sympathizing, to an extent surprising, as the very natural selfishness created in times of extreme suffering, and which, in our case at Sumter, never relaxed, now changed to a bond of closer union; and it was not unusual to see men waiting on each other, as kindly as though they had some important interest at stake.

WILLIAM PITT, *NINETEEN MONTHS A PRISONER IN THE HANDS OF THE REBELS*, 1865

Although William Pitt is listed as the author of this small book, it's actually the story of James S. Anderson, of the 24th Wisconsin Volunteers, Company F, who mustered in on August 21, 1862, and was captured at Chickamauga 13 months later. After the war, Anderson was interviewed by newspaper reporter William Pitt for what was intended to be an article on Anderson's wartime experiences; however, the interview eventually resulted in this book, subtitled, *Experience at Belle Isle, Richmond, Danville, and Andersonville: Some Items with Reference to Capt. Wirz with a Map of the Andersonville Prison Camp, Called Camp Sumter.* The 67 page book was published in Milwaukee by Starr & Son Printers in 1865.

The prisoners had to resort to some occupation to pass away time, and it soon became necessary to establish some police regulations for this large population. Characters of every grade were to be found. It finally became necessary to establish courts of justice. In the way of occupation to pass away the weary hours, the men employed themselves in making from the beef bones, rings, toothpicks and trifles of ornament, all being done with no other instrument than the jack-knife, these were in great demand, the purchasers being confederates. A skillful workman could supply himself with tobacco and sundry other articles of necessity or convenience by the manufacture of these and other ornamental trinkets. There is an inborn disposition in the American character to trade, traffic and grow rich, or fail in the attempt. This characteristic, notwithstanding the forlorn condition of these unfortunates soon developed itself. Markets were established, barter commenced and pretty soon among these forlorn people quite a trade was established. It must not be understood that the successful business operator got rich in money. His highest ambition was to get an increased supply of provisions. The highest success attained by which the successful industrious speculator was to get enough to live upon.

The Northern Army has in its ranks men of all ranks, grades, and profession. The Andersonville prisons were an illustration of this fact. If preaching was required, a preacher was at hand. If a lawyer was wanted more than could be retained were instantly on hand.

This city of horrors had in its borders a fair representation of all classes of people. The Christian gentleman was to be found there, and from him down through the grades and shades of character until pickpockets, thieves, robbers, and murderers were included in the list of characters composing this community.

The last mentioned characters followed their professions to such an extent that they became objects of terror to the whole community. They soon became designated and known by the name of Raiders. They seemed to act in combination or separately as the case required. If any fellow prisoner was fortunate enough to save any valuable thing either in money or other personal property, these professionals seemed to find it out almost by instinct. The possessor of any valuable article was sure to become an object of interest to these precious scoundrels, and if he did not become a victim he might bless his own good fortune. These men were experts. They had evidently applied their professions before entering the army. They manufactured instruments by which they could cut open a pocket without detection. They would relieve a man of his valuables in many cases without his knowledge while the victim was asleep, and if he (the victim) was awakened by the operation they knew how to silence him even if they had to go so far as murder. Their operations were finally carried to such an extent that they became objects requiring some combined action to relieve the camp of their depredation. These men were generally from large cities and at home would be known by the name of "Roughs." They numbered from one hundred and fifty to two hundred. When their conduct became so notoriously outrageous that forbearances ceased to be a virtue, their case was taken in hand by their fellow prisoners.

The facts as far as ascertainable were collected and presented to Capt. Wirz who promptly arrested the culprits. A court was at once formed with judge and jury, which proceeded to try them. It has been stated on good authority that this court in point of ability would compare favorably with any other court possessing or assuming the same powers.

About 40 men were on trial. The proceedings were all in regular form, and the case given the jury in the regular form. Then the verdict was given and the sentence followed. Some were sentenced to wear the ball and chain for ninety days and six were sentenced to be hanged. The trial took place outside of the stockade and lasted three or four days. The condemned were in custody of Capt. Wirz. When the time came for the execution of the condemned, Capt. Wirz brought them under guard into the stockade and said, "Now poys you have tried these men by a jury of your own men, and a schudge of your own choosing, now you do schust what you please mit dem, and immediately left the grounds. [sic]

The result was that these men were shortly seen dangling between heaven and earth in accordance with the sentence of the court.

DANIEL KELLEY, *WHAT I SAW AND SUFFERED IN REBEL PRISONS*, 1866

Troubles, it is said, never some singly, and this proved true in our case. Confinement and suffering were attended with a demoralizing effect upon the men. Stealing and fighting were of common occurrence, and quite a number of murders were committed. About sixty of the most abandoned characters had organized a gang to plunder the men of all they possessed which was of value. Money, watches and blankets, which the men had succeeded in keeping from the rebels, were taken from them by this gang. If they were refused, knives and clubs were freely used to enforce their demands, and frequently men lost their lives by endeavoring to resist the raiders and retain their own property.

One night they surrounded some men belonging to our regiment, and searched them. Not finding anything more valuable, they took their cups and a razor and razor-strop. A few days after they were robbed, the man owning the razor, saw one of the men sharpening it on the strop that had been stolen from him, but had no power to regain them.

Finally we organized a police force sufficiently strong to arrest and punish any who should infringe on the rights of their fellow prisoners. Twenty-four were arrested and tried by a jury composed of twelve sergeants. Six of the twenty-four were found guilty of murder, and sentenced to be hung, which sentence was put into execution on the 11th of July.

The scaffold was erected near the south gate, on the hillside, and the execution was witnessed by about twenty-five thousand prisoners. The sentry boxes were also crowded with spectators from outside.

As soon as the scaffold was completed, the police cleared the path to the gate, and the criminals soon appeared, each having his arms pinioned and walking between two men who were the executioners. As they approached the stand, one of the criminals broke from his guard, and, rushing through the crowd, ran across the valley and jumped over the dead-line closely pursued by his guard. The sentries did not shoot him, but his guard was allowed to go and take him. He was taken back, and with the others ascended the platform.

After they had taken their stand by the ropes, they were each allowed to speak a few words. They asked the boys to pray for them, and begged in vain for the mercy they had refused to show to their innocent victims. After they had finished speaking, they were each given a drink of water, then the ropes and caps were adjusted, and the executioners descended from the platform. All the criminals, except one, now stooped, that the fall might be as light as possible; but the other stood erect, and when the prop was withdrawn and the platform fell, he broke his rope and fell to the ground. He now begged, but in vain, for pardon; the rope was re-adjusted, and he was placed by the side of his companions in crime.

Some may think the prisoners did wrong in hanging these men; but what were we to do? They were given a fair trial, and found guilty of murder; and as long as the guilty were allowed to go unpunished, the innocent must suffer at their hands. But this proved a warning to others. I do not think there was another murder committed, and stealing was of rare occurrence.

JOSIAH BROWNELL: *AT ANDERSONVILLE, A NARRATIVE OF PERSONAL ADVENTURE AT ANDERSONVILLE, FLORENCE AND CHARLESTON REBEL PRISONS*, 1867

Besides all our other troubles we were kept in constant fear by a lawless band of our own fellow prisoners, who had joined themselves together to plunder and rob the rest, and steal the rations of their sickly and weaker comrades; they called themselves the raiders, and were about seven hundred strong. They prowled by night, stealing clothing and cooking utensils, and boldly by day knocked down and robbed inoffensive men of their scanty supply of food. They were the terror of us all—by day we feared to meet them, and night was made hideous by the cries of their victims; four men had been killed outright, and many had been badly beaten by these human fiends.

At length we determined that there should be a reform, and a vigilance committee was formed who waited on Capt. Wirz, the next time he came into the prison, and asked him for redress. He listened with patience to the story of our wrongs, and told the committee to bring every one of the rascals that we could catch to the prison gate. This was good enough—we had got the power on our side and the raiders began to tremble.

In less than an hour out committee had caught one hundred of the most desperate of these thieves and cut-throats, and delivered them to the guard at the gate. "Now," called out Capt. Wirz from the top of the high gateway, "let every man who was ever injured by these men, and also the friends of the dead, whom these men have murdered, prepare for revenge. Get each of you a club, and form a double line, and I will turn them loose, one by one, and make them run the gauntlet?

Human nature at Andersonville was very much depraved, and poor, ragged and starving as we were, there were five hundred who armed themselves with clubs and took their places in line, and as they stood waiting for the command that was to deliver their victims into their power, they looked more like hungry wolves than human beings. One by one, at the command of Wirz, the victims were driven by the Rebel guards into the space between the two lines, and thick and heavy were the blows that were rained upon them, for those who held the clubs struck for many a lost dinner, of which these raiders had robbed them, and some for the memory of friends, and even brothers, who had been killed by their brutality.

But see, a bold and daring thief is about to take the run, and the clubs are held by firmer hands, for he was the leader of the gang, and had been a bold, a desperate and a daring man. A smile, or more properly a ghastly grin, played around the ugly mouth of Capt. Wirz, as he saw the anxiety of these revengeful men to have their victim; such a scene as this was just suited to his brutal nature, and with a laugh that seemed to come from the infernal regions, he gave the order: "Drive him out."

Like a gladiator entering the arena to battle with the enraged beasts of the forest, came that desperate thief to face five hundred of his fellow men, nearly all of whom he had personally wronged, and whom he knew were thirsting for his blood. He took one look along the line, then started on a wild run, but was met by many blows given by revengeful hands. With savage desperation he drew a knife that he had concealed about his person, and laying about him to the right and left like a madman, he wounded five men, two of them mortally. In a moment, all was consternation and dismay; the double line was broken, and the friends of the champion gave a cheer of triumph. But their momentary triumph was soon at an end, for Wirz ordered every one of those who had just been released to be again brought to him. When this was done, he told us to appoint a Judge and twelve Jurymen, and examine each of them separately, and punish them just as the Judge should decide. This we did, and after ten days spent in trying their cases, six were found guilty of murder and sentenced to be hung. The proceedings of the trial were all copied and sent to Macon, where our Union officers were imprisoned, and submitted to the examination of Gen. Stoneman, who signed the papers, saying that he highly approved of hanging any who had abused their fellow prisoners as these had done.

Capt. Wirz furnished the timber and ropes, and we erected the scaffold in the centre of the prison, and the day was appointed for their execution. I had never before seen a man hung, and never wanted to, but this time I was determined to see the whole affair, so I secured a place near the gallows.

The prisoners, since their conviction, had been kept under guard outside of the prison. At twelve o'clock they were brought in and marched up to the scaffold, and Wirz made the following speech:

"Here are your fellow prisoners, as fat and as healthy as they were before they were arrested. They have been tried by a Judge and Jury selected from among yourselves, found guilty of murder and sentenced to be hung. Your officers at Macon approved of the whole thing. Now to me it is a matter of no interest. Hang them, or release them; trust yourselves again to their mercy, or, by hanging them, relieve yourselves forever from their oppression,"—and ten thousand voices cried, "hang them! hang them as high as Haman!"

The gallows was all ready; six ropes with the peculiar noose and knot of the hangman were dangling from a strong beam of Georgia pine. Six men who were to officiate as hangmen were making themselves busy running here and there, trying the strength of the ropes and arranging the dead fall. The hour came at last, and the victims were led upon the scaffold; their hands were bound, the nooses were adjusted around their necks, and then they were allowed to speak the last words of farewell to their comrades. In the most light and trifling manner they said good-bye to their friends, asked for a drink of water, which was given to them, and without further delay they were launched into eternity.

It may seem to the minds of some that the hanging of these men was useless brutality, but it was not so. Previous to their execution no man's life was safe, but after their deaths all was peace and harmony, and all were on an equal

JOHN HARROLD: *LIBBY, ANDERSONVILLE, FLORENCE: THE CAPTURE, THE IMPRISONMENT, AND THE ESCAPE,* 1870

I fortunately met with a member of the regiment to which I belonged, and he secured me a place to lie down. I needed rest, and it was a most gracious relief, even there, as I was weary and nearly exhausted. My comrade gave me a detailed account of the rules and regulations which governed the inclosure [sic], and called my special attention to a little rail-line, some twenty feet from the stockade. "As you value your life," said he, "do not step between that and the stockade. It is the dead line." He also cautioned me against a gang of raiders, composed of our own men, who would rob and murder a man for ten cents.

I soon realized the value of this last caution. A companion of mine who had entered the pen with me, having no place to sleep, was compelled to lay down with some others on the only space left for a wagon road. He had not lain there long, when he was seized by the hair of the head and a knife held to his throat, while a fellow soldier rifled his pockets of the little money he possessed. A number of such cases occurred, and so frequent became these outrages that it was found necessary to adopt prompt and severe measures to check the evil. Accordingly, six offenders, who had just participated in a very aggravated assault and robbery, were apprehended by our own men. They were tried in the most impartial manner under the circumstances, condemned and sentenced to be hung. This sentence was carried into effect on the 11th day of July, 1864. After that we had comparative peace, and felt more secure. At least, no more murders were committed, and few, if any, robberies.

I know that some may pronounce this a summary proceeding; but I consider that the necessities arising from our peculiar situation demanded it. Some 22,000 men were there huddled together—victims of every species of privation, and driven to despair with phrensied [sic] minds and craving appetites, every latent feeling of selfishness was awakened into activity, conscience was blunted by suffering, and the love of life destroyed all scruples in regard to the means of preserving it. In this condition, it is not surprising that they should prey upon one another. And yet, it was absolutely necessary to check such lawlessness as the only means of protecting the weak against the strong; and where so many were packed, it was apparent that all must suffer, unless the most rigid discipline was maintained, and the evil-disposed restrained by proper punishment.

Appendix C

Interview with Leroy L. Key

*T*he following newspaper article originally appeared in the *Boston Journal* shortly after Key's exchange. The following transcription is taken from the *New York Times*, December 1, 1864, page 1, column 4.

We have received from Rev. J.M. CLARK, one of the delegates of the Christian Commission, the following particulars of the execution of the prisoners at Sumter Prison who were tried and condemned by their fellow-prisoners for robbery and murder. The statement is made by LEROY L. KEY, who acted as Chief of Police, and under whose direction the execution took place. He says:

When I arrived there were some 4,000 prisoners, but the number increased till in September there were from 32,000 to 35,000. In August and September the deaths were from 75 to 125 per day. For a time the prisoners treated each other decently, but there were some bad fellows among them. These bad men increased in number, and began a series of atrocious wrongs against their fellow-prisoners.

They would decoy men into their tents with the promise of a blanket or an extra ration, or something desirable, and then rob and plunder them, and all resistance was in vain, as they had the victim fully in their power, in their own tent.

They would go out in a body, and meeting a man in the street, would demand of him his money, or whatever he had. If he would not give it up, it was forced from him. If he resisted, they beat him so that he would die of his injuries. The Surgeon declared that not less than 75 men died from this cause alone.

Spotting a tent in the daytime, they would go out at night, five or six in number, enter the tent, and with a knife or razor threaten the victim till he "shelled out." Some men were thus severely wounded before they would "shell out."

Many men traded to make a little money to get an extra ration. These "raiders," going to these petty traders, inquired of them how they got along in their business, and then demanded of them a tax, saying "in two hours you must pay us $100, or more." If the man refused, they beat him.

These things run on and became worse and worse, until we could bear it no longer. "Raiders" numbered, about the 20th of June, 150 or 200, and it became absolutely necessary for the other prisoners to take some measures for defense; for the "raiders" swore that by the 4th of July they would have every cent in camp or kill the resisters.

Up to this time the Confederate authorities kept no order or discipline within the lines. I spoke to a few of my friends to organize a band of protectors against these raiders. We began to organize, and had proceeded to the formation of thirteen companies, with thirty men and a captain in each. Before the organization was complete, I was one day walking on the north side of the camp, when I saw ahead of me the chief of the raiders, and in pursuit of me five men on the "double quick," with knives in their hands. The chief slapped me on the shoulder and turned me round, saying to me, "I understand that you arc getting up a band to clear out the Irish." I replied, "The report is false and you are mistaken." "Well, you are getting up a band for some purpose; what is it for, if not to clean out the Irish?" Meanwhile the five men closed around us, forming a ring around CURTIS and myself.

He again demanded to know the object of the band. Said I to him, boldly, "we are organizing a band to clean out the 'raiders,' and if you are one of them we intend to clean you out." They did not proceed to violence, but the leader put his knife into his left hand and with his right hand offered to shake hands with me. They then let me go. That night much raiding was done in the camp, and we heard in various quarters the cries of men, "help! murder!" The cook-house was on the outside of the camp, on the stream above, and men were detailed from the prisoners on parole of honor to do the cooking. All rations were drawn into the lines of the stockade in wagons—rations of corn-bread, a small piece of pork or beef; sometimes a pint of cooked beans to a man, not amounting in all to enough for one meal a day. Soup was probably allowed once a week, but we did not get it oftener than once in three weeks, and then it was nothing but a little grease on a chip.

The condition of the prisoners was somewhat relieved by the arrival of some men captured at Plymouth, who had just been paid off, and who brought into camp thousands of dollars. By trading and bartering round, most of the men got some of this money. I regard it as an act of merciful Providence that those men were captured and sent to Sumter Prison, for otherwise many more men must have died from starvation.

The day after CURTIS stopped me in the street, word came that no more rations would be sent into camp until we delivered up the raiders into the hands of the rebel authorities; for they had raided upon the wagons, and had stolen the rations belonging to a detachment on the south side of the camp. We then perfected the organization of our band, and commenced seeking for and arresting the raiders. We laid hold of 150 or 200 men, who were known to be engaged in raiding, and turned them over. Out of the number, the worst cases, twenty in all, were retained outside the camp under guard, and the rest returned within the stockade. The arrests within were continued, until the number of bad cases sent out was about 100. Capt. WERZ [sic] selected twenty-four Sergeants from those that knew most of the matters in dispute, and out of this number appointed twelve jurymen and a Judge-Advocate. The attorneys on both sides were appointed by the Judge-Advocate, whose name was PETER MCCOLLAR, of the Eighth Missouri.

The accused had a fair and just trial, and eleven men were proved guilty, but the chief criminality laid upon six men, of whom CURTIS was the leader. These men were sentenced to be hung, and Gen. WINDER approved of the sentence, and ordered me to erect a scaffold and superintend the execution. I procured the lumber where I was directed, and with a detail of men erected the scaffold and made all ready. The time fixed for the execution was Monday, 4 o'clock P.M., July 11, 1864. When the men were brought in and turned over to us, Capt. WERZ took his guards outside and left the prisoners, the convicted criminals, in our charge. My guards were armed with a stout club, fastened to the right wrist by a cord. Six men were appointed executioners, and each took his stand upon the stage behind the criminal.

Most of the criminals were Roman Catholics, and a Priest came in to attend them. He requested us to have mercy upon the men, and earnestly plead for them; and after he had got through CURTIS asked me to spare him as he had never done me any harm. I told him it was not for me to pardon him, I was appointed to see that the men were hung; but if he had anything to say, I would hear his confession on the scaffold. Then he said he would not stand it, and made a break for the lines, and ran about the camp until he was recaptured. He was brought back perfectly exhausted.

While CURTIS was absent, the other criminals were taken on to the scaffold, and the ropes placed around their necks, the executioners standing behind them. Immediately after CURTIS was brought back, he was delivered to the executioner and taken on to the scaffold likewise. No confessions were made, but the men disposed of their property, and CURTIS gave his watch to the priest, Father WHALEN.

A vast number of the 33,000 prisoners-of-war were assembled around the scaffold. At length the order was given to pull the trigger, when five of them swung off and met their death. One rope broke and the prisoner was injured by the fall. He was brought up again, the rope adjusted, and as the drop was disarranged he was pushed off and met his death.

This terrible example put an end to raiding, and the prisoners were no more troubled with, the as—and depredations of the high-handed. There was nowhere a large number of men who—of the trial and execution, from whom trouble was anticipated, and it was feared that at the execution a crowd would arise and at-tempt to rescue the criminals. A stillness as of death pervaded, and it seemed as if the influence of a breath of wind would have let loose the sympathizers with the raiders, and prevented the execution. But the deed of terrible Justice was—completed. The Chief of Police and executioners were immediately removed beyond the lines, and a new Chief of Police appointed.

Selected Bibliography

Although there are hundreds of sources, both primary and secondary, that deal with Camp Sumter Prison at Andersonville, Georgia, this list includes only those that specifically relate to the raiders.

PRIMARY ACCOUNTS

Published Diaries

Anderson, Harmon. *Harmon Anderson Diary.* Transcribed by Margaret Brown. Edited by Richard Anderson. Available online on Kindle as an ebook (2014), and a transcribed copy can be found at the National Prisoner of War Museum, Andersonville, Georgia.

Coburn, Jacob Osborne. *Hell on Belle Isle: Diary of a Civil War POW.* Bryan, OH: Faded Banner Publications, 1997.

Forbes, Eugene. *Diary of a Soldier, and Prisoner of War in the Rebel Prisons.* Trenton, NJ: Murphy & Bechtel Printers, 1865.

Helmreich, Paul C. *The Diary of Charles G. Lee in the Andersonville and Florence Prison Camps, 1864.* Connecticut Historical Society Publication, January 1976, vol. 41, no. 1, pp. 12–28.

James, Frederic Augustus. *Frederic Augustus James's Civil War Diary.* Rutherford, NJ: Fairleigh Dickinson University Press, 1973.

Smedley, Charles. *Life in Southern Prisons: From the Diary of Corporal Charles Smedley, of Company G, 90 Regiment of Penn's Volunteers.* Lancaster, PA: Ladies and Gentlemen's Fulton Aid Society, 1865.

Tritt, William. *The Apple Trees Look Gay in Bloom.* Granville, OH: Tritt Family Research, 1987.

Unpublished Diaries

Grosvenor, Samuel. Connecticut Historical Society, Hartford, Connecticut.

Hoster, John L. Fenmore Museum, Cooperstown, New York (formerly New York State Historical Association Research Library).

Kellogg, Robert. Part of the Kellogg Papers and artifacts at the Connecticut Historical Society

Knight, Adelbert. In possession of unpublished diary of descendant Larry Knight of Maine.

Marsh, Edwin. Navarro College.

Robbins, George. Connecticut Historical Society, Hartford, Connecticut.

Vance, James. Transcription available at National Prisoner of War Museum, Andersonville, Georgia.

Published Memoirs (1865–1870)

Anonymous. *A Voice from Rebel Prisons.* 1865.

Brownell, Josiah. *At Andersonville, A Narrative of Personal Adventure at Andersonville, Florence and Charleston Rebel Prisons.* Glen Cover: "Gazette" Book and Job Office, 1867.

Davidson, Henry. *Fourteen Months in Southern Prisons; Being a Narrative of the Treatment,* 1865.

Goss, Warren Lee. *The Soldier's Story of his Captivity at Andersonville, Belle Isle, and Other Rebel Prisons.* Boston: Lee and Shepard, 1867.

Harrold, John, *Libby, Andersonville, Florence: The Capture, the Imprisonment, and the Escape,* 1870.

Kelley, Daniel, *What I Saw and Suffered in Rebel Prisons.* Buffalo, NY: Printing House of Matthews & Warren, 1866.

Kellogg, Robert. *Life and Death in Rebel Prisons.* Hartford, CT: L. Stebbins, 1866.

Pitt, William C. *19 Months A Prisoner in the Hands of the Rebels.* Milwaukee, MN: Starr and Son, Printers, 1865.

Sabre, Gilbert E. *Nineteen Months a Prisoner of War.* New York: American News Co., 1865.

Published Memoirs, post-1870

Hopkins, Charles. *The Andersonville Diary and Memoirs of Charles Hopkins, 1st New Jersey Infantry.* Edited by William B. Styple and John J. Fitzpatrick. Kearny, NJ: Belle Grove Publishing Co., 1988.

McElroy, John. *Andersonville, A Story of Rebel Military Prisons.* Toledo, OH: D. R. Locke, 1879.

Northrop, John Worrell. *Chronicles from the Diary of a War Prisoner in Andersonville and Other Military Prisons in the South in 1864.* Wichita, KS, 1904.

Ransom, John. *Andersonville Diary.* Auburn, NY: John Ransom, 1881.

Sneden, Robert Knox. *Eye of the Storm: A Civil War Odyssey.* Edited by Charles F. Bryan, Jr., and Nelson D. Lankford. New York: Free Press, 2000.
Urban, John. *Battle Field and Prison Pen; or, Through the War, and Thrice a Prisoner in Rebel Dungeons.* Philadelphia, PA: Hubbard Bros., 1887.

PRIMARY ACCOUNTS, OTHER

Judson, Amos M. *History of the Eighty-Third Pennsylvania Volunteers.* Erie, PA: B. F. H. Lynn, 1881.
Wilmer, L. Alison, et al. *History and Roster of Maryland Volunteers, War of 1861-5*, vol. 1. Baltimore, MD: Press of Guggenheimer, Weil and Company, 1898.

SECONDARY ACCOUNTS, OTHER

Ayoub, Mike. *Campfire Chronicles: The Words and Deeds of the 88th Pennsylvania 1861-1865.* Bloomington, IN: Xlibris Corp, 2010.
Bennett, Brian. *Sons of Old Monroe: A History of Patrick O'Rorke's 140 New York Volunteer Infantry.* Dayton, OH: Morningside Bookshop, 1993.
Davis, Robert Scott. *Ghosts and Shadows of Andersonville.* Macon, GA: Mercer University Press, 2006.
Futch, Ovid L. *History of Andersonville Prison.* Gainesville: University of Florida Press, 1968.
Marvel, William. *Andersonville: The Last Depot.* Chapel Hill: University of North Carolina Press, 1994.

NEWSPAPERS

National Tribune, Washington, DC (multiple issues spread out over the years; John McElroy was the paper's editor).
New York Times, "'Raiding' in Andersonville Prison, An Extraordinary Story of Outrage and It's [*sic*] Punishment, Six Men Hung." December 11, 1864, p. 1.
Sunday Mercury. "Andersonville Prison, Was Captain Wirz Guilty of the Enormities Charged to Him? Thrilling Episode of Prison Life How an Organized Gang of Ruffians Preyed upon Their Fellow-Prisoners, Six of the Sentenced to be Hanged, Detailed Statement of the Whole Proceeding by the Official Reporter of the Court, &c. &c.&c." August 20, 1865, p. 4.

INDIVIDUAL COMPILED MILITARY SERVICE RECORDS

The Compiled Service Records for the men listed below can be found at Compiles Service Records. Civil War. Carded Records, Volunteer Organizations. Records of the Adjutant General's Office, Records of the Adjutant General's Office, 1890-1912, Record Group 94. National Archives, Washington, DC. These are available at the National Archives in Washington, DC, or copies of compiled service records for an individual can be purchased either online or by writing to the NARA

Richard Allen
William Collins
Charles F. Curtis
Patrick Delaney
James Sarsfield
John Sullivan

PENSION RECORDS

Pension records for the following soldiers are taken from the Civil War and Later Pension Files, Records of the Department of Veteran's Affairs, Record Group 15; National Archives Building, Washington, DC:

John G. Doud
Leroy Key
John McElroy

PRISON RECORDS

Camp Sumter Register of Deaths

Andersonville Prison records, v. 114-118, February–April 1865.
Register of deaths and burials of prisoners, v. 41-42, February 1864–April 1865.
Register of deceased prisoners confined at Morning reports, Asst. Provost Marshall Richmond, Virginia, 1863–1864 (NARA Series M1303, Roll 4). This collection is NARA microfilm publication M1303 from Record Group 249 Records of the Commissary General of Prisoners.

Camp Sumter Morning Reports, April 1864–May, 1865

Andersonville Prison records, v. 110, April 1864–May 1865.

Monthly reports, v. 42 April 1864–May 1865.

Monthly provision returns of the prison hospital, v. 51. Prisoners claiming reinbursement for money taken by Confederate officials (NARA Series M1303, Roll 6).

Microfilmed images of the records for Camp Sumter Prison at Andersonville, Georgia, can also be found at https//familysearch.org/ark:61903/3:1:1QSQ-G979-N4J2?cc+2019835&wc+MW44-H23&3A341349601%2C341351701

Index

About the Author

While most spend their time at family reunions by catching up on family news, the Morgan family quickly switches to intense matches of competitive storytelling. So far, **Gary Morgan** is the only one to eschew the family motto of "Don't let the facts get in the way of a good story," and become a nonfiction writer.

A chance encounter with the letters of Civil War sailor and Andersonville prisoner of war Frederic Augustus James sparked an interest in the Andersonville Raiders, and what started off as a planned magazine article exploded into a full-length study with the receipt of a 2017 Friends of Andersonville Grant. This led to a presentation on the Raiders at the National POW Museum in Andersonville, Georgia, on Veteran's Day weekend in 2018.

When not digging through 150-year-old military records, Morgan is a high school history teacher, an avid genealogist, and the proud parent of two adult daughters.